The Soviet Invasion of Czechoslovakia: Its Effects on Eastern Europe

edited by
E. J. Czerwinski
Jaroslaw Piekalkiewicz

The Praeger Special Studies program—utilizing the most modern and efficient book production techniques and a selective worldwide distribution network—makes available to the academic, government, and business communities significant, timely research in U.S. and international economic, social, and political development.

The Soviet Invasion of Czechoslovakia: Its Effects on Eastern Europe

PRAEGER SPECIAL STUDIES IN INTERNATIONAL POLITICS AND PUBLIC AFFAIRS

Praeger Publishers   New York   Washington   London

PRAEGER PUBLISHERS
111 Fourth Avenue, New York, N.Y. 10003, U.S.A.
5, Cromwell Place, London S.W.7, England

Published in the United States of America in 1972
by Praeger Publishers, Inc.

Library of Congress Catalog Card Number: 77-182987

Printed in the United States of America

INTRODUCTION

E. J. Czerwinski
Jaroslaw Piekalkiewicz

The executioners have taken control of Czechoslovakia. After a year during which psychological warfare was more in evidence than physical violence, the liberals, who had tried and failed to impose a human face on a socialistic system, have been purged from the Party and have dispersed throughout the world. Czechoslovakia at the beginning of the 1970's stands where it did in the early 1960's.

The invasion reaffirmed once again the tragedy of Eastern Europe; a tragedy that, simply stated, lies in the failure of the small countries involved to understand their reliance on one another. In 1968, as in 1956 and—thirty years before—in 1938, petty quarrels and divisiveness among the East European nations contributed to their national disasters. Any attack on one or more of the East European states by an outside power (Germany or Russia) has, historically, been used by brother nations within the region to advance their own interests at the expense of the victim. Thus, in 1938 Poland and Hungary participated in the dismemberment of Czechoslovakia; the year 1940 saw Bulgaria benefiting from the collapse of Yugoslavia at the hands of the Germans and Italians; the bloodbath of Hungary in 1956, while stirring sympathy in Poland, produced only aggressive noises in Czechoslovakia; and finally, the invasion of Czechoslovakia in 1968 was accomplished with the participation of Polish, Hungarian, and Bulgarian troops—brother nations again bringing a brother to his knees. "If we are forced to live under the Soviet yoke, the Czechs must also suffer the same fate." The Hungarians had already had their moment and failed. The Poles had also tried, in 1956. Why should the Czech and Slovaks succeed when the others could not?

The jesters and executioners in Eastern Europe often change places as in a giant kaleidoscope. Some of the jesters join the executioners in the execution of other jesters. The beheading is a public spectacle in which the crowd experiences a certain relief: This time their own heads will not roll. So long as the jesters do not unite and, by so doing, end their fiefdom, the executioners will stalk the land, unhindered in their choice of victims. The remaining jesters will merely retreat behind the wall of defensive laughter.

Disunity, it can be argued, is the exclusive property of unrepresentative authoritarian governments such as the dictatorships in Eastern Europe before World War II and the communist ideocracies of the postwar period. Nowhere, however, is the saying "People get the government they deserve" better illustrated than in Eastern Europe. The aggressive, short-sighted actions of these authoritarian governments have been reinforced time and time again by the negative attitudes (sometimes even hatred) of the East Europeans for their neighbors. It is extremely hard to say who despises whom most and why, but the animosity has a tradition of over a thousand years' standing; it goes back to a period during which, at one time or another, practically every East European country had its own moment of glory when it invaded, dominated, and oppressed its neighbors. The irony seems more intensified when the close cultural relations between many of these East European nations is realized.

The eleven essays in this volume were written by scholars who either had first-hand experience in Czechoslovakia and other East European countries during 1968-69 or carefully followed events in the Soviet Union and Eastern Europe at a distance. The contributing scholars represent various ideologies and points of view, and uniformity of opinion is notably absent.

This is as it should be. An event such as the invasion of Czechoslovakia occurs rarely in history. Efforts to equate what happened in Czechoslovakia with what has happened in Vietnam or the Dominican Republic seem somewhat misdirected, though there are certain points of similitude; specifically, each of these situations reiterates an imperative: Violence against any sovereign state should not go unchallenged.

How strange that the world has almost forgotten what occurred in August, 1968, even with the reminder accorded that fateful act on its first anniversary, when the Czechs and Slovaks attempted to break the backs of their powerful executioners. But their efforts proved futile and a month later, in September, 1969, the Czechs and Slovaks were brought to their knees by their new conservative leadership.

The Soviet Invasion of Czechoslovakia: Its Effects on Eastern Europe

PUBLIC POLITICAL OPINION IN CZECHOSLOVAKIA DURING THE DUBCEK ERA

Jaroslaw Piekalkiewicz

Anyone who was present in Czechoslovakia on August 21, 1968, as this author was, has no doubt in his mind of the widespread opposition of the Czechs and Slovaks to the Soviet occupation. The invasion was a terrible shock; unsuspected by most, welcomed by but a few. The Soviet bear came roaring into the peaceful Czech and Slovak lands, basking, as they were, in the sunny summer of their expectation for continued democratization and liberalization and in the exercise of their newly acquired personal freedom.

What were these expectations; what political system had the Czechs and Slovaks envisaged, and what was their reaction to the brutal destruction of their hopes? All these questions are answered with a considerable degree of certainty by twenty public opinion polls taken in Czechoslovakia between April, 1968, and March, 1969.* The polls, conducted with a high degree of technical efficiency and representing, in most cases, a sample corresponding closely to the actual social and political composition of Czechoslovak society, are in themselves a newsworthy event. Never before had the citizens of a Communist

---

*In order to protect those who allowed the author to examine the surveys, the polls are identified only by arbitrary numbers. For specific discussion of the polls used in this study see the Appendix. For a full examination of all the polls see the author's Public Opinion Polling in Czechoslovakia, 1968-69 (New York: Praeger Special Studies, 1971).

country been asked to express freely their political opinions. It is as
if one were suddenly permitted to lift up the cranium and peer into the
unknown of the "communist mind."

The crucial question is: How freely expressed were the answers
and hence how valid were the findings of the polls. In this respect,
the dates of the period covered provide the key. Prior to April, 1968,
the researchers conducted a number of pilot studies that convinced them
of respondents' inhibitions in talking freely. And then suddenly, in
April, with the publication of the Action Program, the pollsters noted
a genuine lack of fear on the part of the respondents and a willingness
to answer all the questions asked.* This was the time, psychologically
speaking, when Czechs and Slovaks found their freedom. The pollsters
continued to conduct surveys even after the Soviet invasion. Not until
March, 1969, did they suspend their activity because of the considerable
danger to the researchers themselves and the growing awareness on
their part that one day they themselves might have to answer for the
questions asked. Even more discouraging was their recognition that
the general public was no longer willing to express itself freely. Fear
again silenced the voices of the Czechs and Slovaks, and the period of
free debate, and hence of public opinion polls, was over.

THE DANGER OF THE COUNTERREVOLUTION

The five participating powers of the Warsaw Pact justified their
invasion by the argument that Czechoslovakia was on the verge of an
antisocialist counterrevolution. The counterrevolution, they maintained,
would have turned the path of development back to capitalism and delivered Czechoslovakia into the Western camp. In the last analysis, of
course, the definition of "counterrevolution" lay with the Soviet tanks.
Nevertheless, it is instructive to hear the opinions of the Czechs and
Slovaks. In a survey conducted on the streets of Prague seven days
after the invasion, only 2 percent of those polled agreed with the following question: "Was there a danger of counterrevolution before the
entry of the armies?" An overwhelming majority (93 percent) of the
Prazans (citizens of Prague) emphatically rejected the possibility of
a counterrevolution, thus negating the Warsaw Pact's justification for

---

*The Action Program is the political program of the new leader-
ship of the Communist Party. For a good translation of this program
see Robin Alison Remington, ed., Winter in Prague (Cambridge, Mass.:
The M.I.T. Press, 1969).

the invasion. Even counting those who gave no answer, only 7 percent either admitted the possibility or refused to deny it.

The poll was taken immediately after the invasion and in Prague, where the direct confrontation between the population and the Soviet army was most manifest and violent. No doubt the respondents were affected by recent memories. The interviews were conducted in the streets, often in full view of the Soviet tanks. Perhaps even those Prazans who previously were concerned with the danger of a counter-revolution now refuted such a possibility. Fortunately, there is further evidence, this time from the whole of Czechoslovakia, demonstrating that this was only partially the case.

The second survey on this subject was taken four weeks after the invasion and more than fourteen days after the announcement of the Moscow agreement that permitted Dubcek's return to power, at least for the time being. The agreement also "legalized" the "temporary" stationing of foreign troops on Czechoslovak soil, a move intended to hasten the process of "normalization." The beginning of the survey coincided with Dubcek's television appearance on September 14, in which he explained some of the terms of the Moscow agreement and reassured his fellow citizens of his determination to continue the pro-cess of liberalization and democratization.

Only a very small group (1.2 percent) admitted without any reservations the danger of counterrevolution and the possibility of a return to capitalism (see Table 1). More people felt that there was some truth in it (6.8 percent), but the outstanding majority (87.4 per-cent) rejected the assumption. Counting those who gave definite af-firmatives with those inclined to answer in the affirmative, one finds a larger percentage of people afraid of counterrevolution (8 percent) among the general population than among the Prazans (only 2 percent). In evaluating this figure the conservative Party and state officials who were against the democratization simply because in many cases it threatened their vested interest have to be taken into account. Dubcek's regime, perhaps to its own detriment, had never carried out a purge of the old Stalinists. There is no significant difference between the responses of the Czechs and those of the Slovaks, except that in Slovakia a larger group chose the "don't know—no answer" category, which in-dicates a lower political sophistication among the Slovaks and corre-lates with their generally lower education level.

In terms of the social and political patterns of the respondents, the answer "This is true" was given more frequently in comparison to others by the members of the Communist Party (2.1 percent) and

TABLE 1 (Survey No. 2)

Question: From some countries we hear the opinion that socialism was endangered here by the international antisocialist forces and that Czechoslovakia was on the road toward capitalism. Would you say, that:

	This is true percent[b]	There is some truth in it percent	This is not true percent	D/K[a] N/A percent
All subjects (N=1,875)	1.2	6.8	87.4	4.6
Czech lands (N=1,320)	1.0	6.8	88.9	3.3
Slovakia (N=555)	1.6	6.8	83.9	7.7

[a]In this and the following tables, D/K = don't know and N/A = no answer.
[b]Numbers in all the tables are expressed as percents unless otherwise noted.

6

by the individuals with only a primary education (2.8 percent). The latter statistic explains the higher percentage of affirmatives in Slovakia. The frequency of the answer "There is some truth in it" increased as the age levels moved up (18-24 - 2.0 percent; 25-39 - 3.8 percent; 40-54 - 9.1 percent; and over 55 - 10.0 percent), and was more often selected by the members of the Communist Party than by nonmembers (15.7 percent against 4.1 percent); it also received a higher percentage among the skilled workers (9.9 percent).

How do these postinvasion opinions compare with the preinvasion attitudes? In a sample taken in the Czech-lands in July, 1968, (see Table 2) again a large majority (82 percent) did not subscribe to the fear of antisocialist tendencies or of a return to capitalism. Only a small group (6 percent) expressed apprehension that a continuation of socialism in Czechoslovakia might be endangered. Most strikingly, the younger people did not share these fears at all (if the answer "Sometimes yes, sometimes no" is regarded as neutral). Much more positive about this possibility were older people, those with a lower education, and members of the Communist Party (KSC). They could be described as individuals more likely to belong to the power elite, but without, at the same time, the security of professional preparation (education) for their jobs.

It is not completely fair to place in a single category all those who were apprehensive about a threat to the continued development of socialism. An analysis of their motivations (Table 3, answered only by those who expressed fear) suggests that only about 21 percent (answers 1 to 6) could be classified as being in positive opposition to liberalization. Transferring these findings to a previous tabulation (Table 2) it is found that only 1.26 percent of all respondents expressed a fear of antisocialist forces and a return to capitalism. This number corresponds very closely to the postinvasion attitudes, indicating that opinions regarding socialist development remained stable. Again older people were more likely to be fearful of the process of liberalization than young individuals (answers 1 to 6—28 percent to 17 percent respectively); those with a lower educational level more than the higher education group (27 percent to 11 percent respectively); and Party members more than non-Party (27 percent to 20 percent). Again, naturally, those who were most likely to lose their privileged positions were more apprehensive. All three surveys show, without any reservation, that only a very small minority were opposed to the development of Czechoslovak democratic socialism, and that, by reason of social and political groupings, this minority would have been expected to oppose such a process. In the last analysis, however, perhaps even among that minority few really welcomed the invasion of their land.

TABLE 2 (Survey No. 16)

Question: Some people talk about the danger of antisocialistic tendencies and express fear of a return to capitalism. Do you subscribe to this fear?

Opinions (N=487)	All respondents	Up to 40 years	Over 40 years	Education		Member KSC	Nonmember KSC
				Lower	Higher		
1. Strongly don't subscribe	33	39	29	29	39	27	39
2. Don't subscribe	49	50	47	49	49	51	48
3. Sometimes yes, sometimes no	11	10	12	14	9	10	12
4. Subscribe	5	–	9	6	2	9	3
5. Strongly sub-scribe	1	–	2	1	1	3	1
6. N/A	1	1	1	1	–	–	1
	100	100	100	100	100	100	105

TABLE 3 (Survey No. 16)

Question: In what do you see the main danger where this fear would be realized?

Possibility of the main danger of the antisocialist tendencies and return of capitalism	All answers	Age Up to 40	Age Over 40	Education Lower	Education Higher	Member KSC	Nonmember KSC
1. Influence and activity of international capitalism	5	5	7	6	3	4	5
2. Former capitalists and the servants of their families	5	1	9	6	4	5	5
3. Rehabilitated political prisoners	—	1	—	1	—	—	1
4. International Jewry	2	2	2	2	1	2	2
5. Collapse of individual organizations (e.g., CSM[a])	2	3	2	4	—	1	3
6. Activization of the non-Communist political parties	7	5	8	9	3	15	4
7. Unsolved (by the government) economic difficulties	36	37	34	33	41	44	34
8. Failure and inability of the Communists to lead this country successfully	19	20	18	18	22	9	22
9. Other reasons	24	26	20	21	26	20	24
	100	100	100	100	100	100	100

[a]Czechoslovak Youth Movement

FOURTEEN MILLION COUNTERREVOLUTIONARIES?

The great majority of Czechs and Slovaks did not see the political developments in Czechoslovakia as a threat to the socialist system. Was this because they wished to reject socialism and to return to capitalism? Were the 14 million Czechs and Slovaks, with a few exceptions, diehard counterrevolutionaries? The truth is contrary to this assumption. About two months before the invasion, an undisputed majority voted for a continuation of socialist development (see Table 4). Only 5 percent put themselves on record as being in favor of a return to capitalism, while a slightly larger percentage were not sure (D/N-6 percent)—and this in spite of the long period of terror and oppression under socialism, in a country that had one of the worst experiences in the whole of Eastern Europe. It must be remembered that some of those voting might have been released from imprisonment for political crimes as late as 1964. Many others may have had members of their families incarcerated for more than a decade.

The study in Slovakia on the same topic generally confirms the findings for the whole country (see Table 5). Some uncertainty is introduced, however, by the wording of the question ("faithful to Marxism-Leninism") as well as by the introduction of yet another question on the independent character of the construction of socialism. Both questions are not specific enough for scientific testing, since the answers must derive from the individual respondent's perception of Marxism-Leninism. Of course the same criticism can be laid against the previous poll (Table 4) in regard to the respondent's perception of capitalism. Indeed after twenty years of propaganda, capitalism—especially as personified by the Western European and American systems of liberal democracy and free competition—is often viewed as a slightly modified version of Dickens' nineteenth-century England. Few people are aware of the extensive social welfare programs of Sweden, Great Britain, or even the United States. From the viewpoint of this study, a definition of capitalism as perceived by Czechs and Slovaks is immaterial, for the concern is with the positive support given to socialism regardless of the personal motivation of the respondents. In these terms the victory of the idea of socialism in Czechoslovakia is complete; the basic assumptions of the system have the widest possible support of the population and are, therefore, irreversible.*

---

*The author's own observations during his year's stay in Czechoslovakia confirm completely the statistical evidence.

TABLE 4 (Survey No. 14)

Capitalism versus Socialism

1. For a return to capitalist development	5
2. For a continuation of socialist development	89
3. Don't know	6
	100

TABLE 5 (Survey No. 9)

Question: Do you want to remain faithful to Marxism-Leninism and to the ideals of the construction of socialism based on the needs of our own people and nation?

1. Agree	65.4
2. Agree, but I doubt if this will be possible	12.0
3. I have reservations	6.3
4. Don't agree	1.4
5. D/K-N/A	14.9
	100.0

WHAT KIND OF SOCIALISM?

Considering the diversification of ideology in the communist world, and the even greater diversification of the human mind, only a simpleton would argue that socialism means the same thing to all people and in all countries. The crucial question here is what it meant, and presumably still means, to the majority of Czechs and Slovaks.

The survey in Slovakia mentioned above partially attempts to answer that question (see Table 6). The great majority of those polled desired an increase in personal freedom within the context of the socialist system. To put the same wish in negative terms, they wanted socialism without political terror and with minimal restrictions on the freedom of the individual. Significantly, no one opposed this desire, although some had reservations (1.5 percent).

TABLE 6 (Survey No. 9)

Question: Do you desire to broaden the measures for (individuals') freedom?

1.	Agree	86.2
2.	Agree, but I doubt if this will be possible	8.6
3.	I have reservations	1.5
4.	I don't agree	0.0
5.	N/A	3.7
		100.0

Further study reveals that the respondents envisioned a socialist system broadly based on popular support and responsive to the demands and wishes of the population. They also affirmed that the construction of a socialist system in Czechoslovakia, and the characteristics of that system, should be exclusively the internal affair of Czechs and Slovaks (see Table 7). There was practically no disagreement with these two political goals of the Party, and the poll itself would have been dull in its uniformity of answers were it not for the secondary question testing the actual achievement of the system up to May, 1968. Here there was a striking difference of opinion between Party and non-Party individuals. A majority of the nonmembers obviously desired a continuing expansion of their role in the formulation of public policies. The majority of the Party members (61 percent), and an even greater percentage among the first secretaries of the District Committees (DC's) of the Party (78 percent), thought the Czechoslovak construction of socialism to be already based on the will of the people. What was significant was not that the majority of these two groups responded affirmatively, for indeed one would expect the ruling elite to be satisfied with its rule, but that such a large minority (39 percent of Party members polled and even 22 percent of the secretaries) were demanding further democratization.

The Czechoslovak desire for complete sovereignty was forcefully expressed by another poll (see Table 8) in which a large majority opposed the use of foreign forces on Czechoslovak soil for whatever purpose, and, therefore, voted clearly against the Soviet invasion. What comes as a shock is the number of answers in the affirmative (10 percent), which again can be attributed to the conservatives who

TABLE 7 (Survey No. 8)

Exact quotation from the resolution of the Central Committee (CC) of the KSC of April, 1968: "The Czechoslovak way of the construction of socialism, which we
seek, is our internal matter, definitely based on the supreme will of our people."

	May, 1968	May, 1968	5-15-68
	Nonmember KSC N=636	Member KSC N=524	Leading secretaries of the CC and the DC's of the KSC N=139
Do you agree that it should be so?	93	96	90
Do you think that this statement corresponds to present-day reality?	38	61	78

TABLE 8 (Survey No. 14)

Question: Do you agree that in order to crush grave
disorder forces of another state should be used?

1. Agree	4	} 10
2. Perhaps, according to conditions	6	
3. Don't agree	84	
4. D/K-N/A	6	
	100	

felt threatened in their secured jobs. The majority, however, voted
for a socialism independent of outside pressure or direction. What
kind of socialism was it to be internally?

According to Zdenek Mlynar, close advisor of Dubcek and the
"official" political scientist of the new wave, "socialism with a human
face" was to be pluralistic and not monistic. The majority of his

TABLE 9 (Survey No. 8)

A quotation from the speech by Zdenek Mlynar to the April plenum of the Central Committee of the KSC: "The new political system has to make possible in the formulation of political decisions free and democratic expression of several wants and desires of different groups and levels of people in the socialist society."

	Nonmember KSC N=636	Member KSC N=524	Leading secretaries of the CC and the DC's of the KSC N=139
Do you agree that it should be so?	91	87	85
Do you think that this statement corresponds to present-day reality?	37	57	71

compatriots agreed with him without any reservations (see Table 9); non-Party individuals in higher numbers (91 percent) than Party members (87 percent), and the latter again in a higher percentage than the leading secretaries (85 percent), although the difference was not that significant (4 and 6 percent respectively). What was striking was the divergence in the three groups' evaluation of the up-to-date achievement, which, after all, reflected on the previous question and made the comparison among the three different groups less meaningful, even casting a shadow on the meaning of Mlynar's statement itself. Only slightly over one third of the non-Communists thought broad participation to be the existing state of affairs, while more than half of the Communists and nearly three fourths of the leading secretaries believed this to be so. The Party members and, more particularly, the secretaries were obviously quite content with the prevailing level of participation.

The core of Leninism (the Soviet brand of Marxism) is the hegemony the Communist Party exercises in propagating one political line that is binding on Communists and non-Communists alike. This is the most crucial aspect of a political system that differentiates

TABLE 10 (Survey No. 16)

Question: At the present time there are expressed many
different and often contradictory opinions as to the development of our society. Do you agree with the opinion that
"in politics there must be one political line valid for all,"
or should there exist, side by side, many concepts and
proposals of individual parties and groups?

Opinions	All	Education		Member KSC	Nonmember KSC
		Lower	Higher		
1. For many concepts	81	79	94	68	86
2. For one political line	17	20	4	31	13
3. N/A	2	1	2	1	1
	100	100	100	100	100

between ideocracy and democracy.* A substantial majority of Czechs
rejected Leninism and hence ideocracy (see Table 10). Strongest in
their desire for the existence of many political concepts were people
with a higher education (94 percent) and, though it is not reflected in
this particular table, people younger than forty (84 percent). It is also
striking that only 31 percent of the Party members felt that there must
be only one political line—the credo, after all, of the Marxist-Leninist
Party.

In all communist systems the single political line is traditionally
formulated by the Central Committee of the Party or, more specifically,
by the Presidium of the Central Committee. There was considerable
dissatisfaction in Czechoslovakia with this concentration of political
power (see Table 11). The greatest number felt that the power of
formulating the political program should rest either with the National

---

*Ideocracy being a system or movement politically motivated by
one monistic ideology; democracy being a system based on the necessity for political tolerance and ideological pluralism.

TABLE 11 (Survey No. 16)

Question: If there should be only one political line valid for all who should create and formulate it?

The political line should be created by:	All	Education Lower	Education Higher	Member KSC	Nonmember KSC
1. National Assembly (the parliament)	18	17	19	19	18
2. The government	6	7	4	3	7
3. The National Front	25	24	27	30	24
4. Public opinion through the press, radio & television	22	19	25	13	24
5. The Central Committee of the KSC	8	8	8	21	4
6. Other political parties	2	2	2	–	3
7. All working people	9	12	5	6	10
8. Others	1	2	1	2	1
9. N/A	9	9	9	6	9
	100	100	100	100	100

Front—the super-Party organization (25 percent), or with public opinion as expressed by the media of communication (22 percent). One third of the Party members desired the Front to be the dominant force. Only a small minority of all the respondents voted for the Central Committee, and only one fifth of the Party members subscribed to this solution. The Central Committee (or, more specifically, its Presidium) had traditionally been the ruling body of the Party and of the state. Only a very small group of the nonmembers voted for such an allocation of power. There was considerable desire for this role to be played by the National Assembly among Party members (19 percent) as well as nonmembers (18 percent).

One of the most important factors contributing to the Communist Party's ability to impose its political line is the limitation of political debate by Party-controlled censorship. In July, 1968, the National Assembly passed a law abolishing all censorship, thereby depriving the Party of its weapon for enforcing doctrinal purity. The great majority of Czechs and Slovaks enthusiastically supported the new law (Table 12). It is no exaggeration to state that the Czechoslovak media became the freest in the world. Only a small minority (5 percent) objected to the condition of noncensorship; a minority slightly greater in Slovakia than in the Czech-lands. Slovakia's vote for non-censorship was lower than the Czech's mainly because of the larger D/K and N/A vote (18 percent), which again reflected the lesser polit-ical sophistication of the Slovaks.

TABLE 12 (Survey No. 1)

Question: A few days ago the National Assembly passed the law abolishing censorship. Do you consider this law right or wrong?

	C.S.S.R. (N=1,772)	Czech-lands (N=1,306)	Slovakia (N=466)
1. Right	86	91	74
2. Wrong	5	3	8
3. D/K-N/A	9	6	18
	100	100	100

TABLE 13 (Survey No. 8)

Question: Some people say that the press, radio, and television assumed the right to address themselves to matters in which they are not competent. Do you agree with this opinion or not?

	N=100	Agreement	Immaterial D/K	Disagreement
March, 1968, C.S.S.R.	1,614	9	18	73
March, 1968, C.S.S.R.	1,440	19	8	73
Nonmembers KSC May, 1968, North Czech-land	636	11	3	86
Members KSC May, 1968, North Czech-land	524	32	6	62
Leading secretaries of the CC and of the DC's and May, 1968	139	89		16

Their attitude toward censorship was motivated to a degree by the respondents' evaluation of the role and performance of the media of communication, which from January, 1968, to a time well after the invasion (around October or November, 1968) were the main spokesmen for liberalization and democratization. The media bitterly criticized Novotny's rule, the country's general stagnation, and what they called "the perversion of socialism." In two separate polls nearly three fourths of the respondents disagreed with the statement that the media had usurped powers that were not within their purview—powers, it is assumed, of social, economic, and political critism (see Table 13). The percentage of disagreement was higher among nonmembers (86 percent), but even among the members of the Communist Party—some of them under bitter attack by the media—only one third agreed with the statement. The reaction of the leading secretaries of the Communist Party was understandable (89 percent in agreement), since many of them were regarded by the media as the main villains in the country's dilemma.

THE ROLE OF THE COMMUNIST PARTY

As stated above, the mainstay of existing communist systems, with the obvious exception of Yugoslavia, is the undisputable hegemony of the Communist Party, the Leninist vanguard of the proletariat. Theoretically, Party rule is based on the assumption that the Party understands the scientifically proven Marxist-Leninist laws for the advancement of a socialist society. The hegemony of the Party results from its claim to exclusive understanding of Marx. In May, 1968, the majority of Czechs regarded the Party's absolute hegemony as undesirable; they were willing to allow the Communist Party its leading political role only if it "served devotedly the free advancement of socialism." They rejected the Party's right to rule the society. They demanded proof of the Party's capability to lead. This ability could be measured by the Party's hard work for the benefit of the whole society within the socialist framework of production and distribution (see Table 14). Only a small minority (15 percent) of non-Party people believed the Party to be leading rather than ruling the nation, and only half of the Party members thought this to be the case. However, nearly three quarters of the Party leaders felt that the Party was already democratically leading rather than ruling. A great majority of Czechs (83 percent of non-Party people) could easily conceive socialist democracy without the leadership of the Communist Party* (see Table 15).

---

*The Party membership stands at about 12 percent of the total population.

TABLE 14 (Survey No. 8)

Question: The Communist Party fulfills its leading role not by ruling the society, but by the fact that it serves most devotedly the free advancement of the socialist growth of the society.

	Nonmember KSC N=636	Member KSC N=524	Leading secretaries of the CC and the DC's of the KSC N=139
Do you think that this statement corresponds to the present-day reality?	15	49	73
Do you agree that it should be so?	68	88	92

TABLE 15 (Survey No. 8)

Question: You can conceive democracy as a socialist democracy only when the Communist Party has the leading role. Do you consider this opinion to be correct?

	Nonmember N=636	Member KSC N=524	Leading secretaries of the CC and the DC's of the KSC N=139
Yes	11	61	97
Immaterial	6	13	1
No	83	25	2

In addition some people felt the question to be of no consequence (6 percent of non-Party and 13 percent of the members). One fourth of the KSC membership did not regard a leading role for their own party to be essential to a socialist democracy. Counting those who did not see the Party's leadership as essential together with those who did not see any connection between the leading role and socialist democracy, it appears that more than one third of the Party members polled did not consider the Party's leading role to be a prerequisite for socialist democracy. Here the variance between Party and non-Party people was considerable. Nearly two thirds of the Party members regarded the leading role of their party as the core of socialist democracy, and the Party leaders presented a unified front on this issue, insisting in an overwhelming majority that socialist democracy in fact means that the party leads (97 percent for and 2 percent against).

A MULTIPARTY SYSTEM?

Dominance of public policy by one political line was rejected, the hegemony of the Communist Party was rejected—what was to be erected in its place? In addition to the Communist Party, there were in the Czech-lands two other parties: the Czechoslovak Socialist Party and the Czechoslovak People's Party. Perhaps the three-party system was to be the answer? There was a considerable sentiment (40 percent—see Table 16) for this solution, especially among men rather than women, older people, or Party members. A small minority voted for one-party rule, with strongest support in this direction among the members of the Communist Party (10 percent). Nearly one third of nonmembers (and, hence, nearly one third of the population) favored the establishment of another party, and over one fifth voted for the creation of other political groups. This sentiment was stronger among the younger people, with men voting more heavily for one extra party and women for many political parties.

If there were to be only three parties, what role should be played by the two non-Communist parties?* First of all, the majority of Czechs did not regard the Czechoslovak Socialist Party and the Czecho-slovak People's Party as truly independent parties with their own self-reliant political programs (59 percent—see Table 17). At the same time, they desired the parties to become fully independent and equal

---

*At the time of the survey both parties had only a few thousand members, but they were growing very rapidly.

TABLE 16 (Survey No. 16)

Question: Political parties are also part of the National Front. Do you think that the system of political parties, which today exists in the Czech-lands, is sufficient for the requirements of socialist democracy?

Number of political parties	All	Men	Women	Age Up to 40	Over 40	Member KSC	Nonmember KSC
1. Is completely sufficient	41	43	37	30	50	63	34
2. There should be only one political party	7	4	11	9	4	10	5
3. There should be one more party established	27	30	23	30	25	16	31
4. There should be other political parties established	23	19	28	28	18	9	27
5. N/A	2	4	1	3	3	2	3
	100	100	100	100	100	100	100

22

TABLE 17 (Survey No. 16)

1. Do you think that today the Czechoslovak Socialist Party and the Czechoslovak People's Party are self-governing and independent parties that have their own independent policies?

2. Should the Czechoslovak Socialist Party and the Czechoslovak People's Party be self-governing and independent political parties and equal partners of the Communists?

| | All answers | | Member KSC | | Nonmember KSC | |
	Question 1	Question 2	Q1	Q2	Q1	Q2
Agree	29	81	39	71	25	85
Disagree	59	14	52	26	62	12
N/A D/K	12	5	9	3	13	3
	100	100	100	100	100	100

to the Communist Party. A considerable number of people (12 percent) did not really know how independent the two parties were; indeed in the first half of August, 1968, the parties' relationship to the Communist Party was hard to assess, but undoubtedly they were growing rapidly in status, membership, and self-governing leadership. The opinions on this point of Communists and non-Communists were not strikingly different though the non-Communists naturally tended to vote more heavily for the two parties' independence. However, nearly two thirds of the Communists were prepared to meet the political challenge of the socialists and the agrarians (People's Party). The sovereignty of the two parties was supported most strongly by the educated (see Table 18), of whom only 1 percent expressed themselves as being firmly against the idea. Definite negative reaction was most evident among the Party members (16 percent not wanting and strongly not wanting); in view of the previous findings this opinion was most likely prevalant among the leading Communist Party secretaries.

In Table 16, half of the respondents indicated a desire for one or more additional parties (50 percent). Who then would decide on the admission of the new party to the existing political system? What procedure should be followed? This time nearly one fifth voted against

TABLE 18 (Survey No. 16)

Question: Do you want the existing non-Communist parties to be really independent parties and equal partners of the Communist Party?

Expression of wants	All	Education		Member KSC	Nonmember KSC
		Lower	Higher		
1. Strongly wanting	40	35	48	23	45
2. Wanting	41	42	40	44	40
3. Sometimes yes, sometimes no	11	15	6	17	10
4. Not wanting	5	5	5	11	3
5. Strongly not wanting	2	2	1	5	1
6. D/K N/A	1	1	–	–	1
	100	100	100	100	100

the new party or parties (see Table 19)—a smaller number than for the previous answer—and among this group 33 percent were members of the KSC and only 14 percent were nonmembers. At the other extreme, more than one fifth would have wished no restriction whatsoever in the formation of a new political party. This opinion was expressed more frequently among the younger people and among the non-Communists. The rest of the voters felt the issue should be assigned either to the National Front (23 percent) or to the Central Committee of the National Front (21 percent)—both groups choosing to lodge the prerogative with the Front (together, a majority of 44 percent). There was no significant difference in the vote for the Front among different ages and party affiliations. Neither the Ministry of Interior nor the Communist Party were thought to be effective organs for the exercise of the registration function—one may say with good reason so. The low vote for the Constitutional Court no doubt reflected a lack of experience with an independent judiciary.

Even more important than the authority to register the new party were the programmatic criteria for the creation of a new political group. Again, the same number spoke against the formation of a new party (see Table 20), although a slight variation among different groups indicated a lack of consistency among some of the respondents (since both tables are from the same survey). The program most favored by the respondents (21 percent) was one which did not contradict human rights or communism and which did not advocate war, racism, or fascism. Clearly, Nazi or Fascist-type parties, as well as highly nationalist-expansionist parties, were to be excluded.

Such a program obviously reflects the general acceptance by Czechs and Slovaks of the "broad" socialist principles. "Broad," since evidence mentioned above indicated that opinions of communism varied, even if only with regard to its political implications, which nevertheless would determine the character of the system itself, e.g., the question of the role of the Communist Party. The above answer was the most unstructured in the category of possible conditions. (This category obviously excludes answer No. 6.) It did not bind the conditions for acceptance of a new party to any of the existing forms or norms, as, for example, the Constitution of the C.S S.R. (Czechoslovak Soviet Socialist Republic). It was in many ways an expression of a desire for a clear break with the traditional communist system. This answer was more popular with the young, the educated, and the non-Party. In complete opposition to this most flexible solution were the individuals who, in choosing answer No. 1, opposed the creation of a new party. A breakdown of the table, distributing those in favor of the new party among six possibilities, shows answer No. 1 to be

TABLE 19 (Survey No. 16)

Question: According to your own opinion, who should decide on the creation of a new political party?

	All	Age Up to 40	Age Over 40	Member KSC	Nonmember KSC
1. No new political party should be created	19	12	24	33	14
2. The government	5	4	5	2	6
3. The National Front	23	23	23	18	25
4. The Constitutional Court	5	6	4	6	5
5. The Central Committee of the National Front	21	22	19	22	20
6. The Ministry of Interior	1	1	1	3	1
7. KSC	2	1	2	3	1
8. To be left to the members of the party itself (no restrictions)	23	28	19	13	26
9. N/A	1	3	3	–	2
	100	100	100	100	100

TABLE 20 (Survey No. 16)

Question: What conditions, according to your opinion, should there be for the permission for the activating of a new political party?

	All	Age		Education		Member KSC	Nonmember KSC
		Up to 40	Over 40	Lower	Higher		
1. I am against creation of a new political party	19	11	26	21	16	36	14
2. Recognition of the leading role of the KSC	6	8	4	5	7	10	5
3. Willingness to join the National Front and to respect its program	15	14	16	17	12	17	14
4. A program that is not contrary to the law and the constitution of the C.S.S.R	18	21	16	20	16	11	20
5. A program that is not contrary to human rights, communism, which does not advocate war, racism, or fascism	21	26	18	20	24	15	23
6. There should be no restricting conditions	6	7	6	4	9	1	8
7. Socialist program	13	12	13	11	15	9	14
8. N/A	2	1	1	2	1	1	2
	100	100	100	100	100	100	100

27

the most popular among Party members, older individuals, and those with a primary education. Second in popularity among the possible conditions for creating a new party was a party whose platform would not be contrary to the law and the constitution of the C.S.S.R. (18 percent). One must admit this to be a normal provision of any democratic system, where, logically, the acceptance of the system in a broad sense is a prerequisite for legal political activity. More young voted for this solution than old, and more non-Party than Party. In a reversal of the previous alignment, more of the primary-educated respondents than the highly educated opted for the law and the constitution. The third popular preference (15 percent) was for the new party to be willing to join the National Front and to accept its program. The answer indicated again the prevailing respect for the institutions of the Front. The composition of the vote located support for the Front among the older, the less educated, and the Party members. A small minority (6 percent) desired no restricting conditions whatsoever. This was again favored rather by younger, better educated, and non-Party individuals. An answer similar in pattern was that of general acceptance of socialism, making a respectable showing (13 percent), with no significant difference with regard to age, but with more popularity among the better educated and the non-Party individuals.

The character of a political system is often judged to be democratic or not on the basis of the existence of an opposition party. The Western concept of opposition includes as a prerequisite for pragmatic effectiveness the desire and right to challenge the ruling party for power. Indeed most Western definitions of a political party include this very precondition; thus a party resigned to a minor status is not really a political party at all. In terms of the above argument, the majority of Czechs and Slovaks were opposed to the establishment of a true opposition party (see Table 21, part A—answers 3 and 4 taken together: 54 percent). The vote against any opposition party was slightly higher than that, previously given, against a new party (21 percent to 19 percent). Here it received more support from older people and from Party members. Taking each answer separately, a plurality of respondents (41 percent) favored an opposition party in coalition with the Communist Party, but in competition with the Communists for leadership of the coalition. Obviously it had to be a socialist party or, though less likely, an agrarian party in order to form such a union with the KSC. This answer also had plurality in both age groups, though with greater support among the younger. The propensity to choose answer No. 2 was more pronounced among non-Party members, but nearly one third of the party members also favored this solution. The respondents opting for the minor status of the "opposition" party (acceptance of the leading role of the KSC) were

TABLE 21 (Survey No. 16)

Question: Often there is talk about the necessity of creating an opposition party as a basic foundation for the democratic control of power. However, regarding the concept of an opposition party people have greatly different ideas. We give you some possible characteristics of the opposition party. Mark the one that corresponds to your idea of what the opposition party should be here, and furthermore:

A. according to the relationship to the Communist party:

Characteristics of the opposition party	All	Age		Member KSC	Nonmember KSC
		Up to 40	Over 40		
1. A party that refuses to share power and to cooperate with the Communists and that wishes to obtain power itself.	2	2	3	—	3
2. A party that wants to share power with the Communists and to cooperate with them by the division of state offices. It does not automatically recognize the leading role of the KSC and attempts to become the leading force of the coalition.	41	45	37	32	44
3. A party that accepts the leading role of the KSC but reserves to itself the right to its own position; at the same time it does not attempt to broaden its power base.	33	35	31	32	33
4. I am against any opposition party	21	15	27	33	17
5. N/A	3	3	2	3	3
	100	100	100	100	100

B. according to its program:

Characteristics of the opposition party	All	Age		Member KSC	Nonmember KSC
		Up to 40	Over 40		
1. A party with an antisocialist program emphasizing a return to capitalism	—	—	—	—	—
2. A party with a program emphasizing a return to the political and economic system of the 1945–47 period	7	88	5	4	7
3. A party with a socialist program but with the concept of socialism differing from the ideas of the Communists	22	22	22	9	27
4. A party with a socialist program in agreement with the Communists but with a different concept for its realization	48	52	44	55	46
5. I am against any opposition party	21	16	26	31	18
6. N/A	2	2	3	1	2
	100	100	100	100	100

29

unified in their age and political composition (one third in each category) with only slight decline among older individuals. A tiny minority expressed a desire for a truly independent opposition party (2 percent).

In the question of the character of any opposition party, as defined by its program (see Table 21, part B), no one expressed a preference for a party with an antisocialist platform emphasizing a return to capitalism. This reconfirms our previous estimate of the deep commitment of Czechs and Slovaks to the basic principles of socialism. Even more significantly, the majority (48 percent) voted for an opposition party with a program in agreement with that of the Communist Party. The majority accepted the program of the Communists and wished the opposition party to challenge the Communist Party not on programmatic grounds, but strictly in terms of the program's realization. More Party than non-Party people were represented in this majority, and, contrary to previous trends, more younger people than older. The second most popular solution (21 percent) was an opposition party with a socialist program different from that of the Communists. There was complete consistency in this answer with regard to the two age groups and considerable variation between the Party members (only 7 percent) and non-Party people (27 percent). The idea of a return to the economic and political system of 1945-47 was not very appealing; only a small minority (7 percent) advocated an opposition party with such a program. Curiously enough, more young people (8 percent), who had little personal experience with the pre-Communist period selected this option than older individuals more familiar with the post-World War II republic. Those who voted against any opposition party (21 percent) again were divided inconsistently among different groupings.

All in all, the two tables indicate a considerable preference for an opposition party sharing power with and having the same program as the Communist Party, but challenging the Communists for leadership on pragmatic grounds. We cannot disregard the strong reaction (21 percent) against any opposition party even though there was a marked preference for this answer among Party members, rather than the general public.

The concept of an opposition party is closely related to the question of free and democratic elections. The opposition could not function meaningfully if the elections were to be controlled by the Communist Party, as is the practice in all Communist states. There was a frank admission in the next poll (see Table 22) that previous elections in Czechoslovakia had been devoid of real representative purpose. Only a small minority (3 percent) felt that elections under

Question: In the past the elections were formal and the influence of voters on the selection of candidates and the results of the elections was minimal. Which of the following possibilities, in your opinion, will contribute most toward democratization of elections?

	Total	Member KSC	Nonmember KSC	Education Lower	Education Higher
1. Free choice of candidates without any restrictions	29	40	26	24	37
2. Real possibilities and rights for the functioning of non-Communist parties	22	12	25	23	20
3. Possibility of the creation of new parties	7	3	9	7	8
4. Possibility of independent participation in elections of voluntary organizations, e.g., ROH (Trade Union Council)	6	4	6	6	6
5. The real possibility of the use of the state media (press, radio) by all the political parties	7	4	8	8	6
6. Insuring secrecy of elections	21	28	19	22	20
7. Other conditions	1	1	1	1	1
8. No need to change; previous elections were democratic	3	5	3	5	1
9. D/K	4	3	3	4	1

the previous system had been democratic. Even 92 percent of those members of the Communist Party questioned did not think so. The most preferred method for achieving democratization of elections was through free choice of condidates without any restrictions (29 percent). Presumably this meant a rejection of the Communist practice of presenting one electoral list compiled by the National Front. Interesting was the support for the free-choice method among the members of the Communist Party (40 percent). The nonmembers were less enthusiastic (26 percent). People with higher education supported it more strongly than did those of a lower educational level. The second most favored choice was that which proposed free activity for a non-Communist (22 percent) and, in view of the previous tables, opposition party. Here was seen a considerable drop in support among the Communist Party members (only 12 percent), while the rest of the groups showed considerable unification. The third strongest vote was for secrecy of elections (21 percent), with no diversification of the vote between the two educational groups, but a larger percentage voting positively among the Party members. Altogether 68 percent of the Party members advocated either the free choice of candidates or secrecy of the elections. Both measures would have ended the Party's control of elections and, thereby, the absolute hegemony of the Communist Party. A plurality of non-Party individuals, as well as of the people with a lower educational backgrounds, chose either the free-choice system or the free functioning of the non-Communist parties (51 percent and 47 percent respectively). Over one third of the respondents with a higher education thought the free-choice system to be the most effective. They gave a similarly strong vote to the other two solutions: the non-Communist Party and the secrecy of elections (20 percent each).

With elections by secret ballot and non-Communist parties functioning freely, participating in campaigns, and advocating their own "socialist" programs, who would have had the right to nominate candidates: independents, political parties, social organizations, some combination of all three, or, finally, the National Front? Most people (26 percent) preferred independent candidacy of the political parties (see Table 23), while a smaller group (21 percent) selected independent candidacy of the political parties and social organizations (such as trade unions). Third in popularity was the combination of independent candidates with the two previous methods (19 percent). In all, over three fifths of all respondents voted for an unstructured, flexible method of establishing candidacy for elections. Only a small minority wished to retain the current, politically unified system within the framework of the National Front. There was a marked division of opinion on this point between Party and non-Party individuals (19 percen

TABLE 23 (Survey No. 16)

Question: What electoral system would best insure expression of the democratic will of the people?

	Total	Member KSC	Nonmember KSC	Age Up to 40	Age Over 40
1. Candidacy and election of independents	15	15	15	21	10
2. Independent candidacy of political parties	26	13	30	22	30
3. Independent candidacy of political parties and social organizations	21	22	20	21	21
4. Some form of combination of independent (groups) candidates with candidates of political parties and social organizations	19	25	18	21	19
5. The present system of National Front candidacy	9	19	6	8	11
6. Other forms	—	—	—	—	—
7. D/K	10	6	11	10	9

and 6 percent respectively). One fourth of the Party members desired
a system of elections that would combine a candidacy of independents
(social candidacy), political parties, and social organizations; more
than one fourth favored independent candidacy of political parties and
social organizations. A plurality of non-Party people, as well as of
older individuals, opted for the independent candidacy of political
parties. The younger group spread itself among the four solutions
outside the National Front framework, with over one fifth voting for
exclusive independent candidacy.

With an electoral system insuring secrecy* and free competition
of the "socialist" parties, with candidates running outside the rigid
framework of the National Front, who would have won the next election?
In July, 1968, the Communist Party would have emerged with a plurality
in a free, general election conducted by secret ballot in the Czech-
lands, with the three existing parties in competition (see Table 24).
While they would not have won a majority, the Communists would have
controlled, assuming multimember electoral districts and some sort
of a proportional representation, about 40-45 percent of the parliamentary seats. A single-member districts system would have been
harder to predict, but could possibly have given the Communists an
even larger representation in parliament. In either case, the Communists, as the strongest party, would have dominated the government.
In order to obtain a complete parliamentary majority, they would have
had to form a coalition government either with the socialists (a combination representing 56 percent of the popular vote) or with the People's Party (52 percent of the popular vote). The unknown factor in
the results was the large undecided vote (27 percent). However, even
if the entire undecided electorate had voted for the second strongest
party, the socialists, the socialist total would still have fallen short
of the Communist plurality (40 percent). It is quite conceivable that
the undecided vote would have been distributed between the socialists
and the People's Party, the two parties which were, up to January,
1968, only junior partners—front organizations of the Communists.
After January, the two parties experienced considerable growth together as they asserted their independence from the dominant Communists.

---

*Communist elections are formally by secret ballot, but voters
are permitted not to use the electoral booths. The open vote is regarded as support for the system and most citizens find it expedient
not to exercise their right to secrecy. Indeed, with only one candidate
for each position, or even with a few candidates, each a Communist
Party nominate, the insistence on secrecy is a futile act of defiance.

TABLE 24 (Survey No. 16)

Question: To whom would you give your vote if there was an election this month, based on the independent candidacy of all political parties?

I would elect the following party:	All	Communists	Non-Communists
1. Communist	43	90	28
2. Socialist	13	1	17
3. People's	9	2	12
4. Blank ballot	6	4	7
5. D/K	27	3	34
	98	100	98

TABLE 25 (Survey No. 16)

Question: To whom would you give your vote if there was an election this month, based on the independent candidacy of all political parties?

I would elect the following party:	All	Communists	Non-Communists
1. Communist	39	85	24
2. Socialist	9	1	11
3. People's	8	2	10
4. New Political party	11	3	14
5. Blank ballot	2	2	2
6. D/K	30	8	37
	99	101	98

The introduction of an unknown variable—the new, undefined
political party (see Table 25)—complicated the issue by decreasing
the vote for the three existing parties and by increasing the undecided
vote (to 30 percent). The hypothetical new party, even without a speci-
fied program, gained more than one tenth of the total vote (11 percent).
This indicated a latent desire for a new political force and, perhaps a
psychological reaction against the three bankrupt parties of the past.
If the large undecided vote were to be added to the vote for the new
party, the new party would have achieved a victory over the Communists
(41 percent to 39 percent); but all this is only speculation. The empir-
ical evidence strongly suggests that the Communists would have gained
a plurality in the three- as well as in the four-party combination. The
victory of the Communist Party in the three-party alignment was assured by the solid vote of the Party members for their own party,
despite the presence in the Party ranks of hidden socialists (1 percent),
agrarians in disguise (2 percent), "protesters" (those who returned a
blank ballot) (4 percent), and undecided voters (3 percent), In the
four-party framework, the Party members still were solidly in their
own corner, but in a smaller proportion. Three percent "deserted"
to the new party; the "protesters" were reduced to 2 percent; and,
surprisingly, the "wait and see" group swelled to 8 percent.

More than a one-third plurality of the non-Communists expressed
themselves as undecided in both combinations, although their undecided
vote was higher in the four- than in the three-party arrangement.
Neither of the non-Communist parties made a decisive showing, but
the 14-percent vote among the non-Communists for the unknown new
party may be considered as potentially significant. However, over
one fourth of the nonmembers voted for the Communist Party, and
this represents the strongest definite vote for any of the three or four
parties. This hypothetical election affirms the solid popularity of the
Communist Party in Czechoslovakia—a popularity acquired after the
January implementation of policies of liberalization and democratization.
If one were to speculate, it would appear that the most dangerous challenge to Communist political dominance would have come from a new
political party, which might, in dynamic fashion, have won over the
considerable undecided vote.

The popularity of the Communist Party, as reflected in the
predicted election victory, can be attributed without any doubt, to the
Party's leadership in the far-reaching process of democratization
and liberalization desired, as the surveys showed, by the vast majority
of Czechs and Slovaks. Before January, 1968, only a small minority
(6 percent) had complete trust in the Communist Party (see Table 26)
with a larger group, still a minority, expressing some trust (17 percent).

TABLE 26 (Survey No. 14)

Question: What was your degree of trust in the Party before January, 1968?

1. Complete trust	6	} 23
2. Trust	17	
3. No trust but not distrust	29	(Neutral)
4. Distrust	28	} 48
5. Complete distrust	20	
	100	

Note: With this question a graphic aid was used—a picture of a thermometer.

TABLE 27 (Survey No. 14)

Question: What degree of trust do you have in KSC? (June, 1968)

1. Complete trust	11	} 51
2. Trust	40	
3. No trust but not distrust	33	(Neutral)
4. Distrust	12	} 16
5. Complete distrust	4	
	100	

Note: With this question a graphic aid was used—a picture of a thermometer.

Altogether, 23 percent of the respondents indicated some trust in the Party—a surprisingly large group in view of the long history of tyrannical oppression by the Communists.* The harm done by the Party

*The membership of the Communist Party was only 20 percent of the adult (over 18) population.

was delineated by the vehement reaction on the distrust end of the spectrum. One fifth expressed complete distrust, while over one fourth of the respondents selected the distrust category. Altogether, 48 percent expressed some measure of distrust (twice as many as those expressing trust), and they constituted a near majority. The Communists could command the trust of only a minority. Slightly higher was the neutral vote (29 percent).

After the assumption of power by the liberal leadership of the Party, and after the innovation of the program of democratization, the attitudes of the respondents shifted definitely in favor of the Communist Party. Now, more than one tenth expressed their complete trust (see Table 27); an impressive 40 percent voted in the "trust" category.

The majority supported the Party (51 percent), with only a small group still mistrusting (together 16 percent). The latter were not necessarily the same individuals who had expressed mistrust in the previous table; perhaps some of the "conservative" Communists joined this group. The increase of the popularity of the Party is easily measured by the 28-percent increase in the trusting category and by a decrease of 32 percent in the distrusting individuals.

The invasion itself did not damage the support given to Alexander Dubcek's leadership of the Party, but on the contrary increased its popularity enormously (see Table 28). In an obvious act of defiance and solidarity, nearly all the Czechs and Slovaks expressed their trust in their liberal leaders. Unqualified support was stronger among the somewhat more emotional Slovaks than among the sober Czechs (90.9 to 82.4 percent). By adding the "complete trust" vote to that of "trust with reservations" category, an incredible statement of support is obtained: 97.4 percent for the total sample, 97.3 percent for the Czech-lands and 97.7 percent for Slovakia. In both countries only a very small minority refused to back the Communist leaders, presumably because of diehard opposition to the Communists in general or, on the other side of the spectrum, diehard opposition to the democratizing and liberalizing Communists. The question on the reason for lack of support (see Table 29) clarifies the position of the respondents in this category by showing that they overwhelmingly supported the process of democratization and that they did not oppose the Party from the conservative point of view.

CONCLUSION

The surveys afford positive proof that there was no chance of a countersocialist revolution in Czechoslovakia in 1968. The one

TABLE 28 (Survey No. 2)

Question: As you consider the development of recent political events do you or don't you have trust in the new leadership of the KSC (the Communist Party of Czechoslovakia) led by Alexander Dubcek?

	Have trust	Have trust with some reservations	Don't have trust	D/K N/A
All subjects (N=1,873)	84.9	12.5	1.1	1.5
Czech-lands (N=1,318)	82.4	14.9	1.3	1.4
Slovakia (N=555)	90.9	6.8	.5	1.8

TABLE 29 (Survey No. 2)

Reasons for the lack of trust:

1. Inconsistency of the individual members of the leadership of the KSC in fulfilling the process of democratization   60.8

2. Lack of trust motivated by the fact that today the leadership of the KSC works under abnormal conditions and is subject to the pressure of foreign armies   23.2

3. Lack of trust because of the opinion that the leadership of the KSC gives in to the anti-socialist forces   .8

preinvasion poll as well as the two postinvasion polls clearly indicate the lack of fear of counterrevolution in the minds of most Czechs and Slovaks. An outstanding majority voted for the continuation of the socialist development of their country. The Soviets acted for reasons of their own, not because of any need to return the Czechoslovaks to the road to socialism. But even if there had been a danger of counter-revolution, the Soviet leaders would have been hard-pressed to find anyone who would invite them to interfere in the internal affairs of Czechoslovakia. The majority of Czechs and Slovaks rejected the use of foreign troops on their territory under any circumstances. The Czech joke that the Soviets needed so many troops in Czechoslovakia in order to find the individual who invited them in is to the point, although no one is laughing. In view of the Czechoslovaks' overwhelming desire for sovereignty—sovereignty for the country and for the Czecho-slovak brand of socialism—and of their wish for freedom to arrange their own affairs, both reflected consistently in the polls, one can only compare the Soviet invasion of 1968 to the Nazi attack of 1938.

Whatever the reason for the Soviet invasion, it could not have been that Czechoslovakia was on the verge of a counterrevolution. In 1968 the great majority of Czechs and Slovaks were for socialism, but for a democratic and liberal system of socialism. They rejected police terror, censorship, and Soviet-type dictatorship by the Communist Party, a system that is more easily compared with fascism than with the socialism of Marx and Engels. The Czechs and Slovaks desired personal freedom. Their socialist system was to be based on broad popular support, and the government was to fulfill, as closely as possible, the wishes and demands of the population; they wanted a socialist government by the people, of the people, and for the people. "Socialism with a human face" was to be, above all, a pluralistic system, with many political lines, no censorship, and a communication media free to function vigorously as political and social critic.

The Communist Party, accustomed in "the old days" to absolute rule by law, was to be leader only so long as it satisfied the led. There was to be no privileged "vanguard," but free political competition among the three or more socialist parties. The new parties would be licensed by the National Front if their programs were in agreement with "socialist principles" however broadly and freely defined. The definition presumably would exclude the advocacy of return to the private owner-ship of sources of production—a program at any rate quite impossible to consummate in view of the existing realities, e.g., no one could have had enough capital to buy back the industries.

The majority of Czechs and Slovaks even opposed the creation of a true opposition party that would compete with the Communists;

they favored, instead, a coalition. They wished not to challenge the Communist political program, but to evaluate and encourage its implementation. The non-Communist party could, however, achieve leadership in the coalition.

The plurality of the system was to be assured, not by an ideological proliferation of parties, but by the political pragmatism inherent in a system of election by secret ballot of freely nominated candidates from independent political parties. Surprising, in view of previous and most recent history, was the predicted victory of the Communist Party in such a free and democratic election. The Communist Party would have remained in power, but not as unchallenged political hegemony. Its complete control over the economy and administration and, hence, its exclusive patronage system would have been destroyed.

The Communist Party would have won because of the popularity engendered by its ideological rebirth after January, 1968. The Czechoslovak Party, alone among the ruling Communist parties, had actually become a vehicle for the fulfillment of popular desires.

There was no rejection in Czechoslovakia of the socialism of Marx and Engels, but only of Leninist "revisionism." The Czechs and Slovaks tried to free themselves of the Russian system of despotism that Lenin had borrowed from Ogaryev and Tkachyev,* and that had little to do with the logic of social and economic development under Marxist socialism. Hence, the prevailing motif after the invasion and, in many ways, the reason for the invasion itself has been not only "Russky Go Home," but, more precisely, "Leniny Go Home."

APPENDIX

Survey No. 1 was taken on July 13 and 14, 1968, by 250 professional polltakers. It covered the whole territory of the Czechoslovak Republic and was based on a representative sample of the Czechoslovak population over 18 years of age. Analyzed were the answers of the 1,772 respondents for the Czechoslovak Republic; 1,306 for the Czechlands, and 466 for Slovakia.

---

*N. P. Ogaryev (1815-70) and P. N. Tkachyev (1844-86) were the two Russian revolutionaries who gave Lenin ideas on party organization and discipline and also on the role of the Party as the vanguard of the masses. See S. V. Utechin, Russian Political Thought—A Concise History (New York: Praeger, 1963), pp. 119-21, 124-27.

Survey No. 2 was conducted between September 14 and 16, 1968, on the whole territory of the Czechoslovak Republic by professional interviewers. A total of 1,987 citizens were asked for interviews by the method of a quota sample; 105 refused to answer, leaving 1,882 interviews conducted. The polltakers felt that 261 respondents expressed some misgiving (about the polls) and 69, fear.

Survey No. 8 the part used in this article, was conducted in April and May, 1968. A newspaper poll supplied answers of 636 non-Communists. The group of 524 Communist Party members was obtained by mail survey of individuals selected at random from the Party membership rolls. Both groups were from the Northern Czech-lands. The 139 leading secretaries were interviewed at a meeting in Prague.

Survey No. 9 the part used here, was conducted between September 16 and 22, 1968, by mail, on the basis of a representative sample of the population of Slovakia, A return of 1,182 (out of 1,400 chosen) replies was obtained: 511 in West Slovakia, 365 in North Slovakia, and 306 in East Slovakia. The respondents from Bratislava were included in the totals of West Slovakia.

Survey No. 14 was conducted between June 30 and July 10, 1968, in the whole territory of the Czechoslovak Republic. A representative sample method was used in interviews by the polltakers. The total number interviewed was 2,000 individuals and for this particular study only 297 questionnaires were selected at random.

Survey No. 16 was conducted between July 8 and 16, 1968, by two methods:

1. A quota sample of 320 respondents was interviewed by 40 polltakers. The average length of the interview was 45 to 80 minutes. The poll was conducted in the East Czech-lands, South Moravia, in the Northern Czech-lands, and partially in Prague and Pilzen. Only 269 questionnaires were used in the final study, with no explanation for the exclusion of the rest.

2. Five hundred addresses were selected from the citizens' rolls for the Czech-lands (Moravia and Bohemia) by a random method (roughly every thirty-thousandth citizen). The poll was conducted by mail with a 56 percent return and a final reduction to 43.6 percent or 218 questionnaires owing to incompletes, errors, etc.

The results of both methods were combined in the final analysis, giving a sample of 487 respondents.

2

Hana Benesova

A number of attempts have been made to identify the forces that in the spring of 1968 led to the liberalization and democratization movement in Czechoslovakia.[1] Practically all were characterized by the emphasis they placed on the role of Czech and Slovak writers whose contribution was important because their appeal was directed not only to the minds but also to the hearts of the people. Almost instinctively the literati sensed the sentiments of the masses and expressed them in a manner that could be understood by all.

BACKGROUND

The role of the Czech and Slovak writers was by no means novel. Many times in the past they had become political spokesmen for a nation struggling for freedom and national independence. They had defended the moral and spiritual foundations of their society and had stood guard over the national honor of the people, assuming the position of the nation's "living conscience."[2] During World War I the writers and poets raised their voices on behalf of the nation and declared themselves in favor of national independence. In their famous Manifesto of May, 1917, addressed to the Czech deputies in Vienna, they requested that the deputies give full support to the liberation movement of Tomas G. Masaryk.[3]

At the time of the 1938 Munich disaster and its even more tragic aftermath, the writers upheld the flame of national consciousness and many gave their lives for the cause of their people in Nazi concentration camps. Even though after 1945 some succumbed to the mirage of Soviet-type "socialism," the writers were the first to revolt against the totalitarian forms of Stalinist conformity. They took a resolute stand against the neo-Stalinist regime of Antonin Novotny, and in 1968 they gave full support to the reform movement led by Alexander Dubcek. The overwhelming majority of the people backed their endeavors, sensing that the writers alone would be capable of giving meaning to Dubcek's "socialist society with a human face."

The struggle of the writers for such a society started as early as 1956 at the Second Congress of the Union of Czechoslovak Writers. Almost subconsciously the younger generation of authors, who came to the fore in the 1950's, began to return to the permanent values of the Czech literary culture of the nineteenth and twentieth centuries. They divorced their writing and poetry from Soviet dogma, proving that "the spring" of Czech and Slovak literature "after the long winter of Communism" could not be too remote.[4] In 1958 Josef Skvorecky's novel Zbabelci (The Cowards) abandoned the precepts of "socialist realism" and returned to the traditional values of Czech realism. Skvorecky delved into the psychological conditions of the post-1945 period of "liberation" during which the Czechs and Slovaks were suddenly thrown into the maelstrom of two competing ideologies. He exploded the Communist-sponsored myth about the role of the Red Army and the heroic behavior of the predominantly Communist partisans and liberators. The publication of The Cowards was of symbolic significance. It infuriated the cultural propagandists of the Communist Party, and they took harsh action not only against the author, treating him as a person afflicted by a dangerous disease, but also against the director of the publishing house.*

But the disease continued to spread and, in the period of cultural thaw inaugurated by Khrushchev's more liberal policies, the Prague neo-Stalinist manipulators of culture could not return to their past practices. Lacking direct instructions from the Soviet Union, the Czech and Slovak publishing houses began to put out works, both domestic and foreign, that only a few years ago would have been regarded as unacceptable. The books of Karel Capek, the outstanding Czech writer of the twentieth century—which until 1953 were rejected as "bourgeois" and harmful to Communism—were not only republished but also analyzed and extolled by literary critics. Liberalizing and

------

*His book was confiscated and reappeared slightly changed in 1963.

humanizing tendencies were expressed in the literary and cultural monthly Kveten (May), which provided at least a temporary platform for a group of young writers whose works the regime-dominated literary reviews refused to publish. In June, 1959, Kveten and the relatively orthodox Novy zivot (New Life), which was the organ of the Writers' Union, were suspended and subsequently replaced by a new literary magazine, Plamen (The Flame), which was to infuse "a more crystalized ideological line" into literary production. Yet the neo-Stalinist offensive was not entirely successful. It failed to snuff out what the regime referred to as the "literary snobbism" of readers who wished to read the books of non-Communist authors and those of the pre-Communist period—works regarded as "bourgeois" by the regime. Despite the police methods of the government, young writers managed to escape the probing eyes of the censors. They started reading circles that met in private homes and maintained the spirit of the Second Writers' Congress. Nor did the repression affect the activities of a number of small theaters which, after 1958, began to emerge in Prague and other Czech and Slovak cities, foreshadowing the beginning of the so-called abstract theater for which Prague became famous after 1963.

The writers took an important part in the de-Stalinization drive that started in September, 1963. Despite repressive actions and petty interferences by the regime, they clamored for more freedom and insisted on the removal of the tragic consequences of the "cult of the individual." In their cultural periodicals—Literarni noviny, Plamen, Host do domu, and Kulturny zivot—they inaugurated a systematic campaign aiming at a more creative approach to the building of socialism, independence of thinking and of criticism, and the reestablishment of centuries-old Czechoslovak relations with the Western world.

The horizons of Czech and Slovak literary life were greatly extended. The writers no longer were forced to seek inspiration in the remote history of their nation or in the lurid experiences of World War II. They began to depict with great skill and imagination the social reality of their country and the problems of modern society common to all nations. In fact, in almost all fields of cultural and artistic activity the Czechs and Slovaks once again had something to offer to the world.[5]

Of course, works of literary value do not appear overnight; they require a long period of growth and fermentation. Nevertheless, a number of Czech and Slovak writers overcame the handicap caused by years of cultural isolation and lack of freedom. They produced literary works whose main quality was their humane and universally valid message. Vaclav Havel, a young dramatist, put his finger on

one of the basic problems plaguing not only Communist, but also other
societies of the world. His first play, Zahradni slavnost (Garden
Party) in 1964 introduced a new genre referred to as "the theater of
the absurd." In it Havel aimed at shocking the audience by revealing
the senselessness and inhumanity of life that had dwindled to a meaningless bureaucratic ritual. The author proved that life in a communist
society in no way prevented him from drawing upon the inexhaustible
sources of European literary heritage. As pointed out by Petr Den,
the exiled Czech essayist and literary critic, "Havel's play is not
really absurd but neo-realistic," its main characteristic being the
description of the "liquidation of Communism as a revolutionary
movement."6 In reviewing Havel's second play, Vyrozumneni (The
Memorandum, 1966), Petr Den concluded that "for the Communist
society Havel plays the same role as Beaumarchais for the declining
aristocracy of the 18th century."7 Another non-Communist opponent
of socialist realism was Bohumil Hrabal, a lawyer who for more than
ten years was forced to work as a manual laborer. Despite his natu-
ralistic and almost cynical tendencies, Hrabal's writings are an outcry
against the crudeness and vulgarity of contemporary life. He became
famous in the West as the author of Ostre sledovane vlaky (Closely
Watched Trains, 1967), from which a scenario for an Oscar-winning
film was created.

Not surprisingly, a number of at least nominal Communists also
joined the ranks of rebelling writers. Among them Ludvik Vaculik,
Milan Kundera, Ivan Klima, and A. K. Liem were most prominent.
Their writings betray bitter disappointment with Communism and its
disastrous effects on the life of the people. Representative of this
trend was the novel Sekyra (The Hatchet) written in 1966 by Ludvik
Vaculik, a former newspaperman. The book deals with the "deforma-
tion" of ideology and character caused by orthodox Communism.
Especially successful was Vaculik's sensitive and highly critical
analysis of the "socialization" of his native eastern Moravia (Valassko).
The Party bosses, Vaculik emphasized, proved incapable of understanding the feelings of the country folk—their close relationship to
the soil, and their aversion to Party dogma. The hero of the novel, a
Prague newspaperman, is Vaculik himself. He accepted his political
and personal coresponsibility for the tragic alienation of the people
from society and sought the solution of their plight in a return to the
traditional moral values of the past.

Milan Kundera wrote early in 1967 a novel entitled Zert (The
Joke) depicting human tragedies in the period of Stalinism. "The
joke" consisted of three ill-advised words written by the novel's
hero, then a student and dedicated Communist, on a postcard to his

girl. "Jokingly," the correspondent referred to himself as a "Trotsky-ite." This "crime" landed him in an army penal unit. His tragic plight was used by the author to depict the barren dogmatism and inhumanity of the regime. In the end the hero voiced his disillusionment with Communism, which now appeared to him to be nothing but a tragic error.

New literary periodicals also reflected and, to a considerable degree, exceeded the cultural fermentation within the Czech and Slovak literary communities. Since the middle of 1963 the Union of Czecho-slovak Writers had published the literary review Tvar (The Face), whose board of editors included those who contributed to the banned review Kveten. Increased literary activity was accompanied by the reestablishment of connections with the Western world. This was most evident in the enormous increase in translations from Western literatures and in the staging of a great number of Western plays.[8]

Being unable to suppress the anti-Stalinist intellectual movement, the KSC (Czechoslovak Communist Party) leadership assumed a defen-sive position, hoping that it might be able to hold the mounting dissent within bounds and gain time for a counteroffensive. It was clear, how-ever, that the Party was unwilling to assist passively the growth of intellectual and literary opposition. The duel between the writers and the Party continued, and at the end of 1965 began to assume ominous overtones. The regime's change of attitude resulted in the sudden banning of Tvar, allegedly because of its antisocialist tendencies. This action was protested in a public letter addressed to the KSC leadership by more than 300 Czech and Slovak writers.

By 1966 Czech and Slovak literature had all that was necessary for further development. In talent, determination of purpose, original-ity, and sophistication it could hold its own in competition with other world literatures.[9] This fact greatly contributed to the feeling of frustration over those restrictive policies of the regime that prevented the Czech and Slovak literatures from becoming a permanent and inte-gral part of European culture. It was then that the writers turned their attention to the overall conditions of the society in which they lived. They opened the pages of their periodicals to articles by econ-omists, philosophers, and political writers, hoping to inspire a national revival. Responding to the wishes of the democratically minded majority of the nation, they began to return to the traditions of prewar Czechoslovakia, with its atmosphere of freedom and human happiness, and its sense of social justice.

Alarmed over such developments, Novotny spoke harshly about
the writers at the Thirteenth Party Congress in the spring of 1966.
He warned against "the writings of certain cultural magazines which
were false and foreign to socialism" and urged the Party to increase
its vigilance against cultural subversion.[10] In midsummer of 1966 the
writer Jan Benes and the film director Karel Zamecnik were arrested,
the former because of his initiative in preparing the letter dispatched
to Moscow protesting the cruel punishment meted out to Sinyavski and
Daniel. A number of other measures bore witness to the stepped-up
ideological campaign against the writers. Control over all cultural
matters was entrusted to the newly created ministerial post of culture
and Karel Hoffmann, a close associate of Novotny, was appointed to
this position.

1967 FOURTH CONGRESS OF WRITERS

For a variety of reasons the 1967 Fourth Congress of Writers
was destined to become an important landmark in post-1948 history.
It was the precursor of the momentous events which now are generally
referred to as the "Czechoslovak Spring." Characteristic of the period
preceding the congress was the writing in the literary periodicals,
especially Literarni noviny, which disregarded all the regime's pro-
hibitions and dealt frankly with basic issues having a bearing on the
spiritual and intellectual life of the nation. The great majority of the
writers, including those who were KSC members, became entirely
alienated from the Party, its methods, and even its aims. What took
place was an ever-increasing congruence of the ideas and thinking of
the intellectual elite and the disillusioned masses of the nation.

Much has been written in the last two years about the congress
that met in Prague between June 27 and 29, 1967. At first little was
known about its dramatic proceedings and the speeches delivered
there. This lack of information was due to the endeavor of the KSC
to suppress news about events that, because of their liberal character,
by far exceeded the limits of Communist gatherings.[11] The representatives of the Czechoslovak literary community originally did not plan
to stage what their orthodox Party opponents later labeled as "cultural
conspiracy."[12] The working paper, which was to serve as the basis
for the congressional discussion, while critical of the post-1948
Czechoslovak cultural policies, paid more than lip service to the
importance of the Great October Socialist Revolution, the writings of
Lenin, and the struggle raging in a divided world.[13] But the fact that
the writers attempted to combine loyalty to the regime with absolute
autonomy in cultural affairs and insisted on a free and critical

discussion of the fundamental problems of Czechoslovak literary life, infuriated the narrow-minded cultural apparatchiki of the KSC.

The tone of the congress was set by the first speaker, Milan Kundera, who noted the disastrous consequences of the Nazi and Stalinist interruptions of Czech literary traditions. "The Czech nation," Kundera stated, "was again in danger of being relegated to the cultural periphery of Europe."[14] It was the militant speech of the Party Presidium and KSC Secretariat member, Jiri Hendrych, that called forth a wave of indignation among the writers. He combined a clumsy defense of the Party mistakes with an attack against the writers. Identifying their humanism with political reaction, he insisted that they should accept "class approach" as the main criterion of all literary and cultural activities.

None of the leading writers paid any attention to the "admonitions" of the Party dignitary. The congressional discussion became the first public analysis of the main issues of Czech and Slovak literature. The reading of the famous letter of Alexander Solzhenitzyn, which was suppressed in the Soviet Union, was received with great applause. One after another, the writers attacked the oppressive tactics of the KSC used against all cultural and literary activities. Most prominent— because of its firm logic, directness, and honesty—was the speech of Ludvik Vaculik. He addressed himself to the burning issue of Communism, namely that of power. Paraphrasing Lord Acton, Vaculik stated: "Power affects the ruled and the rulers and endangers the health of both."[15] He declared himself in favor of checks and balances that would limit the unmitigated exercise of power. The existence of such regulations—and Vaculik used the term "rules of procedure"—is particularly important in a socialist state. "If the government is allowed to stand permanently, the citizens will suffer." Not all will lose their lives, but the fall of many will be "followed by the relapse of perhaps the whole nation into fear, political apathy, and civic resignation. . . ."

Then Vaculik applied his principles to Czechoslovakia, in which power had become an aim in itself—a "self-perpetuating institution" subverting the fundamental rights of citizens. The strongest passage in Vaculik's address was his discussion of the interwar democratic Czechoslovakia. Its creation, he stated, "was one of the partial successes on the way toward the probably unobtainable dream of a state which would be identical with its citizens." Having thus assessed the achievements of the democratic Republic, Vaculik turned his attention to Communist Czechoslovakia: "It is necessary to realize," he said, "that in our state within the last twenty years no single human problem had been solved—beginning with elementary needs, such as apartments, schools, economic prosperity, and ending with the more sophisticated demands . . . such as subordination of political decisions to ethical requirements, faith in the usefulness even of petty work, need for trust among people, and increase of the educational standards of the masses." The writer Dusan Hamsik, referring later to Vaculik's speech, observed:

> We realized that Vaculik in his novel Sekera, which ap-
> peared only a short time before the congress, dealt with a
> situation similar to the one he was speaking about at the
> congress. His hero had intentionally created a situation
> in which he cut off all avenues of escape so that he would
> be unable to do anything else but what he made up his mind
> to do. . . .16

Vaculik's speech was the expression of the "credo" of the over-whelming majority of Czech and Slovak writers in the approaching moral and political crisis of 1968. On the last day of the congress Hendrych returned to the assembly hall. He attacked the great majority of the congress speakers, especially Vaculik, for "having attempted to misuse the meeting for spreading views contrary to the interests of the people."17

PARTY RETALIATION

The Party proved strong enough to inaugurate a whole series of punitive actions against the recalcitrant writers. Vaculik, Klima, Kohout, and Havel—who were duly elected to the Central Committee of the Writers' Union—were ordered removed. The union's official organ, Literarni noviny, was forbidden to print the speeches delivered at the congress or to report on the election of the Central Committee.18 Amid rumors that even stricter censorship would be introduced, the Party staged a show trial of Jan Benes and Karel Zamecnik, who for several months had been under arrest. Together with them, Pavel Tigrid, editor of Svedectvi (The Evidence), a periodical published in Paris, was tried in absentia.* The reason for this sudden display of strength was to make clear to the writers that their liberal tendencies would not be tolerated. Novotny stepped up the attacks against them in his September 1, 1967, speech to the graduates of military

---

*Benes was sentenced to five years in prison and Zamecnik was acquitted by the court.

academies, stating that "our democracy is a class democracy and our freedom is a class freedom."[19] At the plenum of the KSC Central Committee the writers were accused of "stabbing our society in the back by the preaching of freedom, democracy, and humanism stripped of their class and socialist meanings."[20]

Public censure was followed by sanctions against the main culprits, who were denied the right to publish their works. Censorship was further intensified and finally Literarni noviny, the most influential periodical in the country, was taken away from the Writers' Union and placed under the direction of the Ministry of Culture. The punitive measures against the writers were merely rumblings before the storm that broke out at the end of 1967.

ROLE OF THE LITERATI IN POLITICAL REFORM

The persecution of the writers and their resistance played a key role in the downfall of Antonin Novotny in January, 1968. It helped to mobilize "the best minds in the Czechoslovak Socialist Republic" against his regime;[21] it gave the reform movement its impetus and moral justification and provided the cement that united the forces clamoring for social and political reform.

The political leaders of the Czechoslovak reform were members of the Communist Party, which represented the only organized political force in the country. They would have found it difficult to secure the support of the nation otherwise; the same was true to a large extent of the economic reformers. While everyone recognized the necessity for changes in the economic system, very few people could understand the complexities of the proposals of Ota Sik and his coworkers. Only the writers were able to gain the confidence and understanding of the people. It was to their credit that liberalization, which might have resulted in a more lenient "participatory" autocracy, acquired the characteristics of a democratic movement. In their writings the literati spoke on behalf of the nation: They managed to capture its mood, helped to dispel the two decades of fear, and were able to break through the apathy paralyzing the workers.

Yet the emergence of writers and their organizations as an important element in the public life of Czechoslovakia was only a gradual process—as gradual as the liberalization itself. The first action was taken at the end of January, 1968, when the Central Committee of the Writers' Union met and elected its functionaries. The selection of Eduard Goldstucker, the Kafka expert and literary critic,

as president was the result of a compromise. The same could be said
of the fact that of the 1967 "rebels" only Milan Kundera and Jan
Prochazka became members of the Central Committee. Its decisions,
however, were much more revolutionary. It declared that "by its
work it wants to contribute to the process of the democratization of
Czechoslovak society and for that purpose to renew the publication of
its weekly review under the name of Literarni listy (Literary Papers)."[22] The new president indicated that the immediate tasks of
the Union would be the assessment of the 1967 congress and the review
of the current press law from the point of view of the freedom of the
press.

Step by step the Writers' Union asserted its moral leadership in
the nation. It took a number of measures aimed at the elimination
of the last vestiges of Stalinism from the public life of Czechoslovakia.
It requested the National Assembly to appoint a committee to deal with
the clearing of the innocent victims of political terror and created,
under the chairmanship of the poet Jaroslav Seifert, a similar commission to take up the rehabilitation of writers who had suffered political persecution in the last twenty years. This immense task was
performed with great determination. Some victims, such as the
publicist Zavis Kalandra, who was executed in 1950, or Jan
Zahradnicek, who died shortly after his release from prison in 1960,
could be cleared only posthumously.

The first issue of Literarni listy appeared on February 22, 1968,
under the same editorial board as its predecessor Literarni noviny.
At the end of March the first plenary session of the Czech members
of the Writers' Union took place. The discussion at the meeting was
absolutely free and resulted in a number of interesting statements
and proposals. Jan Benes, who had been released from prison,
stressed the duty of the writers to establish contacts with the people;
some members of the union came very near to what could be described
as self-criticism (Jan Drda), and others called for an extraordinary
conference of the union which would democratize its rules of procedure
and the manner in which new members would be admitted (Vaclav
Havel). The renewal of the banned review Tvar was also requested.
Of special importance was the announcement of twenty members of the
union that they had founded a "Circle of Independent Writers," uniting
those who were not members of the KSC.

Literarni listy stood throughout 1968 in the forefront of the
democratization movement, taking up the cause of all those who were
wronged by the Stalinist practices of the previous regime. Gradually
it became a general forum for all issues having a bearing on the

protection of human and civil rights and the defense of the principle of freedom and decency in the public life of the country. Typical of its interests was the notice relating to two University of Warsaw professors, Bronislaw Baczko and Leszek Kolakowski, who were expelled from their teaching positions by the Gomulka regime. They were invited to lecture at Charles University so that "they would be able freely to develop and spread their progressive socialist views."

Inter arma silent musae! Despite this feverish activity, which helped to forge "the Czechoslovak way to socialism," the writers had little time left for actual literary work. They fought against those who stood in the way of progress toward greater freedom, and took a prominent part in the dialogue between the liberal reformers and the dwindling group of their orthodox opponents, discussing the essence of democracy and socialism, the meaning of true freedom, and the mission of the writers. In their literary periodicals the literati guided the public life of their nation along three fundamental concepts: return to the old traditions of Czech and Slovak spiritual and intellectual life, genuine patriotism, and uncompromising defense of democracy and humanitarianism. Their main weapons were essays and short articles dealing with the ideology and day-to-day developments of the democratization process. Literarni listy increased its volume and was printed in several hundred thousand copies. Voices were heard requesting that it be changed into a daily newspaper.

The first task was the reestablishment of the continuity of Czechoslovak cultural and literary life. Whenever strictly literary matters were discussed, the works of the nineteenth- and twentieth-century classical writers served as the decisive criteria. Men who in the period of Stalinism had been condemned to oblivion, such as Josef Palivec and the exiled writers, Egon Hostovsky and Jan Cep, were fully rehabilitated. Above all, the writers returned to Tomas Garrigue Masaryk, the President-Liberator of Czechoslovakia, whom they recognized as the main source of the internal strength, national self-confidence, and belief in the future of the Czech and Slovak nations. Typical was the statement of the writer Alexander Kliment. When asked about the direction the writers should follow, he said:

> The social problem—the "Czech Question"—the relationship of Russia to Europe—problems of a small nation—humanitarian ideals—methods of work. These issues were placed by T. G. Masaryk into the foundation of our independence. It is from them that we must start our work.[23]

At the beginning of the liberalization process a number of leading authors changed almost overnight into political polemicists, stating in plain language thoughts that before they had been allowed to express only indirectly in their literary works. Thus Vaclav Havel, whose plays demonstrated the monstrosity of the Communist system, participated in the discussion of the freedom of political organization. Attacking the half-baked concepts of those who envisaged political pluralism within the confines of KSC, Havel spoke in favor of the reestablishment of the political practices of prewar Czechoslovakia. He expressed himself quite unequivocally against the political monopoly of the Communist Party and in favor of political opposition:

> Very often a strong and specifically Czechoslovak demo-
> cratic and humanitarian tradition is being emphasized. At
> the same time people forget what this really means: it
> means that in our society there are many people who are
> inclined toward a genuinely democratic and humanitarian
> viewpoint but take no part in political life . . . especially
> because for them the political practice of KSC is not suffi-
> ciently democratic and humanistic.[24]

For these people Havel claimed the right to organize an independent political party. He rejected the idea that the nation should be viewed "through the eyes of the February conflict" and declared himself in favor of reconciliation with the post-1948 non-Communist and anti-Communist exiles who, according to the U.N. Declaration on Human Rights, had committed no crime.

Another writer, Ivan Klima, devoted his interest to the analysis of the essence of socialism and approached it from the point of view of modern democracy. He attacked the very substance of Communism by questioning the assumption "that socialism was the best social system ever put into effect by man." He emphasized its ever-recurring "deformations" and insisted that they cannot be explained in terms of the imperfections of man. "Does not the root of the tragedy lie in the 'socialist project' itself?" While Klima did not speak expressly for political pluralism, he attacked the idea of "false unity." Unity, he stated, was necessary only in times of crises, which are only transitional:

> As long as there is no real danger, this false unity, the
> unity of careerists and morally unstable people with nor-
> mal and honest people, the unity of the indifferent with the
> committed, of the conservative with the progressive, can-
> not but demoralize, dissipate, bring to a standstill any
> social progress and any development in any community.[25]

Another voice was that of Zora Jesenska, a well-known Slovak woman writer. Warning against the misuse of the word "democratization" by the introduction of some form of sham democracy, this prewar Communist defined democracy in its Western sense. It is, she stated, a rule of the majority over the minority, which at the same time provides for the protection of the minority from the arbitary and tyrannical rule of the majority. Democracy cannot exist without "societies, associations and clubs whose origins are free and spontaneous." Jesenska sharply criticized the dissolution of "all kinds of organizations and interest associations" after February, 1948.[26] These and similar opinions were the subject of public discussions in which a large number of writers took a prominent part. The Circle of Independent Writers, by its declaration of July 6, 1968, embraced the program of pluralism with regard to writers' organizations.

The authors were the first to abandon the dubious concept of "proletarian internationalism" in favor of true patriotism. Return to national traditions and expression of loyalty to the great men of the Czech and Slovak past was one way by which the writers demonstrated their loyalty to their people. The most eloquent expression of patriotism was the insistence on Czechoslovak independence—both political and spiritual—from the Soviet Union and its ruling party. Jan Prochazka, writing on the special Czechoslovak road to socialism, stated almost prophetically that "no one can foresee what awaits us in the future." He warned that "small nations should not idealize any of the large and highly centralized powers." Addressing himself to the Soviet Union, he insisted that "socialism does not necessarily require nations to be mere followers." For "even to Rome—as is known—there is more than one road."[27]

The same fear motivated the writer Pavel Kohout, who stated that "the second largest power ruthlessly defends its interests and begins its defense ten thousand kilometres from its borders." Referring to the relations of Czechoslovakia with the Soviet Union, Kohout stated that "each meeting that appears to be a meeting about us takes place without our representatives being present."[28] Later, when a regular discussion developed between the Soviet and Czechoslovak press, the Czech and Slovak writers defended their government and people. Typical of this dialogue was a short article written by Milan Jungmann and published under the meaningful title "Lost Illusions." It appeared after the meeting of the Warsaw Pact powers and voiced disappointment with their decision. Not only "their conception of friendly cooperation," Jungmann wrote, but also the continuously repeated word internationalism were "in deep crisis."[29]

Once again, Czech writers assumed the time-honored role of the previous generations of Czech literati. They acted as the "living conscience" of their nation. In a situation in which the KSC began to falter and vacillate, fearing the consequences of its defiance of the dictates of the "brotherly" workers' parties, Ludvik Vaculik wrote the now famous "Manifesto of Two Thousand Words" (also called "2,000 words"). This was a unique document in its content, in its moral indignation, and in its solemn form. It mercilessly criticized the KSC for having changed from a reform movement into an organization that "exchanged the confidence of the people for the control of offices." Having taken control of the government apparatus, "it had nothing else left." Beginning in January, 1968, the Party made a serious attempt to return to its former ideals by adopting a program of liberalization and democratization. Unfortunately, this process had not been unanimously accepted, and so it appeared that the regeneration process had been arrested. In order to stop this ominous development, the "Manifesto" submitted to the Party a number of demands. Of these the most important one was the insistence that the Dubcek regime not allow itself to be intimidated by the interference of foreign forces into internal affairs.

"The Manifesto of Two Thousand Words"—which subsequently was declared to be a reactionary document attacking the very existence of the people's government—was welcomed by the writers and printed in the Literarni listy of June 27. It was subscribed to by a large number of Czech writers and thousands of others, including the foremost representatives of the national life. On the eve of the meeting between the representatives of the KSC and the CPSU (Communist Party of the Soviet Union) at Cierna and Tisou, Literarni listy brought another appeal of citizens to the Central Committee of the Czechoslovak Communist Party. It asked the Czechoslovak delegation to insist on a program that was expressed in four words—socialism, alliance, sovereignty, and freedom. "Negotiate and explain, but remain united and make no concessions in your defense of the road which we have chosen and which we shall not abandon alive."[30]

REACTION TO THE INVASION

Only a handful of Czech and Slovak writers, who in the past had been the most enthusiastic friends of "Slavonic Russia," visualized the possibility of an invasion. When it came, its utter brutality struck them as a bolt of lightning and caused them to shrink in horror. On August 26, the Union of Czechoslovak Writers issued a proclamation in which it accused the Soviet Union of "returning to the tried and tested traditions of Cossack diplomacy." The Soviet Union was described as "retrograde and Fascist-like, unworthy of the right to play a leading role in the international Communist movement." But, the declaration emphasized, "armies of tanks cannot suppress the yearning of nations for freedom; ideas cannot be shot. . . ."[31]

The next day Rude pravo, the official mouthpiece of the KSC, published a statement by Jan Drda, a writer who, with full justification, had acquired a reputation as the most pliable tool of Communism and its representative, the Soviet Union. What he wrote was a bitter condemnation of the Soviet act of violence:

> The pen is shaking in my hand, my voice is breaking. For 45 years I have taught children to love the Soviet Union, to regard Moscow as the guarantee of our national and state independence. All this now lies in ruins . . . . The number of crimes committed in these days in the streets of Prague call to high heaven . . . . They have given rise to something dreadful in our hearts: hatred against ruse and betrayal, the burning sentiment of humiliation, the unextinguishable flame of hate. . . ."[32]

Even more eloquent was the unsigned poem printed in Literarni listy of August 22:

> So you are here . . . . Welcome!
> Welcome, summer guests
> from the depths of frost
> be welcome
> according to the old custom
> with a shield of bread
> with this crystal of tear-producing salt
> which corrodes everything that fell from heaven.
> Welcome in a tender embrace
> in which bones crack,
> blood soaks
> from the fruit
> as the sunlight fades.
> And again
> deaf-mutes with deaf-mutes.
> And again aspens
> aspens which tremble
> with the simple thought of Judas.
> At dawn a rooster roared.
> I deny that I ever knew you.
> I deny the second time,
> the third time.[33]

Soon after the occupation the Writers' Union paper, <u>Literarni</u> <u>listy</u>, was discontinued in protest against the Soviet act of violence. When it reappeared, in November, 1968, under the simple title <u>Listy</u> (<u>Papers</u>), the Czech writers proved that they had not changed their views. Jaroslav Seifert paid special attention to those of his colleagues who had left the country. He claimed that every author had the right "alone to decide whither he wants to take his pen and his writing pad." He stated that the decision of those who left the country must be respected: "We trust that they will return. And we shall welcome them with open arms." Turning to the political situation Seifert said: "It was promised and guaranteed to us that nobody will interfere with our internal affairs. It doesn't seem that this promise was really meant. For us, writers, there is no other way . . . . After what we have lived through since January no return is possible. We want and must speak up . . . . We cannot and will not lie. . . ."[34]

The increased book production at the beginning of 1969, which emphasized the works of those writers who had been persecuted, imprisoned, or silenced for their opinions, bore witness to the steadfastness of the Czech writers and poets. They endeavored to confirm their determination to have faith in the power of truth, "the truth of freedom and decency, the truth of reason, the truth of all of us, the truth that makes a man a human being. . . ."[35]

Nor did the Czech writers sever the renewed relations with their colleagues and friends who had gone into exile after the February, 1948, coup. In the early months of 1969 the Memorial of National Literature, which is located in the ancient Strahov monastery in Prague, organized an exhibition of Czech literature in "exile." It was welcomed with great enthusiasm despite the intervention of the regime, which tried to eliminate some of the more radically "anti-Communist" writers. This attempt was only partially successful. The books that were found objectionable were placed behind the locked glass doors of bookcases, so that they could be seen by all visitors. Other works, especially those of Egon Hostovsky (now living in New York) and Jan Cep (residing in Paris), were fully exposed to the view of the public. The exhibition was given the meaningful title "Navraty" ("Returns").

It is too early to assess the degree to which Czech writers and their Slovak colleagues, who are now organized in a separate union, will find strength to remain faithful to the promise made on their behalf by the poet Jaroslav Seifert. A new period of darkness has descended upon the Czechs and Slovaks and their cultural and literary life. Again a wall has been erected to separate them from contacts

with the outside world. The fact, however, that at this moment a
number of literary periodicals, including the mouthpiece of the Writers'
Union, Listy, and the leading magazine Plamen have been banned is
an indication that the writers have not given up.

NOTES

1. A number of books and pamphlets on the "Czechoslovak
Spring" have appeared and others will appear within a short period of
time. Perhaps most successful are: Pavel Tigrid, Le printempts de
Prague (Paris: Editions du Seuil, 1968); the 1969 edition of the Paris
periodical Svedectvi (The Evidence), IX., Nos. 34-36, which present
in a systematic fashion documents and commentaries relating to the
1968 events in Czechoslovakia; Aspects of Intellectual Ferment and
Dissent in Czechoslovakia, prepared by Dr. Joseph G. Whelan for the
Internal Security Subcommittee of the Senate Judiciary Committee,
91st Cong., 1st Sess. (Washington: U.S. Government Printing Office,
1969); Pavel Kohout, Tagebuch eines Konterrevolutionars (Lucerne:
Bucher Verlag, 1969); Premysl Pitter, Geistige Revolution im Herzen
Europa's (Zurich: Rotapfel Verlag, 1968) approaches the events in
Czechoslovakia from the point of view of the spiritual traditions of
the Czechs. Other volumes worth mentioning are: Z. A. B. Zeman,
Prague Spring (London: Hill and Wang, 1968); Philip Windsor and
Adam Roberts, Czechoslovakia 1968: Reform, Repression and Resis-
tance (London: Columbia University Press for the Institute of Stra-
tegic Studies, 1969); Viva Dubcek: Reform und Okkupation in der
CSSR (Cologne: Kiepaenheuer und Witsch, 1968); Harry Schwartz,
Prague's 200 Days, (New York: Praeger, 1969).

2. The importance of writers for the very existence of the Czech
nation was best expressed by the great historian and political leader
of the nation, Frantisek Palacky. In his speech in Svatobor (Journal
of the Writers' Relief Association) of November 27, 1864, he stated:
"It is generally recognized that it was the Czech writers who prevented
the extermination of the nation, revived it to new life, and gave noble
aims to its endeavors." See Dr. Bohus Rieger et al., eds., Palackeho
spisy drobne (Collection of Palacky's Short Works), 3 vols, (Prague:
Bursik a Kohout, 1968), Vol. I, Spisy a reci z oboru politiky (Political
Speeches and Writings), p. 204.

3. See Cyril Merhout, Dokumenty naseho osvobozeni (Documents
Relating to Our Liberation) (Prague: Bedrich Koci, 1919), pp. 47-53.

4. Ladislav Radimsky, Rub a lic naseho narodniho programu v atomovem veku (Two Aspects of Our National Program in the Atomic Age) (Rome: Krestanska akademie, 1959), p. 140. Among those mentioned by Radimsky were Miroslav Holub, Milan Uhde, and Milan Kundera, all of whom played an important role in the 1968 crisis.

5. John Dornberg, "The Nettles of Prague," The Nation 206, No. 2 (January 8, 1968), 50.

6. Promeny (Metamorphoses) II, No. 1 (January, 1965), 57.

7. Promeny II, No. 2 (April, 1966), 64.

8. A listing of novels translated from English can be found in the official Czechoslovak Life of June, 1968. Leading American authors like Ernest Hemingway, William Faulkner, J. D. Salinger and many others are included. American playwrights such as Arthur Miller, Edward Albee, and Tennessee Williams were staged in Czechoslovakia much earlier. See The Atlantic Report: Czechoslovakia 214 (November, 1964), p. 12.

9. See Pavel Tigrid, "Frost and Thaw: Literature in Czechoslovakia" East Europe XV, No. 9 (September, 1966), 10.

10. East Europe XV, No. 7 (July, 1966), 43.

11. The most elaborate discussion of the congress and its repercussions can be found in Svedectvi, Nos. 32-33 (Autumn-Winter, 1967) entitled "Czechoslovak Summer 1967." In 1968 the proceedings of the fourth congress were published under the title IV. Sjezd Svazu ceskoslovenskych spisovatelu. Praha 27-29. cervna 1967 (IVth Congress of the Union of Czechoslovak Writers. Prague 27-29 June, 1967) (Prague: Ceskoslovensky spisovatel, 1968).

12. See Dusan Hamsik, Spisovatele a moc (The Writers and Power) (Prague: Ceskoslovensky spisovatel, 1969), p. 62.

13. The working paper was published under the title "The Draft of the Point of View of the Central Committee of the Union of Czechoslovak Writers on Certain Questions of Czechoslovak Literature" in IV. Sjezd Svazu ceskoslovenskych spisovatelu. Praha 27-29. cervna 1967, op. cit., pp. 7-13.

14. Ibid., pp. 24-25.

15. The quotations from Vaculik's speech are taken from ibid., pp. 141-51.

16. Dusan Hamsik, Spisovatele a moc, op. cit., p. 96.

17. IV. Sjezd Svazu ceskoslovenskych spisovatelu. Praha 27-29. cervna 1967, op, cit., p. 169.

18. Dusan Hamsik described the long negotiations with the organs of the Central Publications' Administration (censorship office) which tried to force the individual writers to accept far-reaching changes in what they actually said. When this attempt failed the censorship forbade the publication of the speeches. They came out only in 1968. Spisovatele a moc, op. cit., pp. 89-111.

19. Rude pravo, September 2, 1967.

20. Dornberg, op. cit., p. 51.

21. Radoslav Selucky, Reformmodell CSSR—Entwurf einer sozialistischen Marktwirtschaft oder Gefahr fur die Volksdemokratien (Reinbeck bei Hamburg: Rowolt Taschenbuch Verlag, 1969), p. 70.

22. "Ceskoslovensko 1968. Dokumenty a komentare," Svedectvi IX, Nos. 34-36.

23. Literarni listy I, No. 1 (March 1, 1968).

24. Literarni listy No. 6 (April 25, 1968).

25. Literarni listy I, No. 9 (April 25, 1968).

26. Zora Jesenska, "The Rights of the Citizens," Kulturny zivot, May 4, 1968.

27. Jan Prochazka, "Nase cesta" ("Our Way"), Literarni listy I, No. 9 (May, 1968).

28. Pavel Kohout, "Obcane—a co ted" ("Citizen—and What Now?"), Literarni listy I, No. 12 (May 16, 1968).

29. Literarni listy I, No. 21 (July 18, 1968).

30. Literarni listy I, Special Edition (July 26, 1968).

31. Rude pravo, August 27, 1968.

32. Rude pravo, August 28, 1969.

33. The English translation of the poem is by Jane Tracy, a graduate student in the Indiana University Department of Slavic Languages and Literatures.

34. Listy I, No. 1 (November 7, 1968).

35. This was the pledge made in the farewell issue of the Literarni listy of August 22, 1968 (special edition).

3

CRISIS
OF
THE
EUROPEAN LEFT

Ivan Svitak

"If you enter a dark room and ask 'Is someone
there?', the eventual answer 'No, no one is
here', would confirm just the opposite of what
was said in reply."
(From a textbook of semantics)

During the night of August 21, 1968, Soviet tanks entered a small
country of Central Europe. All that was said by the late-night visitors
was in contradiction to the reality of invasion, occupation, and aggression, most particularly their statement (which they continue to reit-
erate) that their military action would not interfere with sovereignty
of Czechoslovakia, but, on the contrary, would strengthen that country's sovereignty. A naive man under attack may accept the aggressor's reassurance until the moment when he recognizes his mistake;
in any case, it is difficult for anyone to believe words about nonviolence
when he finds himself at gunpoint. The gun speaks for itself and is
a stronger argument than words. The government of an attacked country which repeats the aggressor's words—"No, no one is here" —and
does not protest against the liquidation of its own sovereignty and
the violation of international agreements is just as naive as those
neighbors who observe the scene dispassionately, satisfied with the
aggressor's assurance that he is really not what, in fact, he appears
to be: a threat to the whole of Europe.

Ideologies that attempt to justify the aggression are false; the
reality of aggression is true. The Brezhnev doctrine, openly publicized

in the Soviet press, provides the Soviet Union with the right to intervene in countries of the socialist bloc, legitimizes the imposition of
the Soviet will upon occupied countries, and violates the basic rules
of international law. Further, the Brezhnev doctrine implies a threat
to West Germany in its assertion that the rights of the victor of World
War II include the right to intervene so long as a peace treaty with
Germany has not been concluded. The overt threat of force, the violation of the United Nations Charter and the Soviet behavior in general
are incompatible with international law and represent an obvious,
though undeclared, challenge to the entire Western world. The
Brezhnev doctrine is a doctrine of Soviet imperialism.

DEFEAT OF THE LEFT

The Soviet intervention in Czechoslovakia marks the defeat of
democratic socialism in Europe for a whole generation to come, and
portends the failure of the humanistic version of Marxist theory
applied by Yugoslavia. In short, it represents a defeat for the
European Left that cannot be retrieved for the next decade. Europe
is directly threatened by the fact that its western and eastern parts
are in decline and have become a buffer zone between the two superpowers. Thus, the independent role of Europe in world affairs is becoming less significant than the role played by some of the newly
emerged states of Africa or Latin America. The Soviet intervention
has furthered the decline of European power; within a few hours it
demolished the controversial results of the policy of bridge-building,
and destroyed the illusions about the possibility of mutual understanding entertained by liberal intellectuals of both East and West
who subscribe to the idea of humanistic socialism.

The Soviet action proved the futility of bridge-building by
showing that the other end of the bridge represents a terminus rather
than a passageway. It is possible to bridge a narrow gap, but one
cannot effectively bridge a sea. The European Left must accept the
bitter lesson of history and recognize the failure of the Yugoslav compromise version of democratic socialism. Without the acceptance of
this hard fact, no further leftist orientation in Europe is possible and
what remains is the possibility of either a rightist or anarchistic
revolt against the status quo. The recognition of defeat, however,
may carry with it the means for overcoming the defeat. This is now
the only way to challenge the Brezhnev doctrine.

From the broader point of view of world policy, the defeat of
the European Left during this year, both in Prague and Paris, is, of

course, just a peripheral phenomenon of the dangerous process of
transformation taking place in the political structures of industrial
societies in the West and the East. A tendency toward aggressiveness
in the power elites of today's superpowers is a fact that is being confirmed both in Czechoslovakia and Vietnam, and, internally, by the
victory of Fascist viewpoints in the Soviet politburo and by the victory
of rightist forces in the presidential elections in the United States.
The Soviet Union's application of the Brezhnev doctrine and the results
of the American elections suggest that a creeping conservatism endangers the political life of the big industrial societies and threatens
all humanistic values. If conservatism, with its accompanying fear,
violence, terror, and local wars, is indeed to become the political
style of the 1970's, the outlook for the European Left is dim. It is
assumed, however, that recognition of this new political reality of the
1970's will lead to a greater awareness of the necessity to defend
those basic human rights and humanistic values that the European
Left cannot, at present, protect. Radical groupings of students and
intellectuals are not now in a position to guarantee such protection
in the face of the prevailing general attitudes; their activity is limited
to spontaneous protests. The only other available choice is anarchistic
action, which easily can be checked by the police. Radical groups
eventually will realize, one hopes, that their protests do not affect
radices—the roots of the evil—but only the policemen.

The immediate consequence of the movement toward conservatism will be the weakening of the Left; in the long run, however, the
Left will be strengthened, as the experience of Vietnams and Czech-
oslovakias results in an awakening of broad masses of people who
live in the consumer inertia of industrial societies. What has sounded
highbrow to the man in the street will become real to him as soon
as he faces the danger against which intellectuals have been warning
for a long time. Until the Czechoslovak citizen faced the muzzle of
a Soviet tank, he had been unable to grasp the reality of the Soviet
totalitarian dictatorship. Now, he understands and he knows. Current
conservative trends are creating exactly what the European Left has
been lacking—a broad basis for protest on behalf of freedom and
specific human rights, and this new base represents a social force
that is stronger than the police force.

The European Left was defeated on both sides of the Elbe, in
Prague and in Paris. In both cases the losers were the intellectuals
who had sought to resolve the crisis of industrial society by promoting human rights, freedom, and socialist democracy. Perhaps
they misunderstood their adversaries—the totalitarian regimes they
were fighting—and thus behaved in a way reminiscent of the futile

attempt of the Luddites (the British rioters of the nineteenth century) to protest against capital accumulation by destroying the machines in factories. Both the European Left of today and the Luddites acted as they did because neither group included a theoretician who would be able to formulate real alternatives—as Karl Marx once did.

If one looks unemotionally at occupied Czechoslovakia, one has to conclude that the major causes of the country's defeat were the illusions entertained by leftist intellectuals—reformists who did not recognize the true nature of Soviet power and were unable to see the real face of the Soviet bureaucratic elite. The principle of force inherent in totalitarian government was able to conquer the ideal of humanism just at the crucial point when the reformist leaders proved unable to act as instruments of the popular will and to defend their country militarily. Their "democratism" must have been considered extremely naive by the commanders of Soviet tank units. One may try to sweeten this hard reality by means of such arguments as "what happened must have happened," but one can hardly conceal the lesson that the Communist Party and its reformist leaders cannot effectively spearhead popular movements for civil rights, national independence, and state sovereignty. As the dialectic of emotion can transform love into contempt when love is expressed only in emotion and not in deed, so a nation's love for its heroes becomes an ambivalent hate-love when the heroes fail in their reforms.

The Paris Left was defeated under similar circumstances; in particular, by the isolation of radical student groups, the inefficiency of Communist leaders, the lack of public support, and the absence of an adequate and theoretically sound program. Students, living at some distance from the actual production activities, could only en-courage criticism and strike movements; they were not in a position to assume responsibility for the movement, nor could they act as its leaders, for they have no clear idea of the real nature of the regime they oppose, and they are not prepared to transform the production system of that regime.

That the movement should end in a blind alley is thus inevitable, since we are all both a part of the problem and a part of its solution. What solution, then, is possible?

SOLUTIONS

"Lenin, wake up, Brezhnev has gone mad!"
(Slogan of Prague students in August, 1968)

The modern world is so small and so interconnected that a defeat of the Left in the East is at the same time a defeat of the Left in the West, and vice versa. An authentic Left movement has to isolate itself from military blocs and set itself in opposition to these blocs and to their power elites if it is not to become merely an instrument of American or Soviet power politics. If the Left does not wish to serve as apologist for the existing division of Germany, Europe, and the world, on the grounds that this arrangement represents the only alternative to war, then it must refuse to accept imperialism of any color and shade. Those intellectuals who condemn just one type of imperialism, become, in fact, an instrument of the other. In the case of Fidel Castro, this inconsistent attitude is particularly evident. Castro fully approved the Soviet occupation of Czechoslovakia, although he must have been aware that the invasion of the Warsaw Pact troops was a blatant violation of sovereignty, completely without justification from any point of view of international law. Instead, he considered the Soviet invasion to be an act of revolution in the field of international law; he defended the Soviet action in the name of revolution and approved the military occupation of Czechoslovakia. What, actually, has his decaying regime in common with the Left when he, the Stalin of Cuba, sees a Fascist act of the Soviet bureaucracy as revolutionary?

Because these were the feelings of its spiritual leader, the American Left—adoring Fidel Castro in a quite incomprehensible way—was unable even to protest, much less to undertake a concrete action. The average intellectual in American university circles responded to the Russian intervention with an obsessive examination of Soviet motivation and, in some cases, proved eager to accept the Soviet statement that Russian fear of Germany was sufficient reason for invading Czechoslovakia. He may also have felt a certain subconscious complacency over the fact that on August 21 the Russians lost the moral superiority engendered by the American intervention in Vietnam. The statement of presidential candidate Eugene McCarthy on Czechoslovakia was as misguided as Chamberlain's evaluation of Munich in 1938.

The NATO generals, having accustomed themselves to the unpredictability of Soviet behavior, did nothing, though the Soviets probably would have been impressed had they rushed a half-million soldiers to the eastern border of Germany. The only intellectual who could tell Americans that it would be better to fight at the Adriatic than at the English Channel was Milovan Djilas, of Eastern Europe. In America, only the scholar and former diplomat, George F. Kennan, who did not join in the game of analyzing Soviet motives, would propose that American armies in Europe be strengthened. Of both it can be said that they knew Russia.

The Soviet intervention revealed that the American Left and the American Right both prefer a policy of disengagement and exposed the inertia of pro-Castro intellectuals as well as of American generals. The American reaction to the Soviet intervention surprises only those members of the Left who have not understood that the desire to preserve the status quo unites the generals of the competing powers. Furthermore, one should not forget that after the Hungarian revolution in 1956 it took Khrushchev and Eisenhower only three years to arrange a meeting at Camp David. A meeting between Nixon and Kosygin and Brezhnev has been temporarily postponed, although the bureaucracies of the industrial superpowers—haunted by the specter of war—share a vital interest in maintaining the present division of power. Nixon's attempt at some sort of detente with China has, for the moment, obviated the inevitable handshake with the organizers of the invasion of Czechoslovakia.

European intellectuals of all political shades eventually will recognize that they are part of a buffer zone. Located as it is between two (or three) powers of imperialism, Europe must develop its own independent policy in order to survive. General de Gaulle understood this well, but the European Left never has. Condemnation of Soviet aggression in Czechoslovakia expressed by West European Communist parties may become a positive step towards the establishment of the European Left as a meaningful political force. In a world divided into spheres of influence, Europe has to defend itself if it wishes to avoid a fate similar to that of Eastern Europe before the end of this century. While a Soviet invasion of Western Europe may seem an impossibility today, it must be remembered that Soviet intervention appeared equally unlikely to Czechoslovakia not long ago. All leftist European intellectuals—and Communists in particular—will, therefore, have to find the courage to acknowledge that Soviet imperialism is their major enemy, and that behind the ideological wall of revolutionary slogans there is a Soviet power elite intent on aggression. The conspiracy of this Soviet power elite against nations, labor movements, and the middle class can be challenged only by effective action, as vigorous as that taken in the cause of labor and civil rights. Acceptance of this position can be seen as the primary duty of Leftist intellectuals in the West and could represent the first step toward a resurgence of the socialist movement.

Marxists of the Left know very well that contemporary socialist problems derive from a specific misinterpretation of Marx. They know that a new socialist society cannot be created by an ideology or by a revolutionary elite, but only by a popular, democratic movement in a given country. Further, any revolutionary elite that claims for itself the prerogatives of a truly democratic-socialist movement must inevitably degenerate into some form of Stalinism.

Contemporary followers of Marx recognize that history has been an evolution of various forms of alienation and that after the period of fetishism of goods, a period of fetishism of alienated institutions— totalitarian power and force—follows. The dialectics of alienation and de-alienation has taken new form in the mechanisms of absolute monopoly of ideology, totalitarian dictatorship, and bureaucratic power elite, and, as such, it represents a threat to human freedom. The history of Europe used to be a history of humanism, democracy, and socialism; if this tradition is to continue, European intellectuals on both banks of the Elbe River must reject the role of buffer zone delegated to European nations located between the two superpowers. European intellectuals must find an independent means for solving the present crisis. Those attitudes that were valid in the past have been made obsolete by the political realities of the 1970's. The stage of industrial societies is set for a conservative intermezzo that will be a prelude to a popular movement for human rights, a move- ment of much broader base than the present labor movement. Human alienation in industrial societies has already passed the point at which solution was possible through increased mass consumption. Today, alienation manifests itself in man himself, in his consciousness, and it is precisely for this reason that the present industrial society will produce greater and greater resistance despite consumer pros- perity. European intellectuals must be in the forefront of this resis- tance by virtue of their adherence to the old ideals of European culture.

The tragedies of 1968 may presage even worse tragedies in the future, affecting the freedom of nations and the exercise of human rights. Yet Europe has to be seen as it is, as the ambivalent and controversial consequence of a world divided by superpowers. At the same time, one should not fail to note signs of hope wherever they appear, as for example in Russia after the demonstration at Red Square. One of the participants, Vadim Delone, told the Soviet attorney later: "For three minutes on the Red Square I felt as a free man. For these three minutes I can take the three-year sentence." What a paradox of contemporary history. Europeans in Moscow—a reality of tomorrow and a symbol of future victory for the defeated Left.

CONSEQUENCES

"Brezhnev is Hitler."

(A slogan of Prague students in 1968)

The occupation of Czechoslovakia means a further step in the disintegration of Communist unity. The long-term consequences of the Soviet action will be ideological in nature and will affect both theoretically and practically the international Communist movement. These consequences will prove more important, over a period of years, than the immediate practical gains resulting from the deployment of several divisions on the Czechoslovakian frontier. The strengthening of the Soviet military position in Europe represents an ideological disintegration and theoretical catastrophe comparable in proportion to that caused in 1914 by German Social Democrats when they voted in favor of the military budget submitted to the parliament by Emperor Wilhelm.

No other event thus far in the history of communism has caused so many independent Communist parties to rally against the Communist Party of the Soviet Union, as they did in the case of the recent occupation of Czechoslovakia. The disintegration of the Communist movement and the ideological divisions, which began with China, are now openly manifest in the rupture between the Soviet and West European Communist Parties. The Soviet Communist Party has been engaged in a futile battle against various "nationalistic deviations" for such a long time that the only weapon now at hand is great-power chauvinism— extreme nationalism.

The Soviet intervention opened dark vistas to the Communist movement. The Brezhnev doctrine negated all former statements on the independence of national Communist parties and the independence and sovereignty of Communist states, to which lip service had been paid in the past. The old doctrines have been bluntly replaced by a new school of legal thought, according to which the United Nations Charter does not apply to the Soviet sphere of influence.

The superpower chauvinism of Soviet Communists will inevitably produce certain nationalistic emotions in Western European Communist parties. The only theory capable of explaining Moscow's aggressive action in "Marxist-Leninist" terms is that offered by China; the Soviet aggression fully confirmed Mao's theory and his accusations regarding "further betrayals of Lenin's principles."

The disintegration of international Communist unity and the emergence of new ideological centers outside Moscow suggest that polycentrism has become the final reality for international communism. Chinese, Soviet, and Yugoslav (or West European) interpretations of communism theory no longer have any common denominator. This fact in itself is of such far-reaching importance and represents such a defeat for Soviet world-power ambitions that the deployment of several new Soviet divisions in Czechoslovakia can have little meaning. Three different versions of communism—Soviet, Chinese and West European—derive not merely from ideological divergences but from the varying and conflicting needs of whole nations, groups of nations, or continents. The gap is permanent and it cannot be overcome.

The invasion of Czechoslovakia revealed a deep crisis in Soviet communism. It showed that Stalinist institutions have remained intact after all those years of peaceful coexistence and that they continue to exert a neo-Stalinist influence in the domestic and foreign policies of the Soviet Union. Soviet communism deliberately blocks its own path to Europeanization and democratization and prevents the solution of its own economic and political problems. Thus, the only way that remains open leads Russia to a sort of social fascism and aggressive imperialism; in short, to neo-Stalinism. Neo-Stalinism, however, is not capable of finding solutions for old conflicts; it can only brush them under the carpet and, by doing this, reinforce the sources of conflict and deepen the crisis.

The growing opposition to such neo-Stalinist manifestations as militarism, nationalism, antisemitism, and anti-intellectualism can be temporarily suppressed, but the crisis cannot be solved, for by their very nature Stalinist institutions reject change and negate the possibility of genuine solution. The only alternative would seem to lie in the government's obtaining for its people such a solid and high standard of living as to enable the forces of social demagogy to curb political opposition and criticism. Such an alternative, of course, will remain unfeasible so long as Soviet world-power ambitions—an element of the neo-Stalinist political line—devour that part of the national income that could be utilized for pacification of rebels and protesters.

Under these circumstances, therefore, the liberal revisionist movement against Stalinist institutions becomes a mortal enemy to these institutions. The Czechoslovak experiment proved that this movement leads to: (1) unity of workers and intellectuals; (2) unity of Communists and non-Communists in a movement for human rights; and (3) spontaneous emergence of demonstrations, decline of the power elite, and strengthening of forces beyond the control of the

Communist Party. Czechoslovakia's experiences in this respect are
absolutely unique in the Communist movement, and they reveal the
dimensions of the crisis of Stalinism. They also indicate the immense
possibilities for spontaneous action in defense of human rights, and
for creating a basis for a reformist, democratic, and liberal movement
by joint efforts of Communist and non-Communist.

The revisionist (or for that matter Yugoslav, humanistic, Western,
or Czechoslovak) type of Marxism was militarily defeated by an action
from outside. It remains to be seen whether this defeat will prove
to have been final or merely temporary and whether the possibility of
a democratic and humanistic socialism is real or just an illusion in
a world dominated by blocs and superpowers aligned against each
other. It seems that if Europe will not emerge to assume its independent role in world policy, the humanistic and democratic movements in world communism are doomed to failure, and Marxism, in its
authentic sense as a theory of human freedom, will be dead. The term
"Marxism" would then refer only to the ideological weapon of the neo-
Stalinist power elite.

On the other hand, the Czechoslovak tragedy may become a
victory if democratic and reformist tendencies can survive in the
Soviet Union and if, in that country, a sort of revisionist orientation
can emerge, for example, in the economic life. Such a possibility is
excluded by most knowledgeable "realistic" politicians. Only those
people with a political imagination capable of seeing in present Soviet
conditions a prerevolutionary situation leading to the fall of totalitar-
ianism accept such a possibility. Nevertheless, when realism and
imagination are combined, one has to accept at least the possibility
that, should democratic trends increase in Russia, brother Mao will
be ready to help brother Brezhnev in the same way that brother
Brezhnev came to aid brother Dubcek. The future may well bring
one of Hegel's "tricks of history," by which Russia will reap the
fruit it has sown: namely, the same injustice and absurdity that the
aggressive elite of the Soviet Union has thus far imposed on others.
This prediction is made today by students in Prague, who have already
learned the lesson that politicians continue to ignore. The students
of Prague understand clearly the truth of what they wrote on walls
and posters after the Soviet invasion: "Brezhnev is Hitler." The
sooner this slogan—combining reality and imagination—is understood
by others, the better for the world.

THE CAUSES OF DEFEAT

"The Soviet revisionist clique is like a
notorious prostitute who insists on having
a monument erected to her chastity."

Radio Peking, 1969

If today's occupied Czechoslovakia is looked at objectively, it
must be concluded that the major causes of defeat were:

1. The Communist Party as a Stalinist institution, as a mono-
polist of political power, i.e., not the responsible leaders or central
committees, but the structure of the political establishment itself,
the political system of Stalinist communism as a whole. The Soviet
occupation was the result of this system, and was not caused by the
Czechoslovak experiment as such.

2. The theory and practice of the leading role of the Communist
Party, which reduces every democratic popular movement to a peripheral phenomenon in changes within the power elite.

3. The illusions about the effectiveness of democratic methods
used against a totalitarian system entertained by the Communist
wing of reformers who did not recognize the true nature of Soviet power
and were unable to understand the real nature of the bureaucratic
elite of the U.S.S.R. The Soviet totalitarian dictatorship was easily
able to conquer the Czechs' defenseless humanism when the reformist
leaders proved incapable of acting according to the public will and of
defending their country militarily.

One may try to make this hard reality more palatable, but one
can hardly conceal the lesson that the Communist Party and its reformist leaders cannot function as the leaders of a popular movement for civil rights, national independence, and state sovereignty.
The theory of the Communist Party as the vanguard of the working
class failed again during the August occupation of Czechoslovakia.
Without any assistance by theoreticians, statesmen, or politcal
leaders, the spontaneous action itself produced an alliance of intellectuals and workers that refuted the theory of the leading role of the

party bureaucracy over the underprivileged masses. The new ideological wave that will try to wash away this relevant revolutionary experience will have to discredit the most valuable part of it, namely, the Marxist-humanist character of a program for socialist democracy based on an alliance of the intelligentsia and workers. At the same time, it has been proven that a Stalinist Communist party is the main obstacle in the way of socialism, democracy, and humanism; that it is the main force of conservatism in our present world; that it is the greatest enemy of elementary European and human values—the enemy of human freedom, east and west, south and north.

The Communist Party of Czechoslovakia was preparing to legalize factions. It was making ready far-reaching institutional changes incompatible with the Soviet concept of democratic centralism. It was revising Stalinism. From the Soviet point of view these changes represented an inadmissible revision of the Leninist concept of the Party—and a revision it was—that was the more dangerous because there was a danger that the Party congress would institutionalize principles by which all would be free to criticize the party openly and would legalize a free press. Against this new concept, completely foreign to the fifty-year existence of the Soviet state, the Soviet Party constructed a new, threatening concept of the Communist Party as an internationally organized gang of military elites. This is Brezhnev's neo-Stalinist, anti-Marxist, and anti-Leninist concept of the function of the Communist Party in its future expansionist plans. Not only their own state, but also every territory occupied by the Soviets is the property of the Soviet Party elite. The power of the local Party elite is derived from the military occupation of the country by Soviet troops, and the dependency is not dissimilar to a feudal fiefdom with limited sovereignty in key matters.

Immediately after the occupation, the Communist Party leaders of Czechoslovakia recanted their earlier concept of a more democratic leadership and restored the phraseology and practice of neo-Stalinism. They again based their action and talk on the old myth of Stalinism, according to which the leading role of the party is a precondition for the development of socialism. A party bureaucracy is obviously unable and unwilling to accept the image of a socialist society without a party bureaucracy and its parasitic members. The leading role of the party is based on another myth, according to which there is no political force in Czechoslovakia able to carry out a program of socialism other than the Communist Party of Czechoslovakia. In fact, of course, there has always been such a force—the people of Czechoslovakia.

Once again the Communists claim their right to be the ruling party; again they introduce the old model of society based on the rule of the elite. This model is different from that of Antonin Novotny in the sense that Novotny <u>managed without the assistance of Soviet tanks.</u>

Regardless of the inner Party struggle at the top, regardless of the existence of various technocratically minded factions within the Party, the very heart of that Party is still an authoritarian elite that was unable to lead the nation and that actually killed the idea of identifying socialism with democracy. The great program of identifying socialism with democracy cannot be revived by any elite, no matter how liberal it may appear to be.

For their struggle with Novotny and their coup d'etat neo-Stalinists in Czechoslovakia needed temporary help and allies from among the democratic forces in the country. At the moment when their own interests were at stake, the neo-Stalinists gave up their allies and labeled them "antisocialist elements." By introducing censorship, by making the Soviet occupation legal, and by liquidating the nucleus of political opposition, they showed in their own way the "socialist character of Czechoslovakia." Thus, indeed, the leading role of the Party became the "basic guarantee" of the further development of socialism, but of a socialism combined not with democracy, national sovereignty, and independence, but with censorship, police brutality, and Soviet tanks. This is the content of what is called "normalization." And in this situation the Party elite has tried to keep its prestige by presenting itself as national martyr, while at the same time expressing its solidarity with the power groups in other Communist countries and with the occupying forces. There is no way out, so long as the leading role of the Communist Party is defended; because it was precisely the "leading role of the Communist Party" that was, is, and will remain the second most important cause of the failure of democratization.

The third cause of failure is to be found in the personal limitations of the leading Communist reformers, in the illusions of intellectuals who had been in practical politics for only a short time, and in the leadership of the Party. Democratization was a movement, a process that shaped itself as time went on and that passed through four stages, taking on a significantly different form in each. The official democratization program of the Communist Party, which was managed in the spirit of the apparatus' totalitarian monopoly of power, must be distinguished from the really democratic movement that constantly overstepped the limits conceded by the Communists. It is this democratic movement for human rights and civil liberties that has constantly pressed the Communist Party to go beyond its own program and that has not allowed it to put an end to democratization, even though the great majority of the leading politicians of the Communist Party—including some of the national heroes—have done their best at every step to check and curb the people's movement and to preserve the elitist character of the state and the technocratic character of the economic reforms.

In the spring the aims of the intelligentsia were confined to matters of particular interest to the middle classes; the intellectuals were tolerated by the new leadership of the Communist Party, which dared not forfeit their support because it was directly threatened by the conservatives. But the objectives of the democratic intelligentsia—if we can use this term to cover both the Communist and the non-Party intellectuals—were not homogeneous. The basic position expressing the common denominator of the various political currents was formulated by the Communist writers, and it is a fact that during 1968 there were no substantive political differences between Communists and non-Communists within the unions of artists; the Communists' line was completely in accordance with the non-Party members' interests. The radical students did occasionally go beyond the generally accepted framework, but the fact remains that a common policy brought together the hitherto strictly divided groups of Party members and non-Party members. At first, there was indeed a considerable difference between the two, but it gradually faded away as the spring continued and as politics grew progressively more radical, so that finally the program of democratization became more and more the real program of the Party members themselves.

The weakness of the Communist intellectuals is most apparent in their failure to make the possibilities of the new democracy a subject of theoretical consideration. Now Communist intellectuals will feel that an intelligent technocracy is the most realistic possibility for the future and represents a good way out of such personal difficulties as the need to commit oneself openly to the radical standpoint. The skepticism of intellectuals concerning the program of socialist democracy will become merely an appendix to those politically conservative attitudes that have accepted Soviet rule, limited sovereignty, censorship, the concept of consumer society, and the formation of an effective technocratic government as a surrogate for socialist democracy.

After the failed experiment of the Communist intellectuals, it must be realized that the people of Czechoslovakia are now waiting for a Godot who is not coming. The game of socialist democracy is stalemated. No solution for the Czechoslovak stalemate presents itself just now, and it would be futile to try to find one. Just as the program of democratization collapsed as a result of external causes, any improvement in the internal situation of Czechoslovakia can be brought about only by external changes. Who will play the actual role of stalemated king is more or less irrelevant now, for the differences among those eligible to play the role will soon become negligible.

The nuclear stalemate between the two great powers, the stalemate between the two halves of divided Europe, and the stalemate in Berlin symbolized by the wall—another "family stalemate" between the power elites in the socialist states—preclude any guarantee of stability for the 1970's. After the prevailing current of conservatism and technocratism in the politics of both superpowers has run its course, Europe will unite under an independent, European, humanistic, and socialist policy. Not even then will Godot arrive; but the absurd game of power elites in totalitarian dictatorships will end.

ALTERNATIVE OF RESISTANCE

"Je revolte, donc je suis."
(I revolt, therefore I am.)

Albert Camus

To be radical means to have faith in reason and not in any new ideology. To be radical means to think clearly and not to be deceived by illusions. To be radical means to act in accordance with the re- cognized truth since a concrete man, reason, and truth form the same unity as science, humanism, and practice. The primary duty of man today is to be radical.

To be radical means to see the reality in its truth—and to re- fuse it. If one is revolting against the given reality, it is not because one would not understand the limitations and the realism of policy makers. On the contrary, it is just because one understands them very well. To resist the existing reality is the only honest attitude that remains now that the alternative struggle has been lost and compromise has failed. The alternative of resistance is thus the only alternative.

To be radical means primarily to be aware of the true nature of reality and to refuse a priori the confusions of an ideology that claims

all of us are responsible for the present situation and that all of us
have a part in the decision-making process. In fact, for the loss of national sovereignty and national independence only some 300 people can
be held responsible—not the whole nation, and not "all of us." Where
there is no common responsibility for the establishment of a government and state power, there is no common responsibility for the
failures of the power elite. The demagogy of the power elite continues.

The resistance against occupation depends on internal and external conditions. The occupation of Czechoslovakia brought to an
end all hopes for overcoming the conflict between West and East, all
hopes for a reconciliation of two different socioeconomic systems,
and all hopes for a permanent peaceful coexistence. The occupation
of Czechoslovakia marks the beginning of an era that will force the
superpowers further apart, that will sharpen tremendously the contradictions between the two contending parties, and that will reinforce
the general trend toward conservatism on both sides. The future of
the Czechoslovak experiment with socialist democracy will depend
on developments in the whole world scene, rather than on those internal forces in Czechoslovakia that have already been defeated.

It is necessary also to recognize the changed character of the
Warsaw Pact alliance, the changed nature of relations between members
of the socialist bloc. The openly claimed right to intervene in and
occupy friendly countries, the liquidation of the principle of mutual
recognition of sovereignty and independence means a transformation
of the Warsaw Pact alliance into a criminal organization and a tool of
Stalinist neocolonialism. The Soviet Union has become the last im-
perialistic, neocolonial power. Unless there are changes within the
Soviet Union, unless there is democratization within the Soviet power
elite, tanks and secret police will continue to confirm the irreversi-
bility of the state of affairs in Czechoslovakia and the impossibility
of reversing this state of affairs through internal efforts by the
Czechoslovak people.

As to the impact of the Soviet intervention on countries in
Western Europe, it can be assumed that the intervention will lead to
an intensification of efforts aimed at formulating an independent
European policy. Threatened by Soviet imperialism and engaged in a
process of integration, Western Europe will try to find a more definite
solution for problems relating to Central Europe, while the Soviet
Union, threatened by China, will find it more and more difficult to prevent such a solution or to refuse it. Czechoslovakia is no longer in
a position to liberate itself; it can find an answer to basic questions

concerning the country's existence only in a broader Central European context.

As far as the internal situation is concerned; some hard facts must be stated. The Communist Party did not manage to resolve the basic problems of Czechoslovak society, and it was unable to put into practice the democratization program. Any orientation toward democratic socialism became impossible in the presence of Soviet tanks. Although the Communist Party was quite successful, received mass support, and was, indeed, the leading force in the process of democratization, the power elite of the Soviet totalitarian dictatorship prevented the completion of this process. The Communist Party and its program ended in total failure.

The bureaucratic police system has remained intact and continues to exist with minor modifications as a state system guided by a tiny power elite that cannot be affected by public opinion. The situation has shown again that a totalitarian regime cannot be dissolved by gradual democratization and that modern dictatorships can be uprooted only by revolution or war, but not gradual liberalization. A united nation can force the power elite of a totalitarian regime to make considerable concessions and reforms, but in absence of changes in the very structure of the power system, it was easy for a new power elite to liquidate the previous results of the people's pressure and to keep the centralized executive power out of the hands of the people.

The power elite in Czechoslovakia remains as antidemocratic, bureaucratic, and totalitarian as before; during the past year it has learned that while the assistance of the nation was necessary for the preservation of the regime, the nation could, on the other hand, live without either the elite or its regime in its effort to be free. Under these circumstances, it becomes more and more urgent for the power elite to make a choice between democracy and collaboration with the occupying forces, taking fully into account that in the latter situation the state carries all features of a protectorate: a foreign policy dictated by Moscow, economic dependency, subordination to the activities of KGB agents, and a system of censorship imposed upon cultural life.

Radical opposition to these basic features of the dirty "new reality" is the only honest attitude that can be adopted by Czechoslovak citizens. Only rarely does the future confirm the correctness of so-called realists who justify an existing situation while offering no hopes or perspectives. The future itself cannot solve the problems of today; it can only reveal the problems of tomorrow. The most demonic philosophical category is time. Time will show that, in the long run, it is not the realists who collaborate with the occupation power but those people with political imagination who are right. And it is the latter category of people—the blood and energy of the resistance—who, confirmed in their belief by the contradictions caused by the occupation, can assert with Comenius: "We must see to it that humanity will regain its freedom, the greatest asset which accompanied the creation of man and which cannot be separated from him."

4

NEW APPROACHES
AND
POLITICAL
REALITIES
Ivan Svitak

There are match games based on the principle that the player who is familiar with the basic idea of the game must always win against a partner who does not know the rules. Thus, for example, if two players draw in turn from any number of matches a certain number of matches (one, two, or three), the winner will be the one who is able to determine the critical numbers for his partner. By being able to do so, he actually becomes winner after his first move. In fact, he may even win before his partner has decided on his first move, since the whole game is based on creating in the ignorant partner's mind an illusion that the chances are even for both players.

THE LOGIC OF FRAUD

"We know what we want. We do not want
anything. And this we might get."

Viktor Dyk, Czech writer and poet,
died 1931

The structure of the fraudulent game of Czechoslovak politics is similar to that of the match game. And it can be said that further traps will be set unless the nation realizes that it has no chance of winning so long as it respects the rules of the game and so long as

---

This chapter is dedicated to the students at Charles University.

the ruling power, by virtue of the agreement signed between Czechoslovakia and Russia in Moscow, continues to lead its people into the
traps. Such a recognition is a precondition for any future victory,
and for a solution of the present deadlock. Once the rules of the game
have been imposed from outside, it is necessary to take this situation
into consideration. However, it cannot be denied that it has been the
duty of the nation's leaders to refuse the fraudulent rules and to deny
them a legal status.

The first trap that has been set up is the occupation, or rather
the consequences of the occupation, as reflected in the exclusion of
mass information media from the game, the restriction of human
rights, and the restoration of censorship. Under these circumstances,
there is no justification in saying that "we ourselves are going to solve
our problems" (unless we know what is meant by this tricky "we")
when at the same time—with the exception of the power elite—all
citizens are excluded from participation in the decision-making process
on all key issues. To accept this point of view, which repeats the
slogan of unity of the Party and the people, is to fall into an ideological
trap and to come under the control of a ruling elite that is very much
interested in representing its views as those of the whole nation.

The second trap lies in the so-called new reality which presents
the occupation as an acceptable situation that, after all, can be overcome by various maneuvers designed to achieve the withdrawal of
foreign troops. However, even if all foreign tanks do leave the country,
the situation will not necessarily become acceptable. On the contrary,
the departure of foreign tanks would rather mean that the military
expedition had succeeded and that the old game of censorship, police
terror, and decision-making behind the closed door could continue.
The "new reality" thus illuminates only one thing: that totalitarian
dictatorships cannot be "democratized" —not even after the disappear-
ance of the class struggle, originally the major reason for the establishment of totalitarian regimes.

Just as the trap of occupation became the trap of the so-called
new reality, the new reality will give way to the trap of monopoly of
power. A one-party system with a power elite subject to no controls
is a Stalinist system, regardless of who is in the leadership. This
type of system impedes social progress wherever it is introduced,
no matter what ideological phraseology is used by political parties
adhering to it.

Unless the people begin to understand that the rules of the fraudulent game—on which politicians base their action—have to be refused

and unless they create new rules that insure control by the people and exclude any fraud, they will inevitably fall into further traps. Once it is known that the game of the ruling elites is a fraud, then there are two basic responses available: to accept defeat as something inevitable, or to sweep all the matches from the table and stop the game. If someone knows that he is doomed to failure, but continues to play; if he knows that he is legalizing fradulent rules and does legalize them; if he knows that he is playing with gangsters and still expects that they will act as gentlemen; then such a person may become popular as an ingenious suicide but not as a good politician.

Politicians who express certain interests and claim to represent certain social groups of classes must be judged by these standards rather than by the degree of sympathy expressed by the public as a result of their personal tragedies. The present realists are more competent than those dreamers who were unable to prepare the country for armed resistance against occupation. However, there are politicians who are miles ahead of both the realists and the dreamers. These politicians are able to accept and to refuse the reality at the same time; they are able to understand and at the same time to overcome.

There is no doubt that the factual disintegration of the Communist Party into three major groupings—advocates of terror, centrists, and reformers—reflects the actual political trend in the country itself and thus differentiates opinions within the Communist Party. All these groupings, however, have one common feature: They all agree that the people's authority, the national sovereignty, and the public will should be excluded from consideration in public action, since to all of them the term "public" refers, at best, to Party members. In addition, all three entertain the false views characteristic of any power group: They are convinced of their own importance as a ruling elite; they look upon the intelligentsia as an enemy of socialism; and they believe that the working class could not manage without the leadership of the elite. These mistakes must, of course, result in the setting of new traps.

There is no choice other than to challenge the powerful unity of political monopoly and tanks by introducing new rules of the game—rules that would preclude fraud and that would be based on the strategy and tactics of truth. Although truth as such is not tactful and does not itself require the use of tactics, one should not be concerned with the question of whether priority should be given to truth or to tactics. The only tactic that should be applied under any circumstance is the tactic of truth. The power elite sees truth as demagogy, and regards its own demagogy as truth. The assertions of irresponsible demagogues should be subjected to truth, rational thinking, and reality and then it should be concluded whether the extremism of truth or the cautious lie should be the guide.

There is no defense against fraudulent rules of the game other than a proper understanding of the whole game as a fraud and a complete refusal to play the game. Such an understanding is of vital importance for the next game, for the recognition of the fact that there is no chance of victory with the old rules will lead to other solutions and to new tactics. Once the basic human rights have been lost, once censorship has been restored and the economy of Czechoslovakia taken over by Soviet neocolonialist expansion policy, it would be a fatal self-deceit to think that the mere existence of some critical magazines and newspapers can be a substitute for real resistance.

The policy of the Communist Party leadership reflects an absolute inability to face the new situation. This policy accepts and legalizes the rape of the country and its people, and betrays its own program of April, 1968, as well as the whole popular movement for civil rights. This desperate policy of "normalization" and "new reality" has one aim only: to keep the monopoly of the power elite intact at all cost—if necessary, even with the help of Soviet tanks. The program that the present leadership of the Communist Party maintains can be best expressed in the verses written by Viktor Dyk: "We know what we want. We do not want anything. And this we might get."

THE TACTICS OF TRUTH

"There are truths which were not
created for those who are stupid."

Denis Diderot

We, socialist democrats, want to see civil and human rights as a basis of all social life. Regardless of its ideology, any system that, as a precondition for the citizens' participation in political activities, denies these rights must become and remain a totalitarian dictatorship and an oppressive system in which a power elite sets itself in opposition to the people. We have decided to fight for human rights and to support those politicians and those political groupings or movements which accept the United Nations Declaration of Human Rights as their basis. At the same time, we are resolute in our opposition to any individuals, political groupings, or movements that follow, in their practical activities, different rules of the game.

We, democratic socialists, believe in the indivisibility of socialism and freedom; we see in socialism a theory of growing human freedom and we wish to achieve an international solidarity between workers and intellectuals. If, on the contrary, this great idea of freedom for individuals, social groups, and nations is being transformed into a theory of force, repression, and occupation, then we must conclude that the real antisocialist forces are in the places where they have always been—in the army, in the police, and in the offices of censorship. The criminal elements are those antisocialist forces that subordinate freedom to the interests of power elites and military blocs. There is no freedom without socialism. There is no socialism without freedom.

We, radical democrats, refuse any compromise with totalitarian regimes of any color, since these regimes are foul, inhumane, and aggressive, regardless of the ideologies they promote. These systems—which are instruments of class and group interests within ruling elites—cannot be transformed into instruments of social progress, since ruling elites are used to defending and perpetuating, in a very brutal way, their exclusive class and group interests. Internal forces attempting to change such regimes have had to fight for democratic rights, basic social freedoms, and a humane program for the future. They should not be misled by the idea that a totalitarian regime might be willing to follow the same path or that it might become more moderate or even change into something better. The totalitarian regime will not change because it is based on the interests of the power elite, the new class, which represents a bureaucracy of state capitalism.

We, radical socialists, realize that the current problems of Czechoslovakia have not been caused by individual leaders or by economic difficulties resulting from problems of market and consumption. The problems of Czechoslovakia have not been caused by that theoretical degeneration and dialectical negation that transformed the Marxian theory of freedom into the Brezhnev doctrine of force. All current problems result from the state-capitalistic nature of the social system, from the monopolistic political dictatorship and from the totalitarian ideology of the Soviet neo-Stalinist system. For this reason these problems cannot be solved either by a replacement of leaders or by increased consumption, but only by an expanison of civil and human rights, and by a fight against the state-capitalist structure of society.

We, European internationalists, are convinced that Stalinism, in fact, has produced a restoration of capitalism in the Soviet Union in the form of state capitalism, and has created a new ruling class and a totalitarian monopoly over all economic, political, and cultural activities. State capitalism has been established in Eastern Europe by mere force and police terror, in order to prove that in the building of socialism the most decisive factor is not the form of ownership of means of production but rather the political control of the state. Under state capitalism workers have been deprived of any influence regarding state ownership; they have no reason to defend the system of monopolistic capitalism, since state capitalism has liquidated the independent role of the working class movement in all countries to which it has been exported. State capitalism is nothing other than restored capitalism combined with totalitarian dictatorship and with a fraudulent ideology disguised by socialist slogans.

We, Europeans, who welcomed the October Revolution of 1917 as a step toward making Russia more European, consider the Stalinist state to be a capitalistic system and its new ruling class to be another system of exploitation that is interested in maintaining the status quo, in dividing the world into spheres of influence, and in limiting and liquidating civil and human rights. Today's neo-Stalinism, combined with the efforts of the Soviet ruling class to achieve hegemony, is in direct opposition to those aims promoted by the founders of socialism in the nineteenth century. The problems of occupied Czechoslovakia have been caused by the state capitalistic system and its elite and this system must be changed completely if the world is not to perish. If the state will not die, then humanity must.

We, humanist Marxists, defending the alliance of workers and intellectuals, do not blame the Communist Party for the revolutionary transformation of society, for the creation of the economic conditions of socialism. We never have been and will not be opposed to the socialist system. We blame the Communist Party only for its con- servatism, for its inability to lead the people in defending the national interests, and for its lack of faith in the people. We have learned that the gap between human freedom and industrial society cannot be bridged by the old practices of Communist parties—not even when they advocate reforms, for these parties fear radical change and they fail whenever their power monopoly is at stake.

We, Marxist humanists, who believe in the creative activity of people, are skeptical of any power elite. We can afford to be radic in our demands, our thinking, and our activity for the very reason that the people in their activity are far ahead of the most radical demands and ideas. This is why we do not ask for a restoration of the prewar type of democracy and why we are committed to socialist democracy, a concept as precious to us as totalitarian dictatorship (including a "socialist" one) is abhorrent.

We, Czechs and Slovaks, trying to think and act in conformity with the interests of an independent nation and not with the interests of a political party, bloc, or power elite, can only rely on the alliance of workers and intellectuals that formed the basis for the creation of the theoretical and political platform of spring, 1968. The new Left of Czechoslovakia, the radical democratic intelligentsia, and students, in particular, are more and more aware that the independent existence of the Czechoslovak radical democratic Left is a precondition for any political movement in the country. The independent Left has presented itself, by its strike action, as a spokesman for the nation, the people, and the country.

We, socialist democrats, Marxist humanists, internationalists and advocates of Lenin's idea of revolution know that all conservative forces are trying to accomplish the impossible—they are attempting to hold back historical development in the belief that ballistic laws are stronger than laws of history. Again and again, however, these conservative forces are confronted with the insurmountable obstacle of human freedom. The more force they apply, the more man is forced to claim his authenticity, to commit himself to his personal self-determination, his personality—in the name of freedom. We know what we want and this we will achieve: human rights as a basis of all social life. There can be no retreat from this demand, can be no retreat from the tactics of truth.

SOLUTIONS FOR A DEADLOCK

"Wherever we are not present, there
is a nice place to live."

(Russian proverb)

Our future for the next ten years will be defined by three relevant factors: (1) the nuclear deadlock, which will encourage the two superpowers to divide the world into spheres of influence and to reach an agreement on this basis; (2) the deadlock in Czechoslovak-Soviet relations, which represents neither a full victory for Brezhnev nor a complete defeat for Dubcek but rather a continuation of the present marasmus, which can hardly be solved in the near future; and

(3) the deadlock in the internal situation of Czechoslovakia, in the relationship between the government and the people, which again cannot
be changed without a radical demoralization of the regime. These
deadlocks can be turned into a favorable situation only if the Soviet
Union starts a war against China.

There is no doubt about the possible solutions in this stalemate,
but a resolution may be expected in the late 1970's, when the deadlocks described above will become major issues of world policy.
The present orientation toward the preservation of the status quo will
increase the efforts by both superpowers to achieve some basic change
will provide Europe with a better chance to play an independent role,
and will create favorable conditions throughout the world for the democratic radical Left.

Attempts to find a solution will differ in large and small countries, in the third world and industrial states, and will have different
meanings for the power elites on one hand and for the people on the
other. At present, it is relevant to know that any resolution of the
deadlock in Czechoslovakia will not depend on the internal situation
of the country, but rather on decisions taken by the Kremlin and on
the general international atmosphere. The deadlock in the Czechoslovak-Soviet relationship cannot be solved for the very simple reason
that any new Soviet armed intervention would transform this deadlock into a total defeat of Czechoslovakia. The possibility of a new
Soviet intervention, which would mean bloodshed for workers, is very
real because of the internal situation of Czechoslovakia. Thus, the
deadlock in Czechoslovakia, which affects the relationship between the
government and the people, the elites and the nation, is a very explosive situation and one more dangerous for the new government than
ever before, because the people's indignation will not only be a matter
of liberal television programs or magazines, but will involve the
whole working class. The worsening of the economic situation will
encourage the majority of the population, particularly the working
class, to demand a radical democracy, and this to be extended to
factories, where the awareness of the need for democratization (which
was a weakness in the 1968 post-January developments in Czechoslovakia) will grow.

This explosive situation will exacerbate conflicts and could
result in strikes that not even the national heroes will be able to
handle. Such a situation would mark the end of the fictional national
unity and would increase public awareness of the difference between
the people's interest and that of the elite. The so-called realists
would then be forced to support the Soviet demands more openly, as

the discontent of the public would be turned against them. However, if no political action is taken by the working class, such as a strike or a general strike, then the deadlock will be stabilized and the public will become apathetic. Such a development in the next decade would only mean that the rotten compromises effected in Poland will be repeated in Czechoslovakia.

If no solution can be found in the alliance of workers and intellectuals, then we can expect a continuation of the deadlock. Whether or not a solution can be achieved depends upon what is meant by "solution." Willy-nilly, people will have to ask themselves again whether they should support the realists, or remain neutral, or affirm their opposition. The government will not care very much; it does not expect either support or ideological loyalty. It is satisfied when the state does not fall apart, when the elite manages to retain the power. At the same time, it will justify its political behavior in terms of Soviet pressures.

What will remain of the program of democratization will be the piece of rope on which the butcher hangs up "the sausage with human face"—to quote a joke making the rounds in Prague. What will also be left will be the empty symbols of the formal prestige of leading politicians. Under these circumstances the false technocratic solution will again be presented as a reasonable and acceptable compromise, as a solution for the elites. Technocracy has always offered good solutions for the power elite. So much more so, when naive people in villages, factories, and the Academy of Sciences are deceived by technocratic gimmicks that pretend to offer solutions to problems of our time while these problems, in fact, are getting worse. Technology, after all, is not guided by a democratic movement and is not subject to control.

It can be expected that attempts to present just such a technocratic solution will emerge very soon, despite the fact it was this kind of program that failed during the first period of democratization and that brought the country a tough lesson from the Kremlin. This is also a reminder of the old truth according to which politics is above technocracy. The belief that a sort of caretaker government can dissolve political problems by technical miracles will become a new trap into which intellectuals will be lured by so-called realists.

What is to be done? Don't fall into the trap. If you do happen to fall into the trap, try to understand your mistakes. If you have understood your mistakes, set the trap for your adversary.

5

CZECHOSLOVAKIA
AND
THE FUTURE
OF SOVIET
FOREIGN POLICY

Roger E. Kanet

In the mid-1950's Soviet foreign policy underwent a number of significant changes. In their relations with other Communist states, especially after the suppression of the revolution in Hungary in 1956, Soviet leaders replaced the policy of economic exploitation and political repression with measures designed to achieve a voluntary integration of the various Communist political systems into a socialist commonwealth rather than a Soviet empire held together by military domination. In their contacts with the Western countries, the Soviets turned from the hostile rigidity of the late Stalin era to a flexibility that enabled them to cooperate in lessening international tensions. In their relations with the third major group of states—the newly independent states of Asia and Africa—Soviet leaders indicated a willingness to innovate what would have been inconceivable in the late 1940's. In spite of periodic reversals in one or other aspects of Soviet policy (e.g., the attempt to place missiles in Cuba in 1962) and a number of failures of Soviet policy (e.g., in the Congo in 1960), the basic trend in Soviet relations with the outside world during the decade of Khrushchev's leadership can be viewed as one of a gradual lessening of international

This chapter is a revised version of a paper that appeared in Internationale Spectator under the title of "The Implications of the Occupation of Czechoslovakia for Soviet Foreign Policy." It is reprinted with permission of the Nederlandsch Genootschap Voor Internationale Zaken.

tensions and an improvement of the overall position and influence of
the Soviet Union as a major world power.

However, one major failure of Khrushchev and his associates
concerned the relations of the other Communist countries to the Soviet
Union. The split between the Soviets and the Chinese had become
apparently irreparable by 1964 and Soviet control over Eastern Europe
was significantly weakened. In some respects, this was counterbalance
by increased Soviet activity and influence among the developing countries—in particular, Ghana, Guinea, Mali, Algeria, the U.A.R., and
India—and a gradual erosion of American influence in areas peripheral
to the Soviet Union. By 1965 NATO was in disarray, Iran and Turkey
had lessened their dependence on the U.S., and India was turning
increasingly to the Soviet Union for support against China.

Many Western analysts (including this author) viewed these
developments as an indication that the Soviet Union was behaving
increasingly as a great power interested almost exclusively in maintaining the status quo and unwilling to risk its past gains by supporting
revolutionary movements that might possibly precipitate a direct
confrontation with the United States and a nuclear disaster.[1] With
regard to Soviet policy toward the other Communist states, most
Western scholars (including the author) would have agreed with Jan
Triska and David Finley that

> the growing national independence of the ruling Communist
> Parties, brought about by the reluctant Soviet emphasis on
> "complete" equality, nonintervention in domestic matters,
> and respect for the state sovereignty of the Communist
> party-states, largely eliminated the ruling Parties' sub-
> ordination to the "victorious" CPSU. The end of rule by
> coercion and condemnation, initiated among the Communist
> party-states by Khrushchev, with his emphasis on volun-
> tarism principally on the state level, was carried over to
> the party level and extended to the nonruling Parties.[2]

On August 21, 1968, the military occupation of Czechoslovakia
by troops from the Soviet Union and four of its East European depen-
dencies called into question many of the underlying assumptions of
these analyses. This chapter will examine, very briefly, the meaning
of the Soviet occupation and, in more detail, its implications for
Soviet relations with the rest of the world. How, if at all, has it
affected the Soviet position among other Communist countries—Eastern
Europe in particular? What impact will it have on Soviet attempts
to reassert a dominant role in the "world Communist movement?"

And, finally, what will happen to the gradual improvement of Soviet relations with the West—the United States in particular?

MAJOR FACTORS INFLUENCING THE SOVIET INTERVENTION

A large number of perceptive analyses of the causes of the Soviet occupation have already been published, so only the major factors that influenced the decision of Soviet leaders to intervene militarily in Czechoslovakia will be indicated.[3] The decision apparently was the result of an atmosphere of fear and insecurity that had been increasingly evident in both the domestic and foreign policy of the U.S.S.R. over the three or four years previous to the occupation. Domestically this period witnessed a revival of repressive measures against dissident intellectuals (the writers in particular) who have not only condemned the policies of Stalin, but have called into question the past actions of the very men who now rule the Soviet Union. At the same time Soviet policy toward Eastern Europe evidenced an almost irrational fear of increasing West German economic and political influence, which resulted in Soviet pressure on a number of governments to prevent them from developing official diplomatic relations with West Germany and a propaganda campaign against "German revanchism." Briefly, the Soviet leadership indicated by its policies during three or four years prior to 1967-68 a fear, first, for its continued dominance in the Soviet Union and, secondly, for the maintenance of Soviet hegemony in Eastern Europe.

Against this background, the political developments in Czechoslovakia in 1967-68 represented an additional cause for Soviet alarm. The liberalization process, especially the abolition of censorship and the rise of various political groupings not under the control of the Czechoslovakia Communist Party, found strong appeal outside Czechoslovakia itself. Students in Poland demonstrated in support of the Czechoslovak reforms; Russian and Ukrainian intellectuals were attracted to the new model of Communism being constructed in Czechoslovakia.[4] The danger of decreased Czech dependence on the Soviet Union was highlighted by Western, especially German, willingness to finance some of the economic reforms contemplated by Dubcek and his associates. The Soviet leaders apparently decided that the possibility that the reform and reorientation being carried out in Czechoslovakia might infect the rest of Eastern Europe, as well as the Soviet population, had to be precluded. For this would have meant a reduction of Czechoslovakia's, and possibly other countries', dependence on the Soviet Union and also a threat to the domestic policies being carried out in the Soviet Union itself. In addition, similar fears of the implications of developments in Czechoslovakia for their control in East Germany and Poland led Ulbricht and Gomulka to condemn the Czechs most strongly. In fact, violent accusations against the liberalization in Czechoslovakia appeared in the East German and Polish press earlier than in the press of the U.S.S.R.

Obviously the Soviet leadership weighed the decision to intervene militarily against the possible risks involved—e.g., of antagonizing foreign Communist parties, of stimulating a revitalization of NATO, etc. However, the concern for domestic control and maintenance of the East European empire won out. In the remainder of this paper the actual results and implications of the intervention will be examined.

DEVELOPMENTS IN EASTERN EUROPE

As has already been noted, Soviet policy in Eastern Europe during the decade before 1968 was characterized by an attempt to maintain a dominant Soviet position without the use of military or terroristic methods. Increasing emphasis was placed on the economic and military integration of the area into a socialist commonwealth, but one still dominated by the Soviet Union. At the same time, however, other developments in Eastern Europe were making it increasingly difficult for the Soviet to maintain their position of hegemony.[5]

First, and of greatest importance, has been the revival throughout much of Communist Europe of a sense of nationalism that has been evident especially in Yugoslavia and Romania. This is closely related to an attempt by local Party leaders to build up a domestic political base by stressing national individuality and independence from the Soviet Union. Although Romania has been most successful along this line, Kadar has attempted, relatively successfully, to achieve the same results in Hungary.[6] However, the revival of nationalism and the evolution of a measure of independence have been largely the result of other factors, most importantly the problems of the Soviet Union in maintaining its position of authority in the international movement. The death of Stalin and his subsequent degradation helped to destroy the myth of Soviet omniscience. Khrushchev's willingness to permit different paths of socialism aided in the erosion of the preeminent position of Soviet leadership as interpreter of Marxist doctrine and guide in Communist construction. The eruption of the conflict between the Soviet Union and China has afforded the East European Party-states an opportunity to maneuver between the two giants—although to date only Romania has used it to develop a

significant degree of independence. The moderation of tensions between the Communist world and the West opened up new opportunities
for contacts and for a lessening of economic dependence on the Soviet
Union.[7]

In the light of this gradual movement toward a decrease in Soviet
domination in Eastern Europe, what meaning does the Soviet occupation
of Czechoslovakia have? First of all, it is clear that the Soviet position
in those countries that had already achieved independence—Albania
and Yugoslavia—has been weakened even more. Seven months after
the occupation, at the Ninth Congress of the League of Yugoslav Communists, Tito continued to denounce the "violation of the sovereignty
of a socialist country" and the use of military force to "thwart its
independent socialist development."[8] Besides maintaining their hostile
position on the Soviet occupation, the Yugoslavs have argued that the
growing Soviet naval presence in the Eastern Mediterranean is detrimental to the interests of the smaller countries of the area.[9] In
addition, a significant number of Communist parties refused to endorse
the Soviet position on Czechoslovakia at the Moscow Conference in
June, 1969.[10]

What the Soviet occupation has shown most clearly about Soviet
relations with Eastern Europe is that this area is considered a sphere
of primary Soviet interest or domination that will be prevented at all
costs from significantly lessening its dependence on the Soviet Union.
The elaboration of the new doctrine of "limited sovereignty" is an
attempt to justify Soviet intervention in Czechoslovakia or in any other
Communist state in which developments are viewed as a threat to
Soviet domination.[11] Final determination of the acceptability of
political or economic reform has reverted to Moscow and no longer,
apparently, will "different paths to socialism" be accepted, unless
first approved by the Soviet leadership.[12]

Developments in Czechoslovakia during the year of occupation
have indicated the lengths to which the Soviets are willing to go to
maintain the system they have created in Eastern Europe. When
pressure placed on the Dubcek regime did not accomplish Soviet
goals, he was replaced by Gustav Husak, who is much more amenable
to the Soviet position. The purges of liberal writers, as well as of
government and party officials, the imposition of new laws against
demonstrations are all part of the policy to bring Czechoslovakia
back into line. However, the anti-Soviet demonstration that erupted
on the first anniversary of the Soviet occupation indicated the failure
of the Soviet Union and its puppet government in Prague to reconcile
the Czechoslovak population to the loss of the freedoms and the reforms
of the "Prague Spring."

Although the Soviets have reasserted their military hegemony over Czechoslovakia and have shown their willingness to use coercive measures to maintain their dominance in Eastern Europe, it is unlikely that they will be able to reattain the position of authority that they had under Stalin. In fact, the occupation and the ideological justifications for it have already undermined even further the cohesion of the Party-states. In order to maintain their dominant position in the region, the Soviets have been forced to rely even more than in the past decade on the use or potential use of coercion—either economic or military—and in the future they will probably have even less "voluntary" cooperation. In other words, the attempt to develop a socialist commonwealth based on common interests has failed, and nationalist erosion will force the Soviet leadership to rely even more heavily on the traditional means available to a Great Power to maintain its hegemony in its own sphere of influence.

What this means for the development of sovereignty or independence in Eastern Europe seems quite clear. The Soviets will continue to press forward attempts to reintegrate the area into a bloc dominated by Moscow. The renewed calls for the integration of the Communist economies through a Comecon organization with suprastate power (presumably in the hands of the CPSU) are an example of this attempt. For example, the director of the Institute of Economics of the World Socialist System has proposed integration that would eventually lead to a "single world Communist economy with a single economic plan." Supranational offices would fix national production quotas in such major industries as power, heavy engineering, and chemicals.[13] In spite of Soviet pressures, however, the Comecon meeting held in East Berlin, January 21–23, 1969, apparently resulted in strong disagreements over integration as well as other issues, and no decisions were made.[14]

However, the Soviet pressures for economic integration, the replacing of Dubcek by Husak as leader of the Czechoslovak Communist Party, the reimposition of censorship on Czechoslovak publications, and the efforts to force Romania back into active participation in the military activities of the Warsaw Treaty Organization are all examples of an attempt to maintain control—if necessary by force.

THE SOVIET POSITION IN THE WORLD COMMUNIST MOVEMENT

While the occupation of Czechoslovakia has presented problems for the Soviets in Eastern Europe, they have been and probably will be able to keep these problems under control in the near future, if need be militarily. A much gloomier picture faces the Soviet leaders when they view their position within the world Communist movement. Since the beginning of 1969 the dispute with China has erupted into an undeclared, sporadic border war. Outside the area of Soviet military domination, foreign Communist parties have strongly condemned, and continue to condemn, Soviet intervention in Czechoslovakia.

In spite of Soviet claims to the contrary, it is quite clear that the Moscow Conference did not solve any of the major divisions within the international Communist movement. The list of ruling parties absent (Albania, China, North Korea, North Vietnam, and Yugoslavia) represents almost half of the world's Communist Party members. Of those parties that did attend, a number refused to sign the principal document. For example, the Italians approved only part III, which deals with the struggle against imperialism. They expressed strong disagreement with those sections dealing with Czechoslovakia, China, the interpretation of democracy, political liberties, and, in particular, the leading role of the Soviet Union in the movement.[15]

The Cuban representative, who was present only as an observer, disapproved of that part of the basic document dealing with the role of the Communist Party in the national liberation struggle. He pointed out that this did not correspond with reality in much of Latin America, where many Communists are not willing to support revolution. The delegate from the Dominican Republic supported the Cuban position and refused to sign the document.

Of the seventy-five parties actually represented in Moscow, fourteen signed only a part of the basic document or expressed serious qualifications, and three did not sign it at all. It is clear that one of the major points that divided the conference, and a point of special importance to the European parties, was the Soviet occupation of Czechoslovakia and the claim, as one Soviet writer has put it, that the "Soviet Union is the guarantor of socialism in the East European countries and any attempt against the socialist system in this area will be inevitably resisted by the Soviet Union."[16]

The invasion of Czechoslovakia, although it obviously has not caused the problems that the Soviet Union is having in maintaining its leadership in the international movement, has greatly weakened its position. In fact, it would appear that the most permanent damage wrought by the intervention to the Soviet international position is among the nonruling Communist parties—especially those in Western Europe.

Long before the Soviet decision to intervene in Czechoslovakia, the system created by Stalin had begun to disintegrate. In 1956, Palmiro Togliatti, then leader of the Italian Communist Party, referred to the developing tensions within the movement as polycentrism.[17] In the attempt to reconsolidate the Soviet position in Eastern Europe in the mid-1950's Khrushchev had recognized the possibility of different roads to socialism, and since then a number of Communist parties—both ruling parties and those not in power—have continued to establish their independence from Soviet control. This has been especially true in Italy where the Communist Party has been increasingly successful in playing a role in the national political system. By 1965, the Italian Communists were calling for the creation of a united working-class party that would include Communists and non-Communists alike.[18] They have also been very loath to support the convening of a worldwide Communist conference to deal with the problem of China, and they strongly criticized Brezhnev for introducing the question at the Moscow Conference. Similar tendencies were present in other Western European Communist parties, which have been gradually adapting themselves to the national political environments.[19]

In some respects the Soviet Party is much more dependent upon the international movement than other Communist parties are on the Soviet Union, since much of the justification for the very existence of the CPSU and for the strengthening of the Soviet state apparatus over the past fifty years has been based on the needs of the world Communist movement. The foreign parties, on the other hand, have been increasingly loosening their ties to and dependence on Moscow; while, at the same time, they have participated more in the national political systems of their own countries.[20]

The Soviet occupation of Czechoslovakia represents a major threat to the position that the nonruling European parties have built up during the past decade and adds further to the loss of authority that the CPSU has suffered since Stalin's death.[21] Immediately after the occupation, only three minor European parties (those of West Germany, Luxembourg, and Greece) supported the Soviet action, while the remainder either condemned it or expressed very serious reservations. Even the Finnish Communists condemned the use of a military solution to the problem.[22] The strong condemnations by President Tito of Yugoslavia and Ceausescu, the leader of the Romanian Party have already been noted. For the first time in its history, the French Communist Party openly disagreed with Moscow on a major issue, while the Italians have continued to berate the Soviets for their failure to leave Czechoslovakia. A number of European parties continue to voice their opposition to developments in

Czechoslovakia in spite of Soviet pressure, and in some—e.g., those of France and Austria—Soviet policy in Czechoslovakia has caused a split between those who continue to oppose the occupation and those who have resigned themselves to the Soviet fait accompli.[23]

Even outside of Europe, the Soviets were able to find only scattered Communist support—primarily among the Arab and Latin American parties—and the governments of Asia and Africa have strongly condemned the Soviet action as, in the words of President Kaunda of Zambia, "the most arrogant act of aggression since Hitler's Panzers rolled into Prague thirty years ago."[24]

Front organizations that the Soviets have spent two decades building up as auxiliary instruments of foreign policy implementation have been almost destroyed by the occupation. For example, both the French and Italian sections of the World Federation of Trade Unions condemned the invasion, and the Soviets have attempted to replace both the French secretary and the Italian president of the organization. In Prague, Soviet troops jailed the Czech president of the International Union of Students for participating in anti-Soviet demonstrations. Given the already precarious position of the Soviets in many of these front organizations because of the split with China, the occupation of Czechoslovakia is likely to lead to the further weakening of the organizations.

The long-term effect of the Soviet invasion of Czechoslovakia on the Soviet position in the world Communist movement will probably be to hasten the process of disintegration that began in the 1950's and that has speeded up since Khrushchev's overthrow in 1964. Not only will it become increasingly difficult for the Soviets to gain the support of radicals of the "New Left," as was indicated at the Soviet-sponsored Ninth World Youth Festival in Bulgaria in the summer of 1968, but it will be difficult for them to maintain their influence over "orthodox" Communists, especially in Europe, who are following reformist, rather than revolutionary, policies. The Soviet leadership is well aware of this problem, as their recent increased propaganda emphasis on the need for unity among Communist parties has indicated. However, it is very unlikely that they will be able to reestablish a position of authority over foreign parties in the future.

In Yugoslavia, the Communists have continued their policy of democratization and reconstruction of the Party, in spite of strong Soviet objections.[25] However, since June, 1969, the Soviets have attempted to improve relations with Yugoslavia. In his report to the Supreme Soviet on July 10, 1969, Foreign Minister Andrei Gromyko pointed to the "great importance" of developing "relations with socialist Yugoslavia, although these relations have not always been smooth."[26] In early September, Gromyko traveled to Belgrade for discussions with his Yugoslav counterpart. In spite of this, however, the Yugoslavs continued to oppose the Soviet intervention in Czechoslovakia and the emphasis on a "bloc approach" to international relations. In Italy, the Communists reaffirmed their decision to operate within the existing political system and have stressed the independence of each Communist party.[27] Romania has continued to assert its independence from Moscow, although it is careful not to antagonize its huge neighbor. At the Party Congress held in Bucharest from August 6 to 12, 1969, Ceausescu emphasized that it was the duty of all citizens to be "ready to fight for the defense of the freedom, sovereignty and integrity of the fatherland."[28]

SOVIET RELATIONS WITH NATO COUNTRIES

In addition to the important consequences of the occupation of Czechoslovakia for the Soviet position within the Communist movement, there are also the implications for future relations with the NATO countries, the United States in particular. During the past decade the Soviets have focused their European policy on the disintegration of the NATO alliance and the withdrawal of U.S. military power from Europe. In this, they were at least partially successful, for many West Europeans no longer saw the Soviet Union as a realistic military threat, thereby rejecting one of the bases for the NATO alliance. Besides the focus on the removal of U.S. power from Europe, the Soviet leaders have sought some sort of direct accommodation with the United States that would reduce the likelihood of a nuclear confrontation. In this, too, the Soviets have been partially successful—e.g., the nuclear test-ban treaty and the nonproliferation treaty.

In spite of the tensions between the United States and the Soviet Union created by the war in Vietnam, relations between the two countries did show gradual improvement over the past decade—especially since the Cuban missile crisis in late 1962. What, if any, effect is the occupation of Czechoslovakia likely to have on improved Soviet relations with the United States, as well as on the Soviet attempt to lessen Western European dependence on the United States? In order to answer the question, it will be necessary to distinguish between short-term and long-term results.

The initial response of the West was an attempt to resolidify the NATO alliance and a decision to strengthen NATO's military

capacity. Also, numerous meetings between Soviet and Western officials that had been planned were abruptly cancelled. A NATO declaration calling for Soviet-Western negotiations concerning mutual and
balanced reduction of military forces in Europe was shelved.[29] Overall, the immediate effect of the occupation on Soviet relations with
NATO countries was to halt the movement toward East-West detente.

In late November, 1968, the Soviet news agency Tass issued a
statement that "aggressive NATO circles" were preparing for an
intensification of military activity aimed against the Soviet Union. It
condemned NATO for "expanding war preparations" rather than seeking
to solve existing problems by "a policy of detente." This statement
concluded with the warning that

> Tass is authorized to state that any actions by members
> of the NATO military bloc will certainly be taken into
> consideration by the Soviet Union, in carrying out, jointly
> with other members of the Warsaw Treaty, appropriate
> measures to ensure the security of the states of the social-
> ist community.[30]

However, developments since the fall of 1968, especially since
the outbreak of border fighting between Chinese and Soviet military
units, indicate that the Soviet occupation of Czechoslovakia, by itself,
will not have a major lasting effect on Soviet relations with either
Western Europe or the United States. At the Budapest meeting of
Warsaw Pact members in March, the call for an all-European conference on security and peaceful cooperation was reissued—after two
years of silence on this issue. Since the border incidents with China,
the tone of Soviet relations with the West has greatly improved.
Given the minimal response of the United States and other NATO
members at the time of the invasion, it would appear that it will not
have a lasting impact on East-West relations. The U.S. government
seems to be resigned to recognizing a Soviet sphere of influence in
Eastern Europe in which the Soviets have a more or less free hand,
although President Nixon's visit to Romania in 1969 was an indication
of U.S. interest in minimal support for East European countries that
are attempting to achieve some degree of autonomy. The desire for
a detente is still present in the West, and, although some initial moves
toward the refurbishing of NATO military strength were made in the
fall of 1968, Western governments seem to remain seriously concerned
with the improvement of relations with the Soviet Union.

By January, 1969, France was willing to sign an agreement that
will double Soviet-French trade by 1975. In assessing the implications

of the agreement, Tass correspondent V. Sedykh saw this as an indication of improvements in Soviet-French cooperation.[31] In addition,
the United States, early in 1969, resumed discussions with the Soviet
Union on various levels, and in November discussions on questions of
mutual interest, especially those concerning nuclear weapons, took
place in Helsinki. The Soviets have been anxious to show that, as long
as their dominance in Eastern Europe is recognized, relations with
the West can go on as usual.

CONCLUSIONS

In conclusion, then, it appears that the invasion and continued
occupation of Czechoslovakia will probably be most detrimental to
the Soviet position within the international Communist movement and
that relations with the West will continue to develop outside the context
of developments in Czechoslovakia. The invasion itself was an indication of the desperate position in which the Soviet leaders found
themselves in attempting to maintain an empire in Eastern Europe
and preeminent status within the Communist movement. No longer
can Soviet leaders rely on support from foreign Communist parties,
and only in areas like Czechoslovakia, where Soviet leadership can
exert economic and military pressure—i.e., where it can behave as
a "great power" protecting its own sphere of domination—can it hope
to influence events. West European parties, which no longer depend
on the CPSU for support and are increasingly attracted to reformist
policies, will continue to develop their independence from Moscow.

Even in Eastern Europe, as events in Czechoslovakia since
August have shown, the Soviets, in spite of military dominance, have
been unable to achieve their political goals without direct intervention—
e.g., the eventual replacing of Dubcek by Husak. The occupation of
Czechoslovakia will not prevent the development of nationalist attitudes—in fact it has probably stimulated them. Romania continues to
carry out an independent foreign policy. In Hungary a cautious reform
of the economic system is being carried out. Unless the Soviet
leadership is willing to revert to the terror and brutality of the Stalin
era, it will be unable to completely control events in the area. Soviet
authority is crumbling and, although military force may ensure continued Soviet dominance, it will not and cannot stop the development
of nationalistic attitudes that are opposed to Soviet control and to the
creation of a "Socialist Commonwealth" along Soviet lines.

On the other hand, the Soviet leaders are unwilling—as are their
counterparts in the West—to risk the dangers of a nuclear confrontation.

Both sides seem anxious to get back to the business of increasing contacts and, in particular, of preventing the spread of nuclear weapons throughout the world, as is seen in the widespread approval of the Finnish suggestion for a European security conference and the meetings in Finland between U.S. and Soviet representatives.[32]

NOTES

1. See Robert C. Tucker's discussion of this point in "United States-Soviet Cooperation: Incentives and Obstacles," The Annals, American Academy of Political and Social Science, CCCLXXI (1967), esp. pp. 2-4.

2. Jan F. Triska and David D. Finley, Soviet Foreign Policy (New York: Crowell, Collier and Macmillan, 1968), p. 167.

3. Among the better studies are Richard Lowenthal's "The Sparrow in the Cage," Problems of Communism XVII, no. 6 (1968), 2-28; Vernon V. Aspaturian's "The Aftermath of the Czech Invasion," Current History, CV (November, 1968), 263-67, 305-10; and Adam Bromke's two articles in Canadian Slavonic Studies, X (1968), pp. 581-91 and XI (1969), pp. 23-30.

4. For example, the Soviet nuclear physicist, Andrie D. Sakhorov, in his essay entitled "Thoughts on Progress, Peaceful Coexistence and Intellectual Freedom," referred favorably to developments in Czechoslovakia. See The New York Times, July 22, 1968, p. 15.

5. For an excellent analysis of the changing relationships within the international Communist movement see Pio Uliassi and Erik Willenz, "Origins and Limits of Communist Pluralism" in Dan H. Jacobs, ed., The New Communisms (New York: Harper and Row: 1969), pp. 74-102.

6. See J. F. Brown, "Rumania Today, I: Towards 'Integration,'" Problems of Communism XVIII, No. 1 (1969), 8-17.

7. Total NATO country trade with Communist countries increased from $6.18 billion in 1964 to $8.56 billion in 1967. U.S. Department of State, Department of Intelligence and Research, Trade of NATO Countries with Communist Countries, 1964-67, Research Memorandum, REV-71, December 26, 1968, p. 2. See also the

interesting study of P. Terrence Hopmann on the effects of the moderation of East-West tensions on the cohesion of the "Communist Bloc" in "International Conflict and Cohesion in the Communist System," International Studies Quarterly XI (1967), pp. 212-36.

8. Quoted in The New York Times, March 12, 1969, p. 8.

9. Andro Gabelic, "Strategical Aspects of European Security," Review of International Affairs (Belgrade) XVII, No. 388 (June 5, 1968), 12.

10. Both the British and Italian delegations condemned the continued occupation of Czechoslovakia. See, for example, Rocco Astori, "Le Parti Communiste italien a la conference de Moscow," Est et Quest, No. 430 (July 16-31, 1969), pp. 10-12.

11. The new doctrine was first expounded by Sergei Kovalev in an article entitled "Suverenitet i internatsional'nye obiazannosti sotsialisticheskikh stran," Pravda, September 26, 1968, p. 4.

12. In connection with this reversion to Soviet control over developments in the Party-states, Soviet theoreticians have elucidated a new concept of counterrevolution to justify intervention. Accordingly, it is now argued that counterrevolution can be peaceful by "working from within, not speaking openly against socialist achievements, but at the same time pouring on dirt, falsifying, demoralizing and impairing." See S. Kovalev, "O 'mirnoi' i nemirnoi kontrrevoliutsii," Pravda, September 11, 1968, p. 4.

13. G. Sorokin, "Problemy ekonomicheskoi integratsii stran sotsializma," Voprosy ekonomiki, No. 12 (1968), pp. 77-86.

14. For an interesting discussion of the meeting see "Setback for Moscow's Comecon Plans," Radio Liberty Dispatch, February 20, 1969.

15. See Astori, op. cit.

16. Yuri Davydov, "Washington's East European Doctrines," New Times, No. 31 (1969), p. 8.

17. Palmiro Togliatti, "Nove Domande sullo Stalinismo," Nuovi Argumenti, No. 20, (May-June 1956), pp. 136-39. Cited in Uliassi and Willenz, op. cit., pp. 83-84.

18. See L'Unita, April 30, 1965 and May 31, 1965.

19. See the discussion of the evolution of Western European parties presented in Pio Uliassi, "Communism in Western Europe," in Jacobs, ed., op. cit., pp. 274-98. See also William E. Griffith, ed., Communism in Europe, 2 vols. (Cambridge, Mass.: The M.I.T. Press, 1964-66).

20. I am indebted to Erik Willenz for this observation.

21. For example, the Swedish Communist Party, which had been gradually increasing its electoral support, in part as a result of increasing independence from Moscow—which included a condemnation of the Sinyavski-Daniel trial— suffered a serious setback in the September, 1968, parliamentary election in which they lost five of eight seats and received less than 50 percent as many votes as they had in the local elections of 1966. See Est et Quest, No. 411 (October 1-15, 1968), pp. 7-8.

22. See Branko Lazitch, "La Finlande et l'agression contre la Tchecoslovaquie," Est et Quest, No. 411 (October 1-15, 1968), p. 6.

23. See, for example, the editorial in the Morning Star (London), October 3, 1969, and the comments of Ernest Fischer, recently expelled from the Austrian Communist Party, quoted in The Christian Science Monitor, November 5, 1969, p. 1.

24. Cited in The Interpreter, (September, 1968), p. 15.

25. See the report of Yugoslav reforms in The Christian Science Monitor, March 18, 1969, p. 10. For the Soviet criticism, see P. Kostin, "On Some Erroneous Concepts of the Political and Legal Development of Socialist Society," Sovetskoe gosudarstvo i pravo, No. 2 (1969). Condensed translation in Current Digest of the Soviet Press XXI, no. 15 (April 30, 1969), 3-7.

26. Pravda, July 11, 1969, pp. 2-4.

27. See The New York Times, February 16, 1969, p. 12.

28. Scinteia, August 7, 1969. Cited in East Europe XVIII, No. 8-9 (1969), 59.

29. See the interesting discussion of NATO reaction to the

occupation in Harlan Cleveland's "NATO after the Invasion," Foreign Affairs XLVII (1969), especially pp. 261-63.

30. Pravda, November 24, 1968, p. 4.

31. Pravda, January 10, 1969, p. 4.

32. See Gromyko's statement, Pravda, July 11, 1969.

**HUNGARIAN
AND POLISH
ATTITUDES
ON CZECHOSLOVAKIA,
1968**

George Gomori

Hungarian and Polish attitudes and reactions to the 1968 reform movement and the Warsaw Pact military intervention in Czechoslovakia should be investigated in the context of the power-political interests and antagonistic social forces of both countries. Apart from the viewpoint of the Communist Party and the state organs, the attitudes of the intellectuals, students, and of the "man in the street" should be presented in the light of available facts and personal experiences. As a rule, every political question that has significant international implications creates a conflict between the ruling strata and the rest of the population, the intellectuals often acting as a transmission belt between the two, or as nonconformist exponents of popular views. This is what happened after the Cuban crisis, after the Arab-Israeli war in 1967, and again in the days and months following August 21, 1968.

HUNGARIAN ATTITUDES

The leaders of the Hungarian Socialist Workers' Party were not overtly dismayed or frightened by Novotny's fall in January, 1968. The general impression made by their statements coming soon after Dubcek's assumption of power was encouraging: They were, on the whole, in favor of such personal changes as would complete the process of "de-Stalinization," long overdue in Czechoslovakia. Novotny was, by association, implicated in the crimes of the 1950's and should have stepped down earlier in order to speed up "normalization" (an emotive word in Kadar's vocabulary) and the restoration of Party unity. At the same time, however, the Hungarian leadership had probably underestimated the force of pent-up political dissatisfaction and frustration in Czechoslovakia; consequently, by the spring of 1968 it had begun to sound a note of caution. Support for the Czech program of political reform became qualified, and after the publication of "2,000 Words" and an article in Literarni listy on Imre Nagy (in May, 1968) in which the man whose name is still anathema to all Moscow-fearing Kadarists was mentioned not without sympathy, articles began to appear in the Hungarian press warning the Czech comrades to abstain from "going too far" in their democratization. The words "counterrevolutionary forces" began to appear frequently and Nepszabadsag, the Party's official paper, openly referred to the "Hungarian experience" of 1956, which had resulted from a similar drive to correct and eliminate past mistakes. Nevertheless, Kadar even at this point did not seem to be as aggressively impatient with Dubcek's efforts to regain control of the democratization process as Gomulka or Ulbricht. Himself a former victim of Stalinist abuses of legality, he had, after the cruel interlude of 1957-58 (during which he reestablished the Communist status quo in Hungary) initiated in the early 1960's a more tolerant, conciliatory political line, summed up in the slogan "he who is not against us, is with us." Although "Khrushchev's man" in Budapest, Kadar was still sufficiently trusted by the new Russian leaders to be allowed to continue his relatively "liberal" policies and to go ahead with his economic reforms. Gomulka, on the other hand, was fighting for his political life in March, 1968, and was greatly worried by the possible long-term effects of the independent internal and foreign policy toward which Dubcek's Czechoslovakia was edging in these months. He could hardly have forgotten the popular slogan of the Warsaw students in the March days: "Cala Polska czeka na swego Dubczeka!" ("All of Poland is waiting for her own Dubcek!"). Kadar did not have to face such problems and this is why he volunteered or was chosen by the Russians for the role of a go-between; he could serve as a biased but still acceptable mediator between themselves and the Czechs.

The Russians obviously attached little hope to these efforts of mediation, but they knew that, apart from Romania's Nicolae Ceausescu, whom they did not particularly trust, Kadar was the only East European statesman with whom Dubcek might discuss his plans openly and whose advice might influence the Czechoslovak leader's course of action. Dubcek visited Budapest in the early spring of 1969, and after the visit repeated consultations took place between him and Kadar, the last secret meeting occurring on August 15 or 16 in the border town of Komarno. If Kadar knew about the impending invasion of the "Five," he certainly did not reveal this to Dubcek, but he may not have known about it at all. After the Cierna meeting and the Bratislava Declaration this possibility seemed to be ruled out in any case.

Once the decision to intervene was taken in Moscow, Kadar had no choice but to go along with the Russians and send in his troops as requested. Since the first of his ideological "ten commandments" is that "there can be no Socialism which is anti-Soviet" (that is, against the Soviet Union), Kadar took part in the intervention for both ideological and tactical reasons. Hungary's role, though, was not very important in the whole operation: It involved sending two divisions mainly into South Slovakia, providing support troops and river-crossing equipment to the Russians and furnishing transportation for the token Bulgarian regiment taking part in the invasion.[1] There is a strong Hungarian minority of approximately 650,000 in Slovakia that had suffered a great deal in the past from national discrimination; it might have been thought that the population in this area would greet the Hungarian troops with sympathy and enthusiasm. According to eyewitnesses, however, this response somehow failed to materialize; the Hungarians in Czechoslovakia felt as cheated and depressed by the invasion as their fellow-citizens and many of them identified themselves with the Czechoslovak Republic for the first time in their lives. Some reports stated that the Hungarian chief of staff had to ban fraternization between the troops and the local population because many local Hungarian Communists used all their eloquence on the officers of the Hungarian Army in trying to convert them to the "Dubcekist" point of view. Hungarian troops stayed for two months altogether in Czechoslovakia; they began withdrawing on October 21, 1968, and by October 31 all were reported to have returned to Hungary.

The Hungarian population, or at least the inhabitants of Budapest, reacted to the news of the occupation with shocked surprise. Because of the vague and skimpy information put out by Tass and faithfully regorged by MTI and Radio Budapest, in the first three days following August 21 the majority of Budapest's adult population remained glued to its radios, listening to the uninterrupted flow of Hungarian-language newscasts of Radio Free Europe relayed from Munich. This fact, by the way, was openly admitted by Politburo member Lajos Feher, who, in his televised speech a few days after the invasion, blamed "poor coverage" of the events for the sudden popularity of foreign radio stations.[2] Another top functionary, Istvan Szirmai, claimed that the intervention of Warsaw Pact forces took place only when "the proletarian dictatorship . . . was violently attacked" in Czechoslovakia. The Politburo stressed that while the decision to intervene had been difficult to take and had been much debated among Party members, it was "unavoidable and necessary." In order to defend the decision against Yugoslav and Western attacks, Hungarian journalists were busily digging up any scraps of "evidence" that would show that the democratization process in Czechoslovakia posed a threat to the "essential interests" of the socialist camp. The Hungarian press, however showed some restraint in its reluctance to condemn Dubcek by name (in this not taking its cue from the Moscow Pravda), and after August, when "normalization" was going well (from the Russian point of view) in Czechoslovakia, the press demonstrated its relief, no doubt reflecting the feeling prevalent in Hungarian Party circles.

For a couple of days after August 21, 1968, all Western newspapers—including the Communist ones—disappeared from those few Budapest hotels where they had been on sale previously. Police patrols and guards at Soviet war memorials were doubled but no preventive political arrests took place. In fact, the reactions of the average Hungarian were much more muted than those of the Party activists or of certain groups of intellectuals. To quite a few people who have found the Kadar regime vastly preferable to Rakosi's sycophantic brand of Stalinism, the Czechs seemed to be a nuisance: "That's what they deserve, why did they rock the boat?" Another malicious remark heard not unfrequently in those days was, "At last the Czechs have had it as well!" (This kind of Schadenfreude, characteristic of an emotionally colored and rather primitive political thinking, was not absent in the Poland of 1968 either.) Some people, among them members of the "technical intelligentsia," in order to justify their lack of indignation, pointed to the unjust and tough treatment the Hungarian minority had suffered between 1945 and 1949 or to Prague's cold-shouldering of the Hungarian uprising in 1956: though the invasion of the "Five" could not be regarded as a tit-for-tat for mistakes committed in different political circumstances.

The three groups most shocked by the "preventive occupation" of Czechoslovakia and Dubcek's brutal kidnapping by the Russians were the social scientists, the writers, and the students. Of these, only the first expressed its opinion publicly by signing a protest against the invasion at the summer conference of Yugoslav philosophers at Korcula The Hungarian signatories to this protest, published in Knjizevne novine on August 31, 1968, were philosophers Zador Tordai and Gyorgy Markus, sociologists Vilmos Sos and Agnes Heller. Maria Markus, also a sociologist (of Polish birth), apparently did not sign the protest, but as party secretary at the Sociological Research Group (Szociologiai Kutatocsoport) of the Hungarian Academy of Science, she declared her complete agreement with the Korcula signatories. Another well-known protester was Andras Hegedus, who from a Stalinist ex-premier of 1956 evolved into an intelligent and well-read sociologist and was, at the time of the "Czechoslovak events," director of the Sociological Working Group. Hegedus sent a memorandum to the Party's Central

Committee in which he registered his strong protest against the Soviet action and Hungarian participation in it. At Party meetings in research institutes and offices all over Budapest, people demanded clarification of the events, openly expressed their doubts about the wisdom of the Soviet action and, in some cases, wanted to hand in or actually handed in their Party membership cards.

The sequel to the "revolt" of the sociologists and philosophers was highly characteristic of the balancing tactics and "two-front struggle" of the Kadar regime. Hegedus was removed from his post and the four Korcula protesters were expelled from the Party (with the exception of Heller, who had been expelled earlier), though they were allowed to keep their jobs. "Rightist" tendencies in the Sociological Research Group were condemned in a Party document, but both Hegedus and Markus were permitted to continue publishing controversial articles in the Hungarian literary and sociological press. Moreover, the purge among sociologists coincided with a purge in another institute of the Hungarian Academy—the Philosophical Institute. The director, Jozsef Szigeti, a diehard conservative, was dismayed by Kadar's "lenience" toward "rightists" and sent a long memorandum or denunciatory letter to Moscow. Brezhnev, so the story goes, returned the letter to Kadar who immediately sacked the overzealous Szigeti. The Party secretary of the Philosophical Institute was dropped at the same time. In this manner a certain balance was struck between disciplinary actions against right- and left-wing opposition to Kadar's present policy.

As for other intellectual figures, Gyorgy Lukacs was known to have spoken against the intervention in private, but did not express his disapproval in any printed text or letter. At the end of 1968, false rumors reached the West about Tibor Dery, who, according to this rumor, was pressed by the authorities to sign a statement supporting Hungarian government policy on Czechoslovakia.[3] The complete lack of truth in these allegations was revealed to the author by Dery himself in the summer of 1969. In fact, there was no such statement circulated among the writers; the party was, as it were, relieved that the writers did not initiate a public protest against the intervention. Such plans did exist among the younger writers and film directors, but after some inconclusive discussions they were quietly dropped because no elderly writer of real distinction would sign such a statement. These writers advised caution, believing that it would be unreasonable to disturb the compromise or modus vivendi that had been reached between them and the government, and, thereby, jeopardize their creative freedom and publication prospects. Only one elderly writer, the doyen of Hungarian literary historians, Aladar Komlos,

went so far as to ring up the Hungarian Writers' Association and deliver a verbal protest to the secretary. The writers' inability to organize their protest did not mean that they were not sympathetic with
Dubcek's reforms or even with the "2,000 Words". The Warsaw Pact
intervention had been a blow to their hopes as well. On the other hand,
the restraint showed by the writers in what the regime considered to
be the "critical period" paid off later in the form of continuing official
encouragement of discussions on internal problems, relatively liberal
publishing policies and a statement made by Jeno Fock, the prime
minister, to the writers in October, 1969: "We do not wish to influence
the freedom to create by administrative measures."

The third group that might have been expected to react to the
intervention was the students. The "Czechoslovak events" shattered
their illusions—based on ignorance or faith—in the possibility of a
renaissance of communist doctrine. Idealists suffered most: They
were young men and women or children in 1956 and had only a distorted
and vague understanding of the Hungarian uprising; they had not realized
the enormity of Soviet lies justifying the intervention at Budapest.
They believed that Khrushchev had managed to eliminate the worst
features of Stalinism and that now a peaceful road to socialist evolution
lay ahead for all countries of Eastern Europe. The intervention of the
"Five" showed them that as far as the Soviet leaders were concerned,
nothing has changed since Stalin's death. Although most students did
not show their feelings openly, their mood was discussed in an article
on the ideological situation of Hungarian university youth: "When the
Czechoslovak events were discussed some students raised—though in
a responsible manner—certain fears with regard to the further perspectives of changes taking place in that country."[4] In plain language
this means that they questioned the political wisdom of the Soviet
decision and expected strong reactions from the Czechoslovak population and, possibly, from Western Communist parties. The same
article points to the existence of a variety of "leftist"—i.e., romantic-
radical and pro-Chinese—groups at Hungarian universities, particularly
at the Faculty of Philology and Modern Languages in Budapest. These
groups, though isolated or numerically weak at present, are potentially
dangerous for the regime. Perhaps one is not mistaken in detecting
in the growing radicalization of Hungarian students—whether they ex-
hibit pro-Maoist, Guevarist, or quasi-Trotskyist tendencies—signs of
a deep disillusionment not only with Hungary's "little stabilization"
under Kadar but with the "progressive" character of Soviet policies as
well. For many students Soviet attitudes toward the Middle East conflict had already proved an eye-opener; for many more, Czechoslovakia
was the turning point. Although no spectacular changes can be expected
in Hungarian student politics, the Warsaw Pact intervention in

Czechoslovakia dispelled certain false hopes and illusions among the students and gave an impetus to those groups that want "to reform Socialism" in one way or another.

POLISH ATTITUDES

When sampling and analyzing Polish attitudes to the military intervention in Czechoslovakia in the summer of 1968, one very important fact must be remembered: Namely, that Poland was not the same in August, 1968, as it had been six months earlier. The so-called March events—as the Polish press euphemistically called the chain of official provocations that led to student demonstrations and, in their wake, to a country-wide purge of "Zionists, Revisionists and other unreliable elements" —broke the back of the Polish opposition that had looked toward Czechoslovakia with hope and expectation. The post-March repressions did, among other things, eliminate the possibility of such a wide emotional response to August 21, 1968, as that inspired in Poland by the Hungarian uprising in 1956. While the principal aim of General Moczar and his colleagues in provoking the March demonstrations was certainly to secure a tactical gain in the internal power struggle, which would give them a free hand in purging their real or potential enemies in the Party and State apparatus, the rapid progress of the Czech reform movement in the first two months of 1968 might have been a factor in the timing for this carefully mounted provocation.

After March the Polish press followed events in Prague with undisguised suspicion and hostility. No wonder, for some of the student leaflets distributed during the March demonstrations made explicit references to the success of the Czechs and Slovaks in changing their political leadership. "Faced with an economic crisis . . . far-reaching changes are inevitable in our country. Let us prepare ourselves to carry out these changes!" says one leaflet; "The Czechs and Slovaks showed us that it is possible."[5] In the first week of May the veiled attacks against and unfriendly references in the Polish press to Czechoslovakia were followed up by a diplomatic note in which the Polish government protested against "the anti-Polish and antisocialistic forays" in the Czechoslovak press, radio, and television.[6] The tone of this note was unusually hostile and threatening, and the phrasing of its contentions leaves no doubt about its aim: It is a grave warning— "It is clear that events in Czechoslovakia are not only the internal affairs of a brotherly country. . . . The course of events in Czechoslovakia has a fundamental bearing upon the security as well of Poland, the German Democratic Republic, and other socialist countries as upon the position of socialist forces in Europe. Consequently, in no case can we accept that counterrevolution should gain the upper hand in Czechoslovakia."[7]

In the internal Communist dispute about the relative merits of military intervention, apart from Ulbricht, Gomulka took the most orthodox line. At a certain point his vote might have been decisive in tilting the balance in favor of intervention: Kadar, as has been pointed out earlier, was not especially keen on it, and as for Zhivkov, he would have voted with the majority in any case. In the summer of 1968 Gomulka might have found his position shaken both by the March demonstrations and the nearly successful bid of the Moczar group and its allies for complete control of the Party. Partly out of fear for his own position, partly through fear of a Czech-West German rapprochement, Gomulka emerged as a stubborn defender of the status quo. As he demanded some sort of action against the Czechs, there can be no doubt that he readily agreed to support the Soviet intervention with Polish troops. With regard to power politics, his decision was correct in that it assured him powerful Russian support against any contender or pretender. Brezhnev, in his speech at the Fifth Congress of the Polish United Workers' Party (PUWP) (November 11-16, 1968), gave his full endorsement to Gomulka's "proletarian internationalism" and warned his listeners that the military action of the Warsaw Pact powers would be repeated in any country where the socialist system might be in danger. This was a blow to the Moczar group. After this speech any attempt to oust Gomulka or his closest colleagues could be interpreted by the Russians as an attack on the integrity of the system. This meant, in effect, that "national-communist slogans, even if used for exclusively tactical reasons . . . found themselves in the same dock as . . . revisionism."[8] Gomulka's support for the Russian adventure in Czechoslovakia guaranteed him continued Soviet support, and it paralyzed his internal opposition. On the other hand, it tied him even closer to the Brezhnev leadership; thus any change in Moscow might give his opponents a better chance to remove him. Although both Gierek and Moczar supported the intervention in Czechoslovakia, the man personally responsible for Polish participation in this shameful action was Gomulka.

Protests against the military intervention—in which four mixed Polish-Soviet divisions took part, with Polish military headquarters in Hradec Kralove—came mostly from the most articulate and best educated strata of society: students and intellectuals. While most "liberal-minded" Party members, still reeling from the savage purge that followed the "March events," were passive and watched the intervention with helpless sadness and dismay, the average Pole had mixed feelings about the whole affair: bewilderment and shame, possibly a wish for justification that was hard to find. The account of an English journalist, according to which "most Poles accept the official line that intervention was necessary to protect the security of Poland, " is unfair and misleading.[9] It is more correct to say that people simply lacked the will to act and that, after March, 1968, they were too intimidated, or too preoccupied with their own problems, to make any sort of protest against government policies. Further, traditional anti-Czech prejudices and antipathies as well as more recent political experiences (Zaolzie* anti-Polish attitudes in 1956) may have played a part in their passivity.

Student protest was mainly expressed in writing pro-Czech slogans on walls in Warsaw and in an extensive distribution of leaflets. The Polish press reported only one such incident, that of September 24, 1968, when four young Danish tourists distributed leaflets in front of the Central Department Store in Warsaw. The text of these leaflets "presented events in Czechoslovakia in a false and, to our country hostile, light," said Zycie Warszawy.[10] The Danes were promptly expelled but this did not stop the peddling and distribution of leaflets by students. Scores of them were arrested in the second half of 1968 and put on trial in 1969; a report gives six names and states that one, Piotr Zebrun, was sentenced to eighteen months in jail in April, 1969. His trial and the trial of four other students held on the same charge were not reported in the Polish press.[11] In early 1969 there was another wave of arrests: Some students had smuggled leaflets printed in Polish across the border from Czechoslovakia and had formed an illegal network of distributions.[12] Among those arrested was Marek Wlodek, grandson of the loyalist President of the Polish Writer's Association, and Jaroslaw Iwaszkiewicz (this kind of conflict, in which sons and grandsons of leading functionaries are involved in antigovernment action is not at all rare in Poland). There were reports of pro-Czechoslovak leaflets circulating in Wroclaw, where a group of students decided to send an anonymous letter to Radio Free Europe expressing solidarity with the Czechoslovak people.

The text of one such student leaflet, born out of the immediate reaction of Warsaw students to the Warsaw Pact intervention, was published in the West. It is worth quoting, at least in part, for it shows the truly revolutionary and internationalist character of Polish student solidarity with Czechoslovakia:

---

*Section of Czechoslovakia annexed to Poland in 1938, after the Munich Pact.

The same forces which massacred workers in Poznan and suppressed the 1956 revolution in Hungary in blood, which carrying out an anti-Socialist internal policy eliminated in the years that followed the achievements of the Polish October, those forces which in March of this year brutally struck out against the movement of students and workers— today are trying to suppress the process of general renewal in Czechoslovakia.

The occupation of Zaolzie by the Polish army at the time of the Hitlerist partition of Czechoslovakia was shameful—the participation of the Polish People's Army in the recent aggression is shameful.

Shame to the aggressors!

Czechoslovakia, you are not alone![13]

The ideological affinity between the forces active in the Czechoslovak political renaissance of 1968 and those working in the March movement in Poland was also noted by Brigadier General Jan Czapla, the deputy head of the Chief Political Bureau of the Polish Army, who pointed out the similarity in an article published in Trybuna Ludu soon after the invasion took place. Czapla, however, true to his "partisan" sympathies, trod much too heavily in claiming that "the common characteristics of all antisocialist forces (in Czechoslovakia) was the same unusually expansive fusion of Revisionism and Zionism (as in Poland)."[14] This accusation was never brought up either by Gomulka or by Cyrankiewicz, both of whom might have felt that the anti-Zionist campaign in Poland had gotten seriously out of hand; both based the justification for the Warsaw Pact intervention mainly on the alleged danger from West Germany—Gomulka's "traditional" propaganda monster.

Neither explanation was fully accepted by all Party members. At numerous Party meetings the official interpretation of events was challenged by dissenters, mostly intellectuals, some of whom demonstratively returned their Party cards. Among those leaving the PUWP voluntarily in the weeks that followed August 21, 1968, were the philosopher Wladyslaw Krajewski, the historian Tadeusz Lepkowski and the well-known writer and translator Witold Wirpsza. Again, the fact should be stressed that the Polish United Workers' Party had already lost most of its "freethinking" writers and intellectuals in 1967, in connection with the Kolakowski affair, and in March-April, 1968, as a result of the "anti-Revisionist" purge. Intervention in Czechoslovakia was for the Party only one in a series of debacles resulting in the almos

total alienation of Marxist or leftist intellectuals from the ruling group,
from the seat of political power.

Although the students' protest was, by its very nature, clandestine
and the protests of individual Party members did not get much publi-
city abroad, the stand taken by a number of Polish writers and artists
in and outside Poland against foreign interference in the affairs of
Czechoslovakia made a strong impact on world opinion. The Paris-
bound Polish periodical Kultura, in its October, 1968, issue, published
the text of protest letters by Jerzy Andrzejewski, Slawomir Mrozek,
the painter Jan Lebenstein, the composer Zygmunt Mycielski, and the
architects Maria Paczowska and Bohdan Paczowski. Andrzejewski
and Mycielski wrote from Warsaw, addressing their letters to the
president of the Czechoslovak Writers' Association, Eduard Goldstucker, and to the members of the Czech and Slovak Association of
Composers respectively. Andrzejewski's letter to Goldstucker, which
was first published in the Yugoslav daily Borba, assures the Czech
and Slovak writers of his feelings of the "deepest solidarity" and "a
real brotherhood," adding that though he expressed "only his own
thoughts and feelings, nevertheless believes that in this he is supported
by the overwhelming majority of Polish writers for whom such words
as truth, love, loyalty, hope, patriotism and progress are not yet dead
or have not yet changed into a heavy stone."[15]

Andrzejewski's letter was attacked furiously two days later in
the Warsaw paper Zycie Warszawy—but as Andrzejewski had already
been blacklisted in March, no further action could be taken against
him by the authorities save an arrest and trial for "treason." Attacks
against him in the press grew nastier, while in liberal circles he was
feted as the hero of the day. Mrozek, on the other hand, who had been
living in the West for years and was not in Poland at the time of the
"March events" was more vulnerable: After the publication of his
letter in the Western press he was declared "unprintable" in Poland
and his plays were taken off the program of Polish theaters. The ban
on both writers was still valid in December, 1969, although Ashes and
Diamonds, Andrzejewski's earlier novel and socialist best-seller, was
recently reissued. The protest of Mrozek and Andrzejewski had an
enormous symbolic value for Polish intellectuals, for it showed that
some writers, their compatriots, had the courage to remain loyal to
the best traditions of the Polish nation, to its love of freedom and independence. The Czechs, on their part, were grateful for the solidarity
of Polish writers (they knew that Andrzejewski was speaking on behalf
of many friends and colleagues) and demonstrated their gratitude in a
practical way—helping some of the Warsaw writers to survive the year-
long period of forced silence through generous fees paid by Czech and
Slovak publishing houses that had continued to publish their works.

Even this somewhat fragmentary analysis of Polish reactions
to August, 1968, in Czechoslovakia demonstrates that for the forces
of reform, for the "intellectual opposition" to the increasingly conservative and authoritarian attitudes of the Gomulka regime, the failure
of the Czechoslovak experiment was a much greater blow than to their
Hungarian counterparts (a reflection, of course, of the greater flexibility of the Hungarian Party leadership). After March, 1968, Czechoslovakia remained the only hope of forward-looking Polish intellectuals,
while for a good many Party functionaries the Prague experiment represented the only serious threat to the maintenance of the political
status quo. Although it also amounted to a setback for the "radical
Right" within the Party, that is, to Moczar and his group, the Warsaw
Pact intervention in Czechoslovakia only deepened the rift in Polish
society that had first appeared in March of the same year; it
solved nothing, and only postponed the satisfactory resolution of East-
West hostility in Europe and of Poland's internal problems as well.

NOTES

1. Sunday Telegraph (London), October 20, 1968.

2. Quoted in East Europe, October, 1968, p. 61.

3. See L. Lederer's article in the Observer (London), December
29, 1968, p. 2.

4. Felsooktatasi Szemle, July-August, 1969, p. 391.

5. Polskie przedwiosnie (Polish Harbinger of Spring), Dokumentc
marcowych T. II. (Paris, 1969(, pp. 42-43.

6. Ibid., pp. 126-28.

7. Ibid., pp. 127-28.

8. Leon Szulczynski in Kultura (Paris), January 2, 1969, p. 127.

9. Nicolas Bethell in The Times, March 20, 1969.

10. Zycie Warszawy, September 29-30, 1968.

11. On The Air (London) VII, 73-74 (April-May, 1969), p. 47.

12. The trial of five so-called Tatra-Climbers took place in February, 1970, in Warsaw. They were accused, among other things, of the smuggling and illegal distribution of such documents of the Prague Spring as the "2,000 Words." The accused drew sentences between four and a half to three years.

13. Polskie przedwiosnie (Paris, 1969), p. 130.

14. Trybuna Ludu, No. 233 (August 25, 1968).

15. The full Polish text is published in Kultura (Paris), No. 253, pp. 209-10.

THE HUNGARIAN
AND CZECHOSLOVAK
REVOLUTIONS:
A COMPARATIVE STUDY
OF REVOLUTIONS
IN COMMUNIST COUNTRIES

Ivan Volgyes

The revolution of 1956 in Hungary and the "Czechoslovak Spring" of 1968 attracted the interest, the attention, and the sympathy of the world. The events of these revolutions have been recorded in detail by the world press, and scholars have added insights through prodigious research in various publications. Unfortunately, however, little consideration has been given to a comparative study of these events. Methodological problems and lack of data have prevented East European specialists from examining these revolutions in the framework of comparative studies. Yet such a task is greatly warranted, for these revolutions were only two in a long series of risings occurring Communist countries. By examining each of them it might be possible to draw some insight into the changing nature of Communist society and, perhaps, to discern the conditions that can cause disruption in Communist political systems.

This study is merely a first step in this direction. In the light of the concepts of political science, the Hungarian and the Czechoslovak revolutions will be examined as the two extremes of revolutionary development in Communist states.[1] The first was quite brief and bloody and attempted to destroy the Communist system in Hungary; the second was relatively bloodless and sought to maintain a form of communism in Czechoslovakia. An examination of the similarities and differences between these two revolutions may suggest conclusions regarding the nature of revolutionary change in Communist countries.

For the purposes of this paper, the Hungarian uprising of 1954-5
and the Czech liberalization movement of 1967-68 will be regarded as
revolutions.[2] "Revolution" will be defined as a certain form of rapid
systemic change, accompanied by or resulting in violence;[3] specificall
to use Chalmers Johnson's phrase, "intrasystemic violence."[4] Both
in Hungary and in Czechoslovakia rapid essential systemic changes
took place during the periods to be discussed. Even though there was
little or no armed conflict in Czechoslovakia, the systemic changes
were of such a nature that, as in the Hungarian situation, events culminated in the forceful repression of a specific kind of political process.

SIMILARITIES

Certain obvious similarities in the two revolutions may be
discerned. Both uprisings were anti-Russian in that their ultimate
aim was independence from foreign control. Both attempted to establish greater internal freedom. Both were revolts against autocratic
regimes whose repressive practices, even though they were clothed
in the cloak of "legitimating ideology," were despised and hated by
the population of the countries.[5] And both revolutions failed.

In addition, there are a number of significant, though less obvious, similarities, many of them related to failures resulting from
the functioning of the sociopolitical systems in the two countries.
Much of the discontent that led to revolutionary activity in both countries can be attributed to the fact that both Czechoslovakia and Hungary
were Communist apparat-states (bureaucratic [Police]-states).[6]
Both were monocracies where political opposition was not tolerated.[7]
In both of these states one or two apparats—namely the party and/or
the secret police—dominated and coordinated all operations of the
polity. The social organization that, in theory, was supposed to be
classless and was supposed to abolish men's alienation from one
another failed to attain these goals. Rather, the social organization
of the two countries was characterized by enormous inequalities in
the allocation of authority and power. Such a situation, according to
Rolf Dahrendorf, is a "lasting determinant of social conflict."[8] As
was pointed out as early as Aristotle's time, the desire to abolish
this inequality has been one of the major causes of revolution;[9] the
Czechoslovak and Hungarian revolutions were no exceptions to the
rule.

A second aspect of the monocratic sociopolitical system that
contributed to rising discontent was the very success of the Communis

mobilization system utilized by the ruling apparats. Both in Hungary and in Czechoslovakia, the mobilization system included a rigorous political socialization process. The success of the socialization process is evident from the fact that in both revolutions the leaders of the revolt were prominent party members and students, with shared "cognitive orientations" and uniform conceptions regarding the goals of their societies.[10] Because of the very success of the process, however, most of them were also people who believed in the idealized Communist value-system. When confronted with the differences between the ideology and reality, they rebelled against those aspects of the system that did not measure up to their internalized values.[11]

A third aspect of the socio-political system that led to discontent in both countries is related to the divergency between the theoretical and the actual locus of power. Both in Hungary and in Czechoslovakia power that theoretically was supposed to reside in the party was, in reality, held by the political police. The orthodox party leaders, Rakosi and Novotny, regarded the political police rather than the party as more useful for the maintenance of power. Consequently, the ruling party leadership viewed any attempts at "democratization" of the political life as an effort on the part of the reformers to make the party the supreme apparat. Since the conservative party leadership held power through the utilization of the police apparat, this orthodox element resisted the efforts of Nagy and his reforming comrades in 1954 and the early efforts of the Czech reformers throughout the years, 1963-66.

Another similarity can be observed in both countries prior to the onset of revolutionary conflict. Both of the monocracies suffered economic setbacks that became obvious to the general public. While direct comparisons cannot be made between industrializing Hungary in 1956 and the industrialized Czechoslovakia of 1968, it is a fact that there were economic crises in both of these countries prior to the outbreak of the revolutions. In Hungary it was the issue of the economic plan submitted by Erno Gero in 1954 that brought Imre Nagy, in October of that year, to push for a higher standard of living, less forced delivery, more incentives, and more consumer goods. These same goals, ably advocated by the economist Ota Sik, were to lead Alexander Dubcek to the apex of his power.[12]

The two revolutions were also similar in goal orientation. They both sought more pragmatic national objectives, rational economic planning, less waste, economic reforms, and other concrete goals. In a speech delivered during 1954, Nagy stressed these rational elements as the real attributes of socialism. The Czech reformers sought similar goals in their attempts to change in 1968.

The political demands of the reformers in both countries also were similar. They included: (1) liberalization of controls over the day-to-day affairs of the citizens; (2) an increasing pluralization of political and economic decision making; and (3) the democratization of the political processes. In each case, the liberalization of controls over daily life was essentially an attempt to rid the country of the oppressive Stalinist system imposed on the polity by the orthodox Communist leaders. It is obvious to anyone familiar with these two countries that both Rakosi and Gottwald, and later Novotny, used terror in excess, and that the daily lives of Hungarian and Czechoslovak citizens of the time were ordered by measures of near total control. The system of totalitarian control was justified by the party as necessary for accomplishing the task of modernization, yet the people of both countries began to doubt that progress was being made. They began to question the legitimacy of the methods of governing and the very existence of totalitarian government. In short, there was a "crisis of legitimacy" in both countries. Rakosi, Novotny, and the policies they followed came to be regarded as unacceptable because they had failed to accomplish the task they were supposed to accomplish. It was felt that if Stalinism and the deprivation of freedom did not accomplish goals of Communism, a liberal alternative might be able to do better. The liberal alternative, however, implied de-Stalinization and de-Stalinization meant the rehabilitation of those who were the victims of Stalinism.

In both countries the rehabilitations focused public attention on the malfunctioning of the political system. The reappearance of released political prisoners and the effects of Laszlo Rajk's, Clementis', Novomesky's and Rudolph Slansky's rehabilitations were enormous. According to Goldstucker, the rehabilitations seemed to raise grave doubts in the minds of the people about the legitimacy of the Communist leadership and Communist policies:

> I don't know whether it is possible to rehabilitate a person who was humiliated as a political prisoner. Freedom can be restored to a prisoner, the charges against him dropped: he can even have his civil liberties restored and receive financial compensation. But reparation for the loss of human dignity to which he was subjected is hardly possible.[13]

Ferenc Munnich's emotional speech, following the rehabilitation of Rajk, his reinterment, and the "ordeal of the bier," attempted to place the blame on the "cult of personality":

He [Rajk] was killed by sadistic criminals who had crawled into the sun from the stinking swamp of the 'cult of person- ality.' This swamp was a breeding ground for the falsifi- cation of history, for careerism, for contempt for tradition and law. . . . Those in whose name I now say farewell to Laszlo Rajk will fight for a strong and inviolable socialist democracy, for socialist humanism and legality.[14]

But the rehabilitation ceremonies not only called attention to the responsibility of individual leaders and to the denigrated concept of the "cult of personality"; they also focused on the failure of the system that could allow such tyranny to exist and flourish.

The silent demonstration of the hundreds of thousands of mourners was a pledge not only that we will preserve the pure memories (of the dead leaders), but will also re- member the dark practices of tyranny, lawlessness, slan- der and defrauding of the people. . . . People were numbed not only by a deep sense of grief . . . but by burning hatred, by the memory that these comrades, these men were ex- ecuted as enemies of the fatherland, of the people! We were led to believe—and were willing to believe—the slan- ders about you![15]

With the attack on Stalinism, the fight for liberalization and "democracy" had just begun. The demands were inchoate, vague, and ill formulated. The people wanted "justice, freedom, truth."[16] They wanted a society characterized by "free and critical expression,"[17] and an "open society governed by humanism."[18] The November, 1955, Memorandum[19] and the "2,000 Words,"[20] while differing in particulars, expressed the same demands.

Furthermore, in both countries there was a demand for the pluralization of the political and economic life. The pluralization of the political process was accepted as a basic goal by both of these revolutions. Both in Hungary and in Czechoslovakia, the first demand was for an end to monocracy and a return to a system where political opposition could exist in institutionalized form. In an interview on October 31, 1956, Kadar envisioned a system where "There will be an opposition and no dictatorship."[21] On October 30, 1956, Nagy informed Hungary that the acting cabinet "has abolished the one-party system and has placed the country's government on the basis of demo- cratic cooperation between the coalition parties reborn in 1945."[22]

Similarly, in Czechoslovakia the control of the Communist Party was lessened. The Czech Party reforms released some of the Party's responsibilities to other bodies, such as the Parliament.[23] This pluralization in decision making was followed by the creation of new interest groups such as the League of Women, the Sokols (youth athletic organizations) and the Union of Collective Farms. Interest aggregation was further fostered by the newly strengthened trade unions and by a permissive attitude toward the creation of opposition political groups such as the KAN, the Club of Committed Non-Party People, the K-231, and even the Friends of Israel. The restoration of opposition political parties including the Czech People's Party, the Czech Socialist Party, and the Slovak Freedom and Renascence Party meant an end to the concept of monocratic rule.[24] Contrary to the protestations by Czech leaders and in confirmation of the Soviet view, the Czech Communist Party was losing its influence and determination as the sole control over the life of the people. But this was a process that perhaps was unavoidable, because, especially in the case of Czechoslovakia, the modernization of the country and its economic achievements created apparats that demanded larger portions of the political power.

Additional similarities in the Czechoslovak and Hungarian uprisings may be found in the apparats that served as the primary agents of revolution. In Hungary the intelligentsia served as the primary agent of revolution and it was the most important vehicle of change. The intellectual ferment began with the debates that started in November, 1953, when Peter Kuczka published his Nyirsegi Naplo. At that time, the intellectuals, led by Tibor Dery, Tamas Aczel, and a multitude of others, began agitating for a change. They slowly began to realize that Hungary was controlled by a dictatorship, unjust and cruel, that had made considerably less progress than it claimed.[25] Many fought against this realization as long as possible for they had invested nearly a lifetime of belief in the socialist ideals of the regime.

In Czechoslovakia the agents of revolution that began the revolt were somewhat different from those that precipitated the Hungarian revolution. In Czechoslovakia it was the intelligentsia, the economic apparat, and the workers who fomented the change. The intellectual battle that began at Liblice in May, 1963, was focused on the issue of Franz Kafka and the Czechoslovak authorities' censorship of his publications. Again, the debate was initiated by intellectuals. They included Eduard Goldstucker, Ludwik Vaculik, Ivan Svitak, and many others.[26]

In addition to the intelligentsia, the modernizing managerial elite and the workers of Czechoslovakia also joined the battle against the system. The managerial elite was advocating a complete overhaul of the economy, which had suffered tremendously under the

centralized direction of leaders who had imposed the Soviet economic
model on Czechoslovakia. Backed by the intellectuals, the managerial
elite began a concentrated attack on the Party's economic policies,
which had virtually ruined the highly developed Czech industries, yet
had failed to develop the industries of Slovakia and Moravia.[27]

There were two additional groups—the workers and the students—
that played important roles in the revolutions of both countries. The
workers revolted against oppression in a state where they were supposed to be the rulers. The arguments of the Workers' Opposition of
1921 were reiterated by the Hungarian workers in 1956 and Czech
workers in 1968. In each case, labor wanted more control over management and production. Deprived of viable channels of expression,
since the trade unions were the "transmission-belts of the party" and
not legitimate protective associations, the workers demanded self-
management through workers' councils or factory councils.[28]

In both of these states the students also played an important role
in fomenting the revolutions. The similarities in their activities in
the two countries is enormous. In the Hungarian and Czech revolutions,
the leaders of the youth were the students who were most active in
politics. In the 1956 Hungarian revolution and the 1968 Czech Spring
a large percentage of the rebellious students were party members,
for in both of these countries the political socialization process had
succeeded in transmitting the desired "values and behavioral patterns"
to the students.[29] It was precisely because of the ideology instilled
in them through the political socialization process that they were able
to realize the dichotomy between doctrine and reality.[30] This realization led the students to demand the establishment of a state that
would more clearly resemble their idealized institution.

There exists another similarity between the two revolutions—
the role the U.S.S.R. played in repressing these attempts to liberalize
orthodox Communist regimes. In both cases, part of the motivation
to rebel stemmed from the desire of the Hungarian and Czechoslovak
people to lessen their dependence on the Soviet Union, the dominant
power in Eastern Europe. In 1956 the Hungarian leaders initially
attempted merely to change Hungary's subordination to the U.S.S.R.
to equal status in order to enable Hungary to act as a "sovereign"
power. Similarly, Czechoslovakia intended to act as a sovereign
power in trying to formulate policies that—at least in the eyes of the
Soviet leadership—were at variance with Soviet interests. In order
to reach an acceptable compromise, both nations attempted to find
an alternative to their status of subordination to the Soviet Union that
would be acceptable both to the U.S.S.R. and to themselves. The

Hungarians, in 1956, arrived at a solution they termed "the third way."
Kadar explained "the third way" in an interview published in Il Giornale
d'Italia on November 2, 1956. He said:

> Our communism is Hungarian. It is a sort of 'third line,'
> with no connection to Titoism or Gomulkaism. . . . It is
> Marxism-Leninism applied to the particular requirements
> of our country, to our difficulties and to our national prob-
> lems. It is not inspired either by the U.S.S.R. nor by other
> types of communism and I repeat that it is Hungarian Na-
> tional communism. This 'third line' originated from our
> Revolution during the course of which, as you know, nu-
> merous communists fought at the side of students, workers
> and the people.[31]

The policies of the Czechoslovak leaders during the 1968 liber-
alizations were strikingly similar to Kadar's solution. Goldstucker,
for example, stated:

> Why shouldn't the third model . . . be possible? Why should
> something be inconceivable because it has not been thought
> of until now? There is absolutely no reason why our so-
> ciety, which has surmounted antagonistic contradictions
> (not conflicts of interest, of course), and therefore stands
> on a higher level, should not be in a position to guarantee
> more freedom than capitalist society. . . .[32]

The policy of "the third way" implied a new kind of relationship with the Soviet Union. According to Kadar, a "friendly" relationship with the U.S.S.R. would be maintained, but the presence in the
government of elements increasingly hostile to the U.S.S.R. made the
Soviet Leaders suspicious. The revolutionary government of Hungary
drifted from the position of maintaining closer relations with the
U.S.S.R. to "the renunciation of . . . obligations stemming from the
Warsaw Pact" and the declaration of neutrality.[33] This action insured
Soviet intervention and the reimposition of Soviet interest over Hungary.

The Soviet leadership interpreted the international implications
of the Czechoslovak reforms on the basis of its experience with Hungary in 1956. The implication that the Czechoslovak reforms would
mean independent action disturbed Soviet military leaders, who saw
in these activities a threat to the effectiveness of the Warsaw Pact.
The desire of the Czech leaders to convince West Germany to renounce the Munich Pact, their willingness to accept much needed

credit from the West, and their attempt to stabilize diplomatic relations with the German Federal Republic, convinced the Soviet leadership that Czechoslovakia really wanted to desert the Soviet alliance.
All of these activities were too closely related to the events in Hungary
during 1956 as far as the Soviet leaders were concerned. They felt
that, like Hungary, Czechoslovakia would opt for neutrality and renounce the Warsaw Pact, a situation they believed they could not permit.

DIFFERENCES

In contrast to the similarities between the Hungarian situation
in 1956 and the 1968 Czechoslovak Spring, there are also a number
of significant differences between the two revolutions. The first of
these differences is related to changes in the international situation
between 1956 and 1968. The Hungarian revolution occurred at a time
when the Soviet Union was still in its semi-isolationist phase, when
cold-war tensions characterized East-West relations, when Khrushchev
had not yet attained full power and when the Sino-Soviet split did not
play any role in Soviet policy formulation. The Czechoslovak revolution, however, occurred when the Soviet Union was encouraging active
contact with the Western powers, when the doctrine of peaceful coexistence with the West had replaced the view that war between the capitalist and socialist system was inevitable, when the Soviet Union was
being threatened by an increasingly hostile China, and when the leadership of the U.S.S.R. was concentrated in the hands of rational, pragmatic men.

Another significant difference between the two revolutions lies
in the nature of the ties binding the countries of the Soviet bloc to the
U.S.S.R. At the time of the Hungarian revolution the U.S.S.R. overtly
or covertly controlled all of the Communist states in Europe except
Albania and Yugoslavia, and the native Communist Party leadership
was heavily dependent on Moscow. The revolution in Czechoslovakia,
however, took place at a time when the ideas of independence and of
national sovereignty were at least tacitly accepted, within certain
limits, by the Soviet leaders.

The resolution of nationality problems was also significantly
different in Hungary and in Czechoslovakia. Hungary in 1956 was a
largely homogeneous nation, with no major ethnic conflict except,
perhaps, a dormant antisemitism; while in Czechoslovakia during
1968 a serious ethnic-national problem threatened the tenuous federation with collapse. Unlike Hungary, Czechoslovakia underwent two
processes of change in 1968: It tried to assert its independence as

a nation, and it transformed itself into a state with greater freedom
granted to its minorities. The pressure of the Slovak minority caused
Czechoslovakia to federalize to a greater extent than ever before.[34]

The roles played by the two communist Parties also differed
significantly in the two revolutions. The Hungarian Workers' Party
simply disintegrated in 1956; only those members of the Party who
could appeal to the people for support on the basis of a program of
national communism were able to act effectively in the revolution.[35]
In Czechoslovakia, however, the Party retained its strength and
actually led the revolt. It was the Czechoslovak Communist leadership
that ousted Novotny and initiated economic reforms and cultural innovations. The Czechoslovak Communist Party leadership was in
charge of the revolt; no real coalition government such as the November 3, 1956, government in Hungary existed.[36]

Another difference between the Hungarian and Czech revolutions
was in the level of development reached by the two nations at the time
when the uprisings occurred. In 1956 Hungary was not nearly as
modernized a state as was Czechoslovakia in 1968. Related to this
difference is the role that the workers played in the two revolutions.
In Hungary there was little or no difference between the attitude of the
workers and that of the technical apparat toward the revolution. In
Czechoslovakia, however, there was a cleavage between the workers
and the managers. The Czechoslovak "new economic model" benefited
the latter to a much greater extent than the former. Consequently,
the reforms were regarded with suspicion by the workers, who remained separated from the managerial, modernizing elite until an
anti-Russian nationalism unified them in a common cause.[37]

Finally, the Czechoslovak revolution was more peaceful, better
controlled, better led, and, therefore, more successful in the long
run than its Hungarian predecessor. Its achievements probably will
be more enduring than the accomplishments of the Hungarian revolution. The government and the Party of Czechoslovakia avoided as
much bloodshed as possible and, instead of declaring a pro-Western
policy, were content to force the Stalinist leadership to relinquish
the reins of power. In the end, of course, in spite of these differences,
both revolutions had to acknowledge what Evgenii Shmurlo called the
"Russian hegemony" over Eastern Europe.[38]

CONCLUSIONS ABOUT THE NATURE OF
REVOLUTIONS IN COMMUNIST STATES

If, then, a comparative examination of the Czechoslovak Spring
of 1968 and the Hungarian Revolt of 1956 may serve as a model,

it may be possible to begin drawing a few conclusions about the nature of revolutions in Communist states. First, it must be observed that, contrary to the theories of Marxism-Leninism, the Communist form of government does not prevent alienation, discontent, and revolution. Second, it can be concluded that, although in theory "politics" was abolished with the establishment of the peoples' democracies, political strife is, in reality, a very viable force even in the Communist states. And third, it is obvious that revolutions in Communist countries generally follow the historical patterns set by other revolutionary upheavals.

It also seems that revolutions in Communist countries have been and will be triggered by a "crisis of legitimacy." These crises apparently occur when the established leadership and its controlling apparats no longer accomplish the tasks they attempted to undertake and when the knowledge of the leadership's failure becomes apparent to the population. The leadership clings tenaciously to the legitimating ideology; the leaders juggle their policies, changing them ever so slightly, a step at a time, but by so doing they eventually create a "credibility gap." Finally, the leadership is forced to move from its extreme position toward the center, only to find that the center has been preempted by some other apparat.

Evidence also seems to indicate that revolutionary change in Communist countries follows a well-established pattern and only occurs after nonrevolutionary change has failed to accomplish the task most urgently at hand. As Chalmers Johnson has stated: "True revolution . . . is the acceptance of violence in order to cause the system to change when all else failed, and the very idea of revolution is contingent upon this perception of societal failure."[39] The Czechoslovak and Hungarian revolutions were no exception to this rule.

Furthermore, revolution in Communist states is inherently connected with the modernizing process. It appears that support for Communist systems is strongest in areas where communism is viewed as a successful model for modernization. The downtrodden masses in developing countries who have "nothing to lose but their chains" accept the Communist system, which claims to have a plan to modernize society, in order to better the lives of the people in their lifetime. In order to undertake large-scale modernization, the Communist states develop their mobilization systems. The Party apparat and the political police apparat, sometimes backed by the army, seem to enjoy a nearly complete autonomy. Following the establishment of the plan, all other apparats become secondary: The "magic criterion of growth" dictates the tempo, enforces the change, and punishes the nonproductive culprits. Yet, with the "success," or at least relative success, of modernization, that magic criterion is replaced by another:

efficiency. As demands for efficiency increase, the importance of the technical strata of society, the managerial apparat, assumes a greater role. The Party and the police, in calling on the apparats of the intelligentsia and the managers, create their own Golem. The demand aggregation process begins, and channels for demand articulation are developed. The Party apparat at this stage has two alternatives available: either to attempt to crush those apparats that are becoming too important, or to co-opt the managers and the intelligentsia into the leadership and hope that the party apparat will be strong enough to retain control. In either case, however, the importance of the political police decreases as the importance of the managerial and intelligentsia apparats rise. Both Czechoslovakia and Hungary attest to this pattern.

Another conclusion may be drawn from this comparison of revolutions in Communist states. In all cases a fervent nationalism must be present—a reassertion of the importance of the nation, followed by a search for a national policy, national communism, or even national socialism—but anti-Communist revolutions do not seek to alter the basic concepts of socialism. Even the Hungarian revolution desired the retention of a form of socialism and attempted to maintain the form of social ownership. The social and economic achievements of the postwar years, such as free education, pensions, free national support, etc., will not be given up. It is highly improbable that future revolutions in Eastern Europe will attempt to return to capitalism.

Finally, one must observe that the demands in the European Communist states where revolutions have occurred have been, and will be, manifestations of a desire to rejoin the European community from which they have been excluded by the cold war. Their wish to be a part of the community from which the artificial line of the cold war has separated them, however, cannot materialize as long as their desire is in conflict with the Soviet Union's interpretation of its need for a sphere of influence in Eastern Europe. It is therefore likely that their enforced separation from and desire to rejoin the rest of the European community will lead to further conflicts with the U.S.S.R. and to revolutions within the European Communist states.

NOTES

1. Reference to the most important works on the Hungarian revolution may be found in I. L. Halasz de Beky, comp., A Bibliography of the Hungarian Revolution, 1956 (Toronto: The University of

Toronto Press, 1963). This work only covers the period 1957-60.
The following volumes published after 1960 are of particular impor-
tance: Tamas Aczel, ed., Ten Years After (London: Macgibbon and
Kee, 1966); Francois Fejto, Budapest, 1956 (Paris: Julliard, 1956);
Peter Gosztony, comp., Der Ungarische Volksaufstand in Augenzeugen-
berichten (Dusseldorf: Rauch, 1966); Ervin Hollos, Kik Voltak, Mit
Akartak?, (Budapest: Kossuth, 1967); Paul Kecskemeti, The Unex-
pected Revolution (Stanford, Calif.: Stanford University Press, 1961);
Richard Lettis and William E. Morris, eds., The Hungarian Revolt
(New York: Scribner, 1961); Jean Jacques Marie, Pologne-Hongrie
1956 ou le Printemps en Octobre (Paris: Etudes et Documentations
Internationales, 1966); Tibor Meray, Budapest, 23 Octobre, 1956 (Paris:
R. Laffont, 1966); Janos Molnar, Ellenforradalom Magyarorszagon
(Budapest: Akademiai Kiado, 1967); Marcel Edmond Naegelen, La
Revolution Assassinee (Paris: Berger-Levault, 1966); Joseph Szikszoy,
The Legal Aspects of the Hungarian Question (Aubilly-Annemasse:
Les Presses de Savoie, 1963); Ferenc Vali, Rift and Revolt in Hungary
(Cambridge, Mass.: Harvard University Press, 1961); Francis S.
Wagner, The Hungarian Revolution in Perspective (Washington, D.C.:
F. F. Memorial Foundation, 1967); Paul E. Zinner, Revolution in
Hungary (New York: Columbia University Press, 1961).

2. The literature of revolutions includes a few excellent studies
that must be mentioned. Hannah Arendt, On Revolution (New York:
The Viking Press, 1963); Arthur Bauer, Essai sur les Revolutions
(Paris: Ciard et Briere, 1908); Carl Brinkman, Soziologische Theory
der Revolution (Gottingen: Vandenhoeck and Ruprecht, 1948); Crane
Brinton, Anatomy of Revolutions (New York: The Viking Press, 1963);
Adams Brooks, The Theory of Social Revolutions (New York:
Macmillian, 1913); C. D. Burns, The Principles of Revolution (London:
Allen and Unwin, 1920); Lewis Coser, The Functions of Social Conflict
(Glencoe, Ill.: The Free Press, 1956); Brian Crozier, The Rebels
(Boston: Beacon, 1960); Harry Eckstein, ed., Internal War (Glencoe,
Ill.: The Free Press, 1964); Lyford P. Edwards, The Natural History
of Revolution (New York: Twayne, 1959); Carl J. Friedrich, ed.,
Revolution (New York: Atherton Press, 1967); Everett Hage, On the
Theory of Social Change (Homewood, Ill.: The Dorsey Press, 1962);
Eric Hoffer, The Ordeal of Change (New York: Harper, 1964);
Chalmers Johnson, Revolution and the Social System (Stanford, Calif.:
Stanford University Press, 1964); Chalmers Johnson, Revolutionary
Change (Boston and Toronto: Little, Brown, 1968); Karl Kautsky,
The Social Revolution (London: Twentieth Century Press, 1909);
Vladimir I. Lenin, "Gosudarstvo i Revoliutsiia," in Polnoe Sobranie
Sochinenii (Moscow: Gos. Izd. -vo Pol. Lit. -ry, 1966, Vol. 33, pp.
1-119, notes pp. 123-340); James J. Maguire, The Philosophy of

Modern Revolutions (Washington D.C.; The Catholic University, 1943);
Max Nomad, Aspects of Revolt (New York: Wayne, 1959); Ortega y
Gasset, The Revolt of the Masses (London: G. Allen and Unwin, 1932);
George S. Pettee, The Process of Revolution (New York: Russell,
1963); Eugen Rosenstock-Huessy, Revolution als politischer Begriff
in der Neuzeit (Breslau: 1931); Pitrim Sorokin, The Sociology of
Revolutions (Philadelphia and London: Lippincott, 1925); Nicholas S.
Timasheff, War and Revolution (New York: Sheed and Ward, 1965).
These are a few of the most important general works on the systematic
study of revolutions, but those wishing to pursue further study must
consult the enormous bibliography in article form that more than equals
the outpouring of books related to this subject.

3. Crane Brinton, "The Nature of Revolution," in Hearings of the
Committee on Foreign Relations, U.S. Senate, 90th Cong., 2d Sess.,
1968, p. 22.

4. Unlike Johnson's model, this essay will not differentiate between conflicts over values and conflicts over interests, for such a
distinction would be artificial in its application in systems where
the political socialization process has tended to enforce the identity
or at least the interrelatedness of these two concepts. Johnson, Revolutionary Change, op. cit., p. 13.

5. David Easton, The Systems Analysis of Political Life (New
York: John Wiley, 1965), p. 291.

6. The phrase will be used here in conformity with its utilization
by Ghita Ionescu, The Politics of the European Communist States (New
York: Praeger, 1967).

7. Georges Burdeau, Traite de Science Politique (Paris: Librairie
General de Droit et Jurisprudence, 1966), Vol. VII.

8. Rolf Dahrendorf, Class and Class-Conflict in Industrial Society
(Stanford: Stanford University Press, 1959), p. 64.

9. Aristotle, Politics, trans. Benjamin Jowett (New York: Random
House, 1942), p. 211.

10. For an interesting discussion on the similarity of motivation
of members of a polity achieved by the socialization process, see
Anthony F. C. Wallace, "Revitalization Movements," American Anthro-
pologist, LVIII (April, 1956), pp. 264-81, especially pp. 274-75.

11. The best account relating to the discovery of the cleavage between ideology and reality is contained in Tamas Aczel and Tibor Meray, The Revolt of the Mind (New York: Praeger, 1959). It is significant that the strongest attacks on the regime always came from Communist writers in both Hungary and in Czechoslovakia, such as Ludwik Vaculik or Tamas Aczel. One of the most strongly worded indictments is contained in Gyula Illyes' poem "Egy mondat a zsarnoksagrol," Irodalmi Ujsag, November 2, 1956, p. 3.

12. Ever since 1963 the Hospodarkse Noviny continually published accounts of the enormous economic difficulties of Czechoslovakia. See Oldrich Cernik, "Prestavba Cs. Hospodarstvi a Jeho Vyhledy," Hospodarske Noviny, January 5, 1968, pp. 1, 6.

13. Kurt Hoffman, "Edward Goldstuecker and the Intellectual in Communist Society," Interplay II, No. 3 (October, 1968), 48. Not only those persons who were in prison were rehabilitated. History also was reinterpreted, the role of leading personalities in the formation of the Czechoslovak state or in Hungarian historical events was made to conform more closely to reality. This type of rehabilitation was most notable in reference to the role of Bela Kun in Hungary and Thomas G. Masaryk in Czechoslovakia. On the latter see Karel Pichlik, "Cesta K Svobode," Literarni listy, March 1, 1968 p. 12; J. L. Fischer, "Zamysleni nad T.G.M.," Literarni listy, March 7, 1968, pp. 1, 3, and March 14, 1968, p. 12.

14. Aczel and Meray, op. cit., p. 438.

15. Szabad Nep, October 7, 1956, as quoted in Paul E. Zinner ed, National Communism and Popular Revolt in Eastern Europe (New York: Columbia University Press, 1956), p. 385.

16. Marian Bielicki, "Dzien Wloczegi po Miescie," Po Prostu, December 9, 1956, p. 4. The article is Part III of a series entitled "Rewolucja Wegierska, 1956," and printed in Po Prostu, November 25, 1956, p. 3, and December 2, 1956, p. 3.

17. See, e.g., Jan Patucka, "O Principu Vedeckeho Svedomi," Literarni listy, June 27, 1968, p. 3; Ivan Korecek, "Demokracie a tzv. Spolecensky Zajem," Hospodarske Noviny, May 3, 1968, pp. 1, 7; Jiri Lederer, "Co Dals Demokracii," Literarni listy, April 4, 1968, p. 2.

18. See, e.g., Miroslav Strafelda, "Prilis Mnoho Demokratu," Literarni listy, March 14, 1968, p. 3; Robert Kalivoda, "Demokratizace

a Kriticke Mysleni," Literarni listy, May 2, 1968, pp. 1, 12, and May 9, 1968, pp. 6-7; Eduard Goldstucker, "Domuluvme se, Pratele," Literarni listy, May 16, 1968, p. 10.

19. Aczel and Meray, op. cit., pp. 344-50.

20. "Dva Tisice Slov," Literarni listy, June 27, 1968, pp. 1, 3.

21. Interview with Bruno Tedeschi in II Giornale d'Italia, November 2, 1956, as quoted in Melvin J. Lasky, The Hungarian Revolution: A White Book (New York: Praeger, 1957), pp. 177-78. See Nemeth Laszlo, "Partok es Egyseg," Uj Magyarorszag, November 2, 1956, p. 1.

22. "A kormany vezetoinek radiobeszedei," Magyar Fuggetlenseg, October 31, 1956, p. 1; "Nagy Imre, az uj nemzeti kormany elnokenek radionyilatkozata," Nephadsereg, October 29, 1956, p. 1; "Nagy Imre beszede," Szabad Ifjusag, October 29, 1956, p. 1. The following major parties were recreated in Hungary during the revolution: Magyar Szocial-demokrata Part, Kisgazda Part, Petofi (Nemzeti Parasztpart) Part, Magyar Szocialista Munkaspart, and several others.

23. Jan Jonas, "Obroda v Parlamente," Praca, March 2, 1968, p. 5; Ludvik Vaculik, "Obrodny Proces v Semilech," Literarny listy, June 27, 1968, p. 5.

24. "Nase Politicka Soustava a Delba Moci," Rude Pravo, February 13, 1968, already hints at the new direction, although the parties mentioned were not formally regenerated until the latter part of the summer.

25. Lajos Kassak, "A diktator," Irodalmi Ujsag, November 2, 1956, p. 2; "Lobogjatok magyar zaszlok," Magyar Nemzet, October 26, 1956 (special issue), p. 1.

26. On the role of the Czech intellectuals see: Ludvik Vaculik, "Tolerancni patent," Literarni listy, March 1, 1968, pp. 1-2; Ivan Klima, "Jeden Projekt a Jedna Strana," Literarni listy, April 25, 1968, pp. 1, 5; Ivan Svitak, "Dusledky Slov," Literarni listy, July 18, 1968, pp. 1, 4.

27. For the ills of the Slovak economy see, e.g., Zderek Skorepa and Miroslav Parkan, "Slovensko Pavna Soucast Ekonomiki," Hospodarske Noviny, February 22, 1963, pp. 1, 3.

28. It is interesting to note that Lenin's observation about the workers' councils as the desired instruments for the fulfillment of higher wages was repeatedly raised by the ruling parties as a reason for the "reactionary" nature of the councils. For Lenin's arguments see: "Proekt Tezisov or Roli i Zadachakh Profsoiuzov v Usloviiakh Novoi Ekonomicheskoi Politiki," in his Polnoe Sobranie Sochinenii, op. cit., Vol. 44, pp. 341-53. In Hungary the workers's councils created in 1956 were eliminated in 1957. In Czechoslovakia, however, the demands for workers' councils were stronger in 1969 than they were in 1968. For a Russian attack see "Tribuna Chekhskikh Kommunistov," Pravda, February 27, 1969, p. 4.

29. Richard E. Dawson and Kenneth Prewitt, Political Socialization (Boston: Little, Brown, 1969), p. 37.

30. It is interesting to note that the young all over the world seem to show a healthy disrespect for what the French call "depolitization," or "deideologization." One wonders if in this pragmatically oriented world of efficiency their reluctance to accept an ideology-less or "hope"-less world may be the only force capable of substaining men's desire for something qualitatively better for all of us. On the literature of "depolitization" see: Georges Vedel, ed., La Depolitisation: Mythe ou Realite? (Paris: Armand Coline), or Daniel Bell, The End of Ideology (Glencoe, Ill.: The Free Press, 1960), among many other important works.

31. Il Giornale d'Italia, loc. cit.

32. Hoffman, loc. cit.; Ludvik Vaculik, "Omulva o 992 Slovech," Literarni listy, July 11, 1968, pp. 1, 2; Ilios Jannakakis, "Socialisticka Demokracie a Internacionalismus," Literarni listy, July 18, 1968, p. 12; Michael Reiman, "Demokraticky Socialismus," Literarni listy, July 11, 1968, pp. 1, 6.

33. "Felmondjuk a varsoi szerzodest, semlegesek vagyunk," Magyar Vilag, November 2, 1956, p. 1; Magyar Nemzet, November 1, 1956, p. 1; Paloczy-Horvath Gyorgy, "Labhoz tett fegyverekkel," Irodalmi Ujsag,November 2, 1956, p. 1. For a Czech view of the problems of Nagy's neutrality see Osvald Machatka, "Take Jedno Vyroci," Literarni listy, June 13, 1968, p. 13.

34. It is interesting to note that the Soviet leadership, according to rumors circulating in the West, actually attempted to bribe the Slovak leadership by promising a "dismemberment" of Czechoslovakia

and the creation of an independent Slovakia. There is some suspicion that Gustav Husak's position as the head of the Slovak wing after the invasion may be attributed to his willingness to cooperate with the "highest bidder"—be he Russian or Czech. Whether the rumor is true or not cannot be ascertained but its existence in Eastern Europe has been observed by several scholars visiting Eastern Europe prior to and after the Soviet invasion. The argument may further be advanced that a federalized Czechoslovakia with greater regional controls may serve as a more powerful integrative force than the previous cohesion accomplished partially by coercion and directed from Prague. However, it must be realized that somewhere along the line in the national socialization process a faulty link must have developed, for the survival of Slovak nationalism and separatism succeeded in weakening the centralized authority of the Czechoslovak state. See, e.g., Miroslav Jodl, "O Ideu Ceskoslovenskeho Statu," Literarni listy, April 25, 1968, p. 5.

35. Janos Kadar, "Partunk vedi nemzeti becsuletunket, a demokracia es a szocializmus ugyet; Megalakult a Magyar Szocialista Munkaspart," Nepszabadsag, November 2, 1956, p. 1; For an English-language account see George Ginsburgs, "Demise and Revival of a Communist Party: An Autopsy of the Hungarian Revolution," The Western Political Quarterly, XIII, No. 3 (September, 1960), 780-802.

36. Perhaps the fact that in Czechoslovakia the Communist Party has deeper national roots and more historical tradition as a mass party may account for the strong leadership of the Czechoslovak Communist Party. The Communist Party membership was higher in Czechoslovakia than in Hungary: 21.00 percent versus 10.90 percent. Clement Gottwald, "International and Internal Situation and the Tasks of Communist Party of Czechoslovakia," (sic!) For a Lasting Peace for a People's Democracy, March 2, 1951, p. 5.

37. For the suspicious attitude on the part of the workers, especially fearful of possible unemployment, see Radoslav Selucky's Priroda a Spolecnost, No. 11, 1967; "Hrozi un Nas Nezamestnamost," "O Vyvoji Mezd a Zasobovani Truh," Rude Pravo, August 31, 1967, p. 1.

38. Evgenii F. Shmurlo, Istoriia Rossii, 862-1917 (Munich: 1922).

39. Johnson, Revolutionary Change, op. cit., p. 5.

8

**HUNGARIAN
INTELLECTUALS'
REACTION
TO THE INVASION
OF CZECHOSLOVAKIA**

Rudolf L. Tokes

Revolution is the most severe test of legitimacy of a political system. This is particularly true in polities whose political, economic, ideological, cultural, and psychological legitimacy rests on foundations of a derivative revolution, that is, on externally imposed and coercively maintained patterns of authority, models of economic development, and methods of ideological, cultural and psychological consensus-building.

In the postwar history of Eastern Europe there have been three notable instances of revolutionary and near-revolutionary crises of legitimacy: Poland and Hungary in 1956 and Czechoslovakia in 1968. All three have climaxed in traumatic confrontations between the people and the Communist Party, which, in the case of Hungary and Czechoslovakia, escalated into an open (violent and nonviolent) clash with the Soviet Union—the ultimate guarantor of the Communist Party's legitimacy.

In all three instances it was the intellectuals—writers, artists, and members of various professional elites—who took the leadership in articulating popular demands arising out of underlying sociopolitical tensions, and challenged not one, but all aspects of the regime's legitimacy, and, through it, that of the Soviet Union.

This chapter is concerned with the Hungarian intellectual's reaction to the Czechoslovak reform program and that country's occupation by the Soviet Union, East Germany, Poland, Bulgaria, and Hungary in August, 1968. Specifically, the following arguments will seek: (1) to explain the reasons for the once-revolutionary Hungarian intellectuals' paradoxical response to the Czechoslovak events: (2) to

offer an analysis of the politically significant properties of the post-
1956 Hungarian elite-consensus; and (3) to suggest a number of tentative hypotheses and propositions concerning the dynamics of post-totalitarian Hungarian and East European politics.

AN UNCONCERNED REACTION
TO THE INVASION

On August 21, 1968, the morning after the invasion of Czechoslovakia, five Hungarian participants of an international symposium
on "Marx and Revolution" held in Korcula, Yugoslavia, issued a declaration concerning the ideological implications of that event:

> We consider that the intervention of certain countries of
> the Warsaw Pact constitutes a serious danger to the pro-
> cess of the renaissance of socialism and to the renais-
> sance of Marxist theory which has been taking place in
> recent times. Regardless of the consequences, our duty
> is to try everything possible in order to further the de-
> velopment of authentic socialism and genuine social de-
> mocracy.[1]

This statement by the Hungarian Marxists Agnes Heller, Maria
and Gyorgy Markus, Vilmos Sos, and Zador Tordai was the first and
only public protest by Hungarian intellectuals in connection with the
occupation of Czechoslovakia. Gyorgy Lukacs and, according to un-
confirmed reports, the prominent revisionist sociologist Andras Hegedu
as well, chose to register their disapproval in private letters addressed
to the Hungarian Party's Central Committee.[2]

But where were the other non-Marxist Hungarian writer-intel-
lectual champions of freedom and advocates of the "community of fate
of the small Eastern European nations?" Where was Gyula Illyes,
the author of the poem "One Sentence on Tyranny," Laszlo Nemeth,
the leading populist spokesman, and the rest of the living veterans
and guiding spirits of the Hungarian October while Soviet tanks were
rumbling on Prague's streets and Hungarian troops occupying central
Slovakia? It appears that these men and their fellow intellectuals chose
to "sit out" the rape of Czechoslovakia in their summer villas or in
one of the rest homes of the Writers' Union. In any event, none of them
came forth to speak for the ideas of the Prague Spring or to add a few
to their Czechoslovak colleagues' "2,000 Words."

A new "treason of the intellectuals"?—one might ask when con-
trasting the five young and two old Hungarian Marxists' anguished

protest to the deafening silence of the former leaders of the Hungarian
October. After all, if in the midst of a Soviet antirevisionist campaign
at least eighty-eight Moscow writers had the courage to sign a statement in opposition to Russia's occupation of a fraternal socialist country, why then did the considerably freer Hungarians remain mute?[3]
Was it a new sense of "political realism," a cynical hodie mihi cras
tibi philosophy of a presumably bygone era of East European chauvinism,
or was it simply cowardice that kept these men silent in the months
preceding and following the Soviet-led five-power invasion of a neighboring country?

        The answers to these and similar questions seem to lie in the
peculiar nature of Hungary's political development since the revolution
of 1956. In attempting to sort out the political, economic, and ideological ingredients of a tentative explanation of the Hungarian intellectuals'
and, we might add, the entire country's apparent unconcern with the
momentous events in Czechoslovakia, certain aspects of Hungary's
post-1956 history—with particular attention to the Party, its leader,
Janos Kadar, his domestic and foreign policies, and the newly emerg-
ing nationalist ideology of Hungary's leading bureaucratic, economic,
and cultural elites—should be considered.

                        THE POST-1956 HUNGARIAN
                          ELITE-CONSENSUS

        In retrospect, Western nonintervention and Soviet harshness in
crushing the Hungarian Revolution in 1956 should be credited in equal
measure for Kadar's success in restoring "socialist law and order,"
rebuilding the party, and reviving the severely dislocated national
economy within eighteen months after Soviet intervention. To be sure,
substantial Soviet economic aid, Khrushchev's personal stake in the
Hungarian party's fortunes, public apathy and the lack of sustained
armed resistance to the restoration of Communist rule also contributed
to the return to normalcy by the spring of 1958. Perhaps more important than these factors were Kadar's astute leadership and his
ability to make himself indispensable both to his slowly growing domestic constituency and to his foreign (Soviet, Polish, and occasionally
Yugoslav) supporters. Having dispensed with Imre Nagy and his friends,
who were secretly tried and executed in June, 1958, and with the un-
popular but politically crucial task of agricultural collectivization,
Kadar called for a battle on "two fronts," that is, against revisionism
and dogmatism, and set out to remold the Party to his image. The latter task involved the selective purging of many middle-echelon techni-
cally and educationally inadequate supporters of the deposed Stalinist
Matyas Rakosi, the reorganization of the internal security apparat and

several waves of "rationalization" within the overstaffed and chroni-
cally inefficient state administration.[4] The party also took great pains
to come to grips with the ideological heritage of the October Revolution,
especially with Imre Nagy's revisionist views, and with the Populists'
literary-political theories concerning a "third road" that Hungary was
to follow between the East and the West.[5]

With the advent of the Sino-Soviet rift and with the fading of the
international disapproval of the ill-begotten Kadar regime, Hungary
began to rise from the status of a docile satellite to that of a Soviet
client state with considerable latitude in domestic policy and practically
no involvement in foreign affairs other than economic. The latter aspect may best be demonstrated by pointing to Hungary's almost complete disinvolvement in the work of the United Nations and other international organizations and to the country's increasingly vigorous com-
mercial and trading ties with Yugoslavia, Austria, West Germany, and
several Middle Eastern and Asian countries.[6] This is not to suggest
that Hungary's economic dependence on the U.S.S.R. for raw materials,
oil and military hardware lessened in any way, or that Hungary's CMEA
(Council for Middle Eastern Affairs) commitments decreased to a
significant extent; rather, these were symptomatic of the Hungarian
economy's diversified productive potential, and through it, the sound-
ness of Kadar's program of economic reconstruction and selective
industrial modernization.

Although the domestic impact of the government's foreign policies
is difficult to measure, it may be argued that by the early 1960's Kadar
had succeeded in developing the public image of a "Hungarian Gomulka"—that of a thoughtful, unassuming man of good will and former
victim of Stalinism who was trying hard to live down the memory of his
responsibility for the Soviet invasion of Hungary and his complicity
in the politically inspired executions of Laszlo Rajk (1949) and Imre
Nagy (1958).

For most people, Kadar's continued leadership and repeated—
and thus far well-kept—promises to eradicate the last vestiges of
Stalinist lawlessness and Rakosi's own brand of cynical terrorism
were sufficient guarantees against the return of the dreaded Rakosi
era in Hungary.[7] Insofar as the Party's rank-and-file membership
was concerned, the Kadar team's crushing of the most visible members
of the Party's Muscovite wing was significant, and, as many hoped,
represented a lasting victory for the generation of native militants
who from the late 1930's on had been suspected, slighted, and persecuted by Stalin's Muscovite Hungarian deputies. That this reemergence of the "natives" also entailed a subtle Semitic purge in the Party,

no one but the affected upper- and middle-level cadres seemed to
notice, and they were in no position to fight the party-inspired resur
gence of nationalism in Hungary.

The Party's gradual reconciliation with the intellectuals was a
far more complex affair than had been the task of internal house-
cleaning among the browbeaten apparatchiki. Kadar's new slogan, "he
who is not against us is with us"[8] and the subsequent amnesty for all
prominent political prisoners—"Octobrist" and Stalinist alike—laid
the groundwork for an extended period of a "live-and-let-live" relationship between the Party's cultural bureaucracy and the intellectuals.
Dramatically relaxed controls on travel and tourism in the West, the
resumption of cultural and scientific contacts with Western intellectuals
and academic institutions, and the publication of record numbers of
hitherto forbidden nonsocialist literary and scientific works clearly
attested to the regime's sense of self-confidence and evident satisfaction with the result of its post-1956 policies.

After the initial excitement over the opening of Hungary's political
and cultural boundaries subsided, after everyone who could afford a
trip to the West had satisfied his curiosity—and his craving for domestically unavailable consumer goods—and after a few thousand young
tourists had defected while abroad, a remarkable period of quiescence
began in Hungary. Perhaps this change was caused by the trauma of
discovery that the vagaries of the capitalist market economy, the threat
of unemployment and the firm work discipline that was the lot of the
average man in the West seemed unacceptable to citizens of a welfare
state with their guaranteed (though low-paying) employment, free
(though often inadequate) medical care, and state-subsidized rent, public transportation, and basic food supplies. Perhaps it was a combination of housing difficulties and shortages of consumer goods, or the
overwhelming drabness of daily life, but the fact remains that in the
early 1960's Hungary enjoyed the unenviable reputation of having the
highest suicide rate and the lowest birth rate in the world. Was it a
belated psychological reaction to the crushing of the 1956 revolution
or perhaps the older and younger generations' respective vote of no
confidence in the Communist-sponsored new sociopolitical equilibrium?

Available evidence seems to point to a somewhat different conclusion: for those who committed suicide included not only the old, the
sick, the victims of broken marriages, but several insufficiently
educated and suddenly demoted work and peasant executives, cashiered
army and secret police officers, and many now politically useless
middle-aged and older Communists as well. On the other hand, the
young generation's widespread estrangement from the Catholic church,

the state's liberal abortion policies, the dilemma of <u>kicsi vagy kocsi</u>?
(a little one or a car?) and the unwillingness of many emancipated
working women to have more than one child or no children at all were
probably more responsible for the low birth rate than the young Hungarians' lack of confidence in the regime's present and future stability.
The political impact of changing life styles in terms of public opinion
and nationally shared political values should, therefore, be placed in
a different and historically more realistic perspective.

The grand alliance of the Hungarian October was made possible
by the catalyst of the revolution, which crystallized in an unprecedented
ideological consensus between the people and the country's elites. The
former had been motivated by sentiments of nationalism, the latter by
a well-articulated program representing a mixture of revisionist
Marxism, romantic nationalism, Populism, and youthful radicalism.[9]
Eight years later this sense of national unity had disappeared practically beyond recall. When the revolution was defeated the workers
were herded back to the factories and the peasants to their collective
farms. Though subsequently benefiting from shorter hours, higher
wages, and generally improved living conditions, the common people
of Hungary were abandoned both by the younger generation and by their
better-educated former leaders.

The defection of the elites and the young from the anti-Soviet
national alliance was a natural and, in some ways, inevitable consequence of the Party's policies of de-Stalinization and selective co-op-
tion of the young, talented, and educated elements into the Party, state,
and cultural bureaucracies. The shift in official emphasis from ideological orthodoxy to technical expertise, from overt terror to a carefully balanced system of material rewards and psychological incentives,
from an inflexible command economy to rudimentary consumer sovereignty benefited not the average worker, peasant, or office clerk,
but the bright university graduate, the ambitious and hard-working
young professional, and all those creative intellectuals who, within
broadly defined limits, were prepared to support the Party's program
of political moderation and economic modernization.

Those who are old enough to remember the politics and social
structure of Hungary in the 1930's may find many similarities between
the life style, the well-developed sense of social identity, and the
economic status of these new elites and those of the radical rightist
middle-class supporters of Gyula Gombos' national-Fascist platform
of economic modernization and spiritual rejuvenation.[10] In both instances the elites were prepared to surrender their political birth-
right to the benevolent autocratic leader in return for nominal

participation in political decision making, the promise of guaranteed social standing, economic security, and the psychic gratification of being regarded as indispensable to the leader's and his party's dynamic scheme of national development.[11]

MUTUAL ACCORD BETWEEN PARTY LEADERSHIP AND THE ELITE-CONSENSUS

The first major test of the stability of this mutual accord between the Party leadership and the elites came with the fall of Khrushchev in October, 1964. Kadar's first public speech in Hungary following the unexpected exit of his political patron—and perhaps personal friend— was a forceful display of independence almost amounting to personal bravado, which was exactly the kind of leadership posture that never failed to impress Hungarians and engender loyalty among the people.

> I think that comrade Khrushchev had great merits in the struggle against the Stalinist personality cult and in the maintenance of peace. The hundreds of thousands of Hungarians who greeted Khrushchev in the recent past and also this year in Hungary—and they did it from their hearts—as the representative of the great Soviet Party and state and people, as well as the unrelenting fighter for peace, did well to do so. There is no need to have afterthoughts about this.[12]

With this defiant affirmation of the Hungarian party's independence from Moscow in matters of such magnitude as the removal of the first secretary of the CPSU, Janos Kadar, the hitherto tolerated and grudgingly supported man, became a national hero overnight. Perhaps the Budapest wit—"he is the best Emperor we have had since Franz Joseph"—missed the point somewhat, but there could be no mistake about the popular acceptance of the man as the legitimate leader of the country. Although Kadar later reluctantly joined the Soviet-led chorus of Khrushchev's detractors, he made a point that no one in Hungary, least of all the intellectuals, was about to forget in the years to come.

Shortly after Dubcek came to power Kadar and the Politburo's foreign specialist, Zoltan Komocsin, met him in the Slovak border town of Komarno in early February, 1968. According to the official Hungarian communique, the meeting had been conducted in "an atmosphere of total understanding" and had resulted in a "complete identity of views" on all matters on the agenda.[13]

By all appearances this summary was accurate—even to the
normally skeptical readers of such Communist protocol documents.
Even at that time it was clear that both Communist leaders were on
record as being committed to de-Stalinization, economic reforms,
and cultural liberalization. They were also motivated by the same
sense of reasoned loyalty to the Soviet Union, hostility to China (or at
least Mao's ideology and leadership style), and a purposefully ambivalent attitude toward Yugoslavia and the West, especially West
Germany.

While Dubcek barely began to realize the demands of his constituency, which included Czech moderates, Slovak nationalists, liberal
writers, students, economists, and Novotny's assorted enemies in the
Czechoslovak party, Kadar was well on his way to developing a politically stable, economically viable, and intellectually flexible new "model"
of socialism in Hungary. Political stability had been won by a combination of steadfast leadership, consolidation of control over the Party
apparat, revitalization of the hitherto neglected parliamentary pro-
cedures (well-publicized, sometimes provocative questions to cabinet
ministers, a modicum of debate on procedural matters and secondary
issues, and the establishment of multiple candidate districts at national
elections), and official support to the reemergence of nationalism.
The latter was especially significant since it involved a widely shared
popular concern over the political equality and cultural freedom of
3.5 million Hungarians living in Yugoslavia, Romania, and Czechoslovakia.[14]

Hungary's economic viability was due to new profit-sharing
schemes in agriculture (the "Nadudvar model") and industry, relaxation
of controls on small producers, craftsman, and service establishments,
imaginative joint ventures with Western industrial firms and to the
overall restructuring of wages, prices, and state subsidies—a policy
better known as the New Economic Mechanism (NEM).[15]

Flexible cultural policies represent the third, and, for purposes
of evaluating the intellectuals' behavior during the Czechoslovak crisis,
the most important facet of the Hungarian political scene. With the
unlamented demise of "socialist realism" as the official yardstick of
artistic achievement, in the mid-1960's a tacit compromise was reached
between the Party and the writers, artists, and academic intellectuals.
The former, through a series of policy statements—some of them
issued by Kadar personally—went on record as not only tolerating
unorthodox experimentation and search for new artistic truths, but
actually underwriting the cost of new literary subsidies and providing
for more generous royalty payments on all published works.

The intellectuals, obviously appreciative of these conciliatory gestures, responded in three ways: To begin with, all established and most young writers and artists suddenly began to produce great quantities of books, poems, musical works, and movies—some highly original, some indifferent, and some simply bad—all that the traffic and the improved royalty schemes could bear.[16] Others, mostly social scientists, economists and sociologists, rather than catering either to the popular tastes or to the still-standing ideological dogmas, began to depoliticize their disciplines through vigorous intellectual house-cleaning and the reestablishment of professional ties with their Western colleagues. The third group of intellectuals included a few self-exiled Left and Right opponents of the regime and a small cluster of revisionist Marxist sociologists and philosophers—most prominently Gyorgy Lukacs and his disciples.

Insofar as can be reconstructed from the Hungarian Party daily, the literary journals, and the official statements during the spring and summer of 1968, the following interesting and somewhat complex consensus emerged concerning the significance and the long-term prospects of the Czechoslovak reform movement. The Party, and particularly Kadar's followers in the Central Committee, viewed Dubcek's efforts with a mixture of sincere sympathy and an "it has been done before" kind of patronizing condescension. Ota Sik's reform proposals evoked only lukewarm reaction among Hungarian economic planners, who felt that Hungary's 8-to-9-percent annual rate of industrial growth, the abundance of consumer goods (particularly foodstuffs that Czechoslovak visitors in Hungary purchased in great quantities) and, generally, the "pay as you go" philosophy of the NEM more than fulfilled those aspects of the Czechoslovak program that were applicable to the conditions of an industrially less developed Hungary.

Although official uneasiness in the form of hints about the necessity to battle on "two fronts" was always in evidence in commentaries on the Czech de-Stalinization campaign, it was clear that Kadar was ready to give his unqualified personal support to Dubcek and his liberal colleagues in the Czechoslovak party. Unlike the suspicious and hostile Ulbricht, or Gomulka and the orthodox Bulgarian leadership, who were apprehensive of the internal consequences of Novotny's fall, Kadar derived domestic political strength and added stature in the councils of the ruling Communist parties as an honest broker between the Czechoslovak Party and its conversative critics, including the Russians, abroad.

According to reliable sources, Kadar's preinvasion policies toward Czechoslovakia were not altogether popular in Hungary. It has
been suggested that Kadar's pro-Dubcek proposals were voted down
in the Politburo at least six times in the summer of 1968. However,
while in the Party the centrist majority was strong enough to uphold
Kadar's leadership, the non-Marxist intellectuals and their specific
demands concerning the Czechoslovak experiment were more difficult
to control. For the majority of the intellectuals and, perhaps not so
paradoxically, for many former Stalinists, the fate of the 700,000 Hungarians living in Slovakia was the most important and essentially the
only issue of interest in the entire Dubcek program.

Offering practically an exact replica of arguments advanced thirty
years before, the newspapers, and especially the literary journals, gave
extensive coverage to stories on the comparative well-being of Hungarians living in Yugoslavia, Romania, and Czechoslovakia. As far
as the none-too-subtle hints in these articles indicated, not much had
changed since the 1930's: The Hungarian minorities were well treated
in Yugoslavia, were experiencing "considerable but hopefully not insurmountable" difficulties in Transylvania, and were struggling for
equal linguistic, educational, and economic opportunities in Slovakia.[17]

There was, of course, nothing new about the officially condoned
low-key, anti-Romanian campaign in Hungary, especially after the
prominent writer Gyula Illyes publicly complained while on an official
visit to Paris about the Romanian government's discriminatory policies
toward the Hungarian minorities, for which, despite vehement Romanian
protests, Illyes received no official or private reprimand whatsoever.
Unlike Ceaucescu, who seemed unresponsive to Kadar's successive
emissaries dispatched to discuss the minorities' problems, Dubcek
was not only a man in obvious need of Hungarian understanding and
support, but one who appeared open to suggestions on this issue.

Kadar's speech delivered in Dubcek's presence on the occasion
of the signing of a twenty-year friendship pact took cognizance of this
still unresolved question by reminding his audience of the "burdensome
past of nationalist passions" that had been exploited "by the Hapsburgs,
German imperialism and the bourgeoisie of our countries as a weapon
to divide and rule" and adding: "Certain remnants of this past are
still in existence today. . .their liquidation is only possible on the basis
of socialism."[18]

As the events of July and early August progressed, Dubcek's
image in Hungary underwent a little-publicized, yet significant change.
Well after the Soviet, East German, and Polish press suggested it,

<u>Nepszabadsag</u>, the Hungarian Party's daily, issued friendly and obviously worried warnings about the increasingly apparent similarities between the Hungarian political situation in the months preceding the 1956 revolution and that of Czechoslovakia in Julym 1968.[19] Although the full text of the "2,000 Words" manifesto was not published in Hungary, enough excerpts were printed in the provincial Party press for one to surmise that the Hungarian party was greatly concerned about the anti-Soviet passages and the likely international consequences of such half-heartedly suppressed provocative statements.

Clearly Kadar was in a dilemma, torn between offering his continued support to the well-meaning but politically imprudent reformers in Prague and protecting his party's hard-won internal stability and its relative freedom from Soviet interference.[20] These doubts, however, were not shared by most Hungarian intellectuals. While applauding in principle their fellow intellectuals' bold struggle for artistic and creative freedom, they felt that Dubcek was no longer the master of his house, and, above all, was unable to restrain the nationalists in the Slovak party from persecuting the leaders of the Hungarian minority for their demands of a "new deal" under the liberal Prague leadership. Rather than passing judgment on the validity of the Hungarian minority's claims, it will suffice to suggest that for the Budapest intellectuals these grievances were genuine and worthy of their support.[21] They had hoped that Kadar, either through Dubcek or directly in Bratislava, would intercede on the Hungarian minority's behalf and arrange a favorable settlement of all feasible claims in return for his support of Czechoslovak aspirations in Moscow, Warsaw, and Berlin.

It is, of course, impossible to tell whether Kadar was fully aware of these hopes or if he himself encouraged this kind of reasoning in order to keep the potentially troublesome intellectuals occupied with a secondary (and foreign) issue and to prevent them from emulating the Czech example in Hungary. On balance, it seems that Kadar was not and did not need to mislead his nationalist constituents in this manner. Kadar not only must have felt more secure than his Polish and German colleagues but probably sensed that the Czechoslovak reformers' ideological, political, and economic program, if not entirely irrelevant, was probably not an attractive alternative for Hungary's intellectuals and other elites.

Whether it was the memory of the defeated revolution of 1956 or the considerable internal progress made since then, or both, the Hungarian elites' reaction to the Soviet invasion of Czechoslovakia may be explained by the emergence of a Hungarian "battle of the White Mountain" mentality, which implied a noncommittal political posture strikingly similar to that displayed by Ferenc Deak and his "cautious progressives" (fontolva haladok) in the years following the Austro-Hungarian Compromise of 1867. In the wake of defeated revolutions (1848-49 and 1956) the intellectuals in both cases resigned themselves to the new status quo, withdrew from active participation in politics, and, with a mixture of self-pity and political realism (the "little Hungary" syndrome), resolved to strengthen the moral fiber of their people with emphasis on cultural—especially linguistic—nationalism, positive attitudes toward economic modernization, and xenophobic distrust of Austria, (U.S.S.R) and of neighbors who actively or passively contributed to the defeat of Hungary's revolution—Romania and Czechoslovakia.

If this historical analogy is valid then it should be apparent why the ideological and political alternatives developed by the Czech reformers (the revival of Thomas Masaryk's philosophy of democratic humanism and plans for a socialist and democratic restructuring of society) failed to generate any kind of response from the Hungarian intellectual and professional elites. It should be remembered that Tito's and Ceaucescu's visits to Prague and comments in both the Romanian and Czechoslovak press on the preinvasion situation in Czechoslovakia could be interpreted in Budapest as tentative suggestions for the rebirth of the "little entente"—which was something that no Hungarian, from Kadar down to the last unreconstructed Stalinist, was prepared to accept, Dubcek's good intentions notwithstanding.22

Whether the reasons for these noncommittal and to some extent hostile attitudes toward the Czechoslovak experiment were justified or not, they go a long way in explaining the sympathetic silence and absence of public protest in Hungary following the five-power occupation of neighboring Czechoslovakia.

CONCLUSIONS

In evaluating the once-revolutionary Hungarian intellectuals' response (rather, nonresponse) to the political, economic, and philosophical aspects of the Czechoslovak reform program and the Soviet invasion that put an end to it, the following propositions concerning the broader implications of the Hungarian case could be generated.

1. It can be argued that if one of the unstated Soviet reasons for the invasion and its subsequent doctrinal justification by Brezhnev rested on an East European "domino theory," then the invasion should be regarded as an example of latter-day Russian imperial paranoia rather than as an expression of a well-founded concern about the politica

stability of Communist Eastern Europe. The domino theory, or a
comparable simplistic scenario, is untenable because of the sheer
diversity of political (viability of party control), economic (develop-
mental unevenness), cultural (liberalization and modes of Party-intel-
lectuals relationship), and psychological (nature of popular consensus
on the legitimacy of the regime) factors, combined with fears of a
Soviet invasion that have resulted in an internally divided Eastern
Europe and, generally, in conditions that effectively prevent any syn-
chronized response to alternative models of socialist nation-building
such as those offered by the very example of Czechoslovakia.

    2. Polycentric tendencies aside, the tragic legacies of East
European history (authoritarian traditions in politics, autarchic pro-
pensities in economics, cultural and linguistic chauvinism in literature
and the arts) and Stalin's "time bombs" (the Oder-Neisse line, unresolved territorial questions between Romania and Russia, Bulgaria
and Yugoslavia, Hungary and Romania, etc.), which, at the discretion
of the Soviet Union, may be reactivated at any time—barring an unexpected shift in the East-West balance of power—are sufficiently
powerful and explosive to assure the maintenance of the status quo in
this divided, hence effectively conquered part of Europe.

    3. In general, the attractiveness of the Czechoslovak model for
the elites of an East European party-state in its post-totalitarian phase
depends on their perception of the legitimacy of the political system
in which they live. In this sense, legitimacy involves the following
aspects: (a) political—the Party's ability to govern effectively; (b)
economic—the nation's continued economic modernization and satisfaction of basic expectations associated with it; (c) ideological—doctrinal flexibility in reconciling inherent dichotomies between the stated
and feasible goals of the party; (d) cultural—the achievement of a viable
synthesis between the socialist form and national content in literature,
arts, and sciences; and (e) psychological—the regime's ability to evoke
supportive or nonhostile responses to its ruling style and political
symbols.

    4. In Hungary's case it may be argued that the sum total of the
Kadar regime's reformist innovations in these five spheres of legitimacy amounted to a de facto revisionist model whose sheer momentum
and apparent success have, in effect, inhibited the elites from going
beyond muted expressions of sympathy with the goals of the Czechoslovak liberalization program. Moreover, the Hungarian elites' potential responsiveness was also conditioned by the outcome of the 1956
revolution and a subsequently developed "battle of the White Mountain"
mentality that effectively prevented the crystallization of a radicalized

elite consensus around specific issues raised by the reformers of
Prague and Bratislava. Therefore, even if the overriding nationality
issue were to be discounted, the fact remains that the Czechoslovak
revisionists' ideological alternative of a socialist democracy rooted
in the unique traditions of Thomas Masaryk's democracy was funda-
mentally alien not only to the Hungarian but to the rest of the East
European elites as well.

In other words, the new Hungarian elite-consensus that rested on
an implicit commitment to modernization, on depoliticization of intellectual life, on officially sponsored cultural nationalism, and on the
revival of traditional social structure and political governing style
under the benevolent autocrat Janos Kadar was sufficiently supportive
of the status quo to remain immune to radicalization and essentially
unmoved by external events, even of the magnitude of the Czechoslovak tragedy.[23]

5. In sharp contrast to this ambiguous posture, Gyorgy Lukacs'
circle of revisionist Marxist philosophers and sociologists had been
on record as supporting the Czechoslovak intellectuals' aspirations
and, in Lukacs' case, as personally intervening, in the form of provocative interviews with Plamen, on behalf of the embattled Czech and
Slovak writers.[24] While there is less known about the specific activities of Lukacs' followers, there is some evidence indicating that many
of the Prague Marxists' key philosophical propositions have found a
way of appearing—without attribution—in their articles and studies
published between the fall of 1967 and the summer of 1968.[25] Unlike
the old Communist intellectuals reminiscing about the old days of Bela
Kun, Admiral Horthy, and Matyas Rakosi; the Populists and their preoccupation with the countryside and the minorities question; and the
"urbanist" writers deeply involved in experimentation with new literary
forms; Lukacs and his followers clearly identified with the ideological
position of the Prague reformers, hence their defeat was a deeply felt
loss to them too.

6. From this it follows that Lukacs, Hegedus, and their small
band of followers are probably the only people in Hungary who had
a significant intellectual stake in the outcome of the Czechoslovak
reforms. For them the Czech revisionist model that called for a
humanist Marxist philosophy and an existentialist ethic, a militant
critique of bureaucratization, and efforts to vindicate "open Marxism"
as a superior alternative to barren orthodoxy had immediate relevance
both for Hungary and Eastern Europe.[26]

In terms of a shared philosophical posture and general intellectual outlook, Lukacs and his circle had more in common with the Czech revisionists Karel Kosik, Ivan Svitak, Milan Prucha, and Ivan Dubsky, the Yugoslav Praxis group, the Polish Leszek Kolakowski, the German Haveman and with the Western Bloch, Haebermas, Goldman, and Garaudy, than with Kadar's dull ideological bureaucrats or with the neonationalist, culturally semiparochial Hungarian intellectuals at large. That is, unlike the last two groups, the Hungarian revisionists were committed to the idea of socialism not merely in terms of relative intellectual freedoms, piecemeal structural reforms, and economic modernization, but in the Marxist humanist and genuinely internationalist sense of the word.

7. The prospects for Lukacs and the rest of the philosophical revisionists seem rather bleak in the foreseeable future. In an age of dying ideologies their role as self-appointed critics of a new class that has no moral philosophy and tolerates none and of the neonationalist intellectuals who raised moral opportunism to the rank of a new nationalist ethic is not only difficult but may be self-defeating as well. Insofar as trends toward limited consumer sovereignty represent a measure of democratization under socialism, then Haveman, Lukacs,[27] and the other ethical purist critics of "goulash communism" are historically irrelevant enemies of economic modernization and are bound to be swept away by the very people whom they are trying to deliver from the danger of embourgeoisement and ideological decadence. On the other hand, while subjectively rejecting Stalinism, the very logic of the ethical socialists' dogmatic righteousness objectively demands the return of precisely such a dialectically clear-cut system, and with it, of course, their own demise.

Whether the Hungarian revisionists should be regarded as a group of politically isolated idealistic philosophical radicals destined to be suppressed and to disappear into oblivion or as the forerunners of a new intellectual elite striving to reconcile Marxist humanism and post-totalitarian empiricism and develop an ideology of a Central European "New Left," it is probably too early to tell at this time.[28] It is worth remembering, however, that it was not the professional philosophers and their intellectual "death wish," but the people of Budapest and Prague and their raw courage that made revolutions and shaped history in October, 1956, and August, 1968. For them the philosophy of the young Marx was not a dogma but a guide to action.

NOTES

1. Figaro (Paris), August 23, 1968. For the text of the letter signed by all seventy Eastern and Western Marxist and radical philosophers, see Studies in Comparative Communism 2, No. 2 (April 1969), 147-48.

2. See "Three Hungarian Philosophers Expelled From the Hungarian Party"(Radio Free Europe) Research H/20 (December 17, 1968) citing wire service reports (Defense Production Administration September 4, and AFP, September 7) on the Hegedus and Lukacs letters.

3. The text of the statement was published in The Times (London) on September 11, 1968. The signers' names were withheld.

4. Kadar's post-October policies are analyzed in Francois Fejto's comprehensive essay, "Hungarian Communism," in William E. Griffith, ed., European Communism, Vol. I (Cambridge, Mass.: The M.I.T. Press, 1964), pp. 177-300.

5. Texts of appropriate resolutions of the Central Committee and the Committee on Cultural-Ideological Questions may be found in A Magyar Szocialista Munkaspart Hatarozatai es Dokumentumai, 1956-1962 (Resolutions and Documents of the Hungarian Socialist Workers' Party 1956-1962) (Budapest: Kossuth, 1964).

6. For a well-documented discussion of Hungary's foreign economic policies in this period see Laszlo Zsoldos, Economic Integration of Hungary into the Soviet Bloc (Columbus, Ohio: Bureau of Business Research, Ohio State University, 1963).

7. The most important step in this direction was the Central Committee's decision of August 12-14, 1962, to expel Matyas Rakosi, Erno Gero, and twenty-three of their former associates from the Hungarian party.

8. Nepszabadsag, December 10, 1961.

9. This dichotomy of revolutionary ideologies is well-outlined in Paul E. Zinner, Revolution in Hungary (New York: Columbia University Press, 1962).

10. This point is discussed in Fejto, op. cit., some detail. For a more comprehensive analysis of the Hungarian radical Right elites'

personality and political style in the 1930's, see Istvan Deak, "Hungary" in Hans Rogger and Eugene Webber, eds., The European Right (Berkeley: University of California Press, 1965), pp. 364-407. See also Andrew C. Janos, "Single-Party Experiments in Eastern Europe." Paper delivered at the 1967 Annual Meeting of the American Political Science Association, Chicago, Ill.

11. Zbigniew Brzezinski makes this point in a more forceful way:

> Indeed, increasingly national Communism in East Europe is beginning to resemble social fascism and we should not forget that the prewar fascist movements, which were not dominant but which had been gaining strength, preached nationalism, chauvinism, anti-intellectualism, certainly, whenever relevant, anti-Semitism, and also modernization of the states, including their economic development and social reform."

The Communist World in a New Phase. Proceedings of the Academy of Political Science at the Spring Meeting on "The Soviet Union Since Khrushchev—New Trends and Old Problems" (April 14, 1965), p. 59.

12. Speech of October 18, 1964, as transcribed in "Communist Reaction to Khrushchev's Fall," Radio Free Europe Research (November 10, 1964). See also, "Kadar Wins Popularity," The New York Times, October 26, 1964.

13. MTI release (in English), February 5, 1968.

14. See Thomas T. Hammond, "Nationalism and National Minorities in Eastern Europe," and Ferenc A. Vali, "Transylvania and the Hungarian Minority," Journal of International Affairs XX, No. 1 (1966), 9-44.

15. See Jozsef Szabados, "Hungary's New Economic Mechanism: Promises and Pitfalls," East Europe 17, Nos. 4, 6 (April, June, 1968).

16. The most exciting products of this controlled cultural explosion have been short stories, semisociological exposes, unorthodox musical compositions, and bold cinematic creations, rather than the political and probably more relevant muckraking journalism or poetry that in 1956 had been the preferred vehicles of esoteric political communication for the Hungarian intellectuals.

17. See issues of Valosag, Uj Iras, Elet es Irodalom, Kortars, and the provincial literary monthlies between early 1967 and the summer of 1969. Here is one typical passage on the nationality issue by Gyula Illyes published in the Hungarian Party's official newspaper:

> Linguistic equality is an empty phrase for many people. Can Walloons, Flemings, South Tyroleans, North Italians, Catalonians, Spaniards, Greeks or Turks do better than that? They should learn each other's language.
>
> But here is something worth pondering: what will happen if some countries discriminate against hundreds of thousands of their citizens on grounds of their native tongue, and push them to the bottom of the social scale so they are not allowed to reach even the level of skilled workers? (Because, to get a professional training they have to attend a technical school which requires a command of the language of the country even in areas where this language is not spoken within a radius of many days' journey.) The point here is that the persons in question are bread-winners, and not just Catalonians, Flemings or Walloons. Or Hungarians.
>
> Nepszabadsag, January 6, 7, 1968.

18. The New York Times, June 15, 1968.

19. Nepszabadsag, July 25, 1968.

20. It did not help matters that Literarny listy (June 13, 1968) chose to commemorate the tenth anniversary of the death of Imre Nagy and called his execution a "discredit to the socialist world."

21. See "Hungarian Minority Tensions in Slovakia Worry Budapest," The New York Times, June 23, 1968.

22. See "Speculation on the Motives for Soviet Invasion," Radio Free Europe Research (August 30, 1968) and Fritz Ermarth, Internationalism, Security, and Legitimacy: The Challenge to Soviet Interests in East Europe, 1964-1968 (Memorandum RM-5909-PR) (Santa Monica, Calif.: The Rand Corporation, 1969), especially pp. 90-117.

23. That the Party was grateful for this display of "political maturity," particularly that of the writers was made amply clear by Peter Renyi, deputy chief of the Nepszabadsag editorial board. See "A Muzsak nem hallgatnak" ("The Muses Are Not Silent") in Kelet-magyarorszag and three other provincial dailies between September 22 and 28, 1968.

24. Plamen (Prague) October, 1967. For an English-language translation of the interview "The Great October of 1917 and Contemporary Literature," see East Europe 17, No. 2 (February, 1968) 29-30.

25. See Andras Hegedus, "A tarsadalmi fejlodes alternativaihoz" ("On the Alternatives to Social Development"), Kortars, June, 1968; Gyorgy Markus, "Vitak es iranyzatok a marxista filozofiaban" ("Debates and Tendencies in Marxist Philosophy"), Kortars, October, 1968; Zador Tordai, "Miert vannak iranyzatok a marxizmusban?" ("Why Are There (Different) Tendencies in Marxism?"), Kortars, October, 1968; and Ivan Vitanyi, "Muveszet es iranyitas" ("Art and Guidance"), Tarsadalmi Szemle, August-September, 1968.

26.For an excellent summary and analysis of the leading Czechoslovak revisionist philosophers' theoretical propositions, see Peter Ludz, "Philosophy in Search of Reality," Problems of Communism 18, Nos. 4-5 (July-October, 1969), 33-42.

27. See Ibid, p. 37 and "Az uj gazdasagi mechanizmus es a szocialista kultura. Beszelgetes Lukacs Gyorggyel" ("The New Economic Mechanism and Socialist Culture. Conversation with Gyorgy Lukacs"), Kortars, April, 1969.

28. Milovan Djilas seems to be more optimistic on this score:

"Just as the termination of the Communist monopoly of power does not mean the destruction of the economic and other foundations laid down during its reign, but it is actually a prerequisite for their greater freedom of mobility, so the disintegration and dethronement of Marxist ideology need not, and probably will not, involve the extinction of all Marx's teachings, his ideas and visionary insights."

Milovan Djilas, The Unperfect Society—Beyond the New Class (New York: Harcourt, Brace & World, 1969), p. 58.

9

ROMANIA
AND
THE INVASION
OF
CZECHOSLOVAKIA

E. Bennett Warnstrom

In response to the Soviet-led invasion of Czechoslovakia the first
and sharpest reaction came from Bucharest the morning of August 21.
Even as Russian tanks were systematically liquidating socialist freedom in Czechoslovakia, Nicolae Ceausescu began taking measures
to prepare Romania for, conceivably, a similar fate. In an act of
genuine concern for the future of his country and the world socialist
movement, the Romanian chief of state denounced, in clearest terms,
the Warsaw Pact occupation of Czechoslovakia as a flagrant violation
of an independent nation's sovereignty and as an event incompatible
with socialist ideals. In his historic speech to the Romanian people,
Ceausescu followed with an unequivocal demand for the immediate
withdrawal of the occupying forces. His vehement stand was impressive, if somewhat precipitous.

ROMANIAN NATIONALISM

By appealing to the nationalistic sentiments of the Romanian people,
Ceausescu was able to consolidate the unanimous support of the population, a feat never previously achieved in the country's history as
a Communist state. Romania was in peril. It stood alone in the
socialist world, and, if forced to, would fight alone to preserve its
new independence. During those several heady days following the
invasion of Czechoslovakia, Romanians seemed to be stimulated by
a patriotic adrenalin that had remained dormant for a generation.
The future, even the next month, was too remote to be pondered. The
Central Committee consented to allow the Romanian people to voice

their frustration. Their expression took the form of blatant anti-
Russianism. As hundreds of screaming youths surrounded the Soviet
embassy in Bucharest, shouting anti-Soviet, anti-Russian slogans,
the facade of fraternal Soviet-Romanian relations crumbled; and the
Western press was there to use the pieces for sensational headlines.

Three years have passed since the events of August, 1968.
Romania has not fallen to the same tragic fate of the Czechs, and
Romanian arms have not been used against neighboring (fraternal)
forces. Significantly, Nicolae Ceausescu has won even more widespread
popularity at home and abroad without having to come to any major
compromise with Moscow. The Soviet leaders tolerate him, but approve
of almost none of his political maneuvers. In Moscow's eyes,
Ceausescu's insistence on "Romania first" borders on ideological
heresy. Putting national interests before those of the socialist camp,
the Romanian president dares to flirt with and do business with whom-
ever he chooses. In August, 1969, less than one year after the dramatic end of the Czechoslovak experiment, President Richard Nixon's
brief but significant visit to Bucharest was a painful reminder to the
Soviet leaders of just how far Nicolae Ceausescu's international image
had evolved, as well as how successful Romania's independent line in
foreign affairs has thus far been.

The events that had been taking place in Czechoslovakia since
January, 1968, when Alexander Dubcek made his ill-fated debut,
were ultimately to have a far-reaching and essentially positive impact on Romania. Already the Bucharest regime, whose liberal
policy of international economic laissez-faire was the envy of the
other East European states, showed some important signs that it too
was eager to embark on at least some type of domestic liberalization
program. Granted, travel abroad was still heavily restricted and
party controls were concentrated more than ever in the hands of the
members of the Central Committee. Yet, in the early months of 1968,
not a single Romanian the author spoke with could honestly deny that
"things have never been so good."

Intensified trade with the West had brought a multiplicity of
new products within the buying power of nearly all Romanian families.
In some instances these included consumer items still lacking in
most of the other Eastern bloc countries and the Soviet Union. Such
brand names as Del Monte, Heinz, Amieux, Schweppes, and many
others had become commonplace in the households of Bucharest and
the provincial cities of Romania. The populace was better dressed
and better fed than it had been at any time over the last generation.
Romania's growing prosperity was parellel to, and, in good measure,

an outgrowth of the country's impressive industrial development of
the 1960's.

With almost all political prisoners freed by 1967, many Romanian writers and intellectuals felt themselves at liberty to begin push-
ing for intellectual reforms. As a result, Romanian literature is
among the most creative in Eastern Europe. On several occasions
the sensitive question of state censorship of the press has been discussed, though with due discretion. In the spring of 1968, Romania
still retained many of the fundamental aspects of the totalitarian
socialist state it had been for the past twenty years. It was still a
society carefully controlled by the top handful of men in the Party
hierarchy. Those in power were not yet ready to match Alexander
Dubcek's experiment in socialist humanism. But this proud Balkan
nation had come a long way since the death of former Party boss
Gheorghe Gheorghiu-Dej.

NEW FREEDOMS

In a relatively new atmosphere of social relaxation, new freedoms—token but significant—were being granted. When the Romanian
delegation headed by Niculescu-Mizil walked out of the Budapest
summit conference in February, 1968, passports were already being
allocated to individuals who, just one year earlier, had no hope of
leaving the country. Western films, books, and fashions were being
imitated in Bucharest as if the regime were encouraging the assimi-
lation of such aspects of the "decadent consumer society." Romanians
who remembered the excesses of Stalinist moralism were amused
by this apparent return to a more familiar joie de vivre. They would
not easily give up this new relaxation for ideological reasons, especially since it had all come about with the wholehearted endorsement
of the Central Committee. No one knew better than Nicolae Ceausescu
that the Romanian character itself would not allow for easy doctrinaire
backsliding. Besides, the new, relaxed social order gained for him
increasing popular support and strengthened his already firm control
of the Party machinery. It was not surprising, then, that the leadership in Bucharest took pains to follow, with not a little self-interest,
the evolution of Dubcek's politics during the first months of Czechoslovakia's "new era of socialism."

As the year progressed and it became evident to everyone that
Dubcek was heading toward a confrontation with the Moscow conservatives, Bucharest made a concerted effort to have its own position
understood in all corners of the world arena. Doubtless, Ceausescu

did not expect to be directly consulted by Moscow on its intentions concerning the Czechoslovakian crisis. He had long been considered the "black sheep" of the bloc and he himself probably preferred to live up to the reputation vis-a-vis Moscow, so long as he could maintain a degree of independence in dealing with the Soviet leadership at a distance. Nonetheless, the refusal of the Warsaw Pact members to inform him of even their most obvious intentions did irritate the Romanian president. It became obvious in Bucharest by late spring that the Romanian party was being scorned as much as the new leadership in Prague, if for different reasons. Already in June, the state newspapers, Scanteia, Romania libera, Informatia, which usually ran semi-informative issues of four to eight pages, were printing ten-and twelve-page editions that gave astoundingly good coverage of the events to the public. The hostile letters delivered to the Romanian state during the summer of 1968 by the respective governments of Poland and East Germany were published in toto, for the readers at large. An accurate account of the surrounding political circumstances was also offered, with a slight Romanian slant, of course. It was an invigorating, politically enlightening summer for the average Romanian, who, for all too long, had been conditioned to think of a political event as something that happened only in the capitalist world. Now, because of its leadership position, Romania was actually in the focus of world attention. In the same summer that witnessed the growth of a new freedom in a fraternal socialist country, and the subsequent destruction of that freedom and the violation of that country, Romanians became acutely aware of themselves as a separate nation and were concerned about their future as an independent socialist state.

WESTERN AND EASTERN
EUROPE BEFORE THE STORM

During June and part of July, 1968, the author (who had been living in Romania) vacationed in Western Europe. Everywhere the headlines were similar. The situation in Czechoslovakia had taken on a new character when it became known that Soviet and Warsaw Pact troops were engaged in "general maneuvers" on the Czech border. Nowhere were perceptions keener than in West Germany; it seemed that the Germans had a realistic, if at that time seemingly exaggerated, understanding of where the political situation was heading. Another "Budapest," staged in Prague in 1968, appeared a remote possibility in the minds of astute Westerners, but for middle-aged Europeans who remembered Berlin, Warsaw, and Budapest, it was no improbability. Granted, the Soviet Union had in the last several years gained a good deal of respect in West European capitals.

Washington, not Moscow, was engaged in an extremely dubious war
in Southeast Asia. The Soviets' apparent "soft pedaling" in world
affairs since Khrushchev's fall and that country's rise to international
prestige were enough to warrant reconsideration on the part of many
West Europeans. A modus vivendi had been achieved with the Eastern
giant. Besides, the recent events in France—the student riots and the
near-revolutionary strikes—were still monopolizing Western concerns
and diverting attention from the Czechoslovakian dilemma. It was the
meeting at Cerna-on-the-Tisa between Dubcek and the Soviet overlords
that, more than any other development, signaled the Czech leader's
supposed success in the eyes of most Europeans. For some reason,
Moscow could accept the "new" Czechoslovakia, even if it did pose a
vital threat to the "security" of the Soviet Union. Few experts, anywhere, then saw this as tactical manipulation on the part of Moscow.
A calculated calm had been decreed by Moscow—before the storm.

Upon his return to Bucharest in late July, the author was immediately impressed by an apparent evolution in the Romanian political, and
social, scene. The daily papers were the prime source of startling
news; there were now "letters to the editor" by articulate citizens
who wished to express their "admiration for and solidarity with"
the Romanian leadership and, more importantly, to state their personal
disapproval of recent declarations made by some of the "fraternal"
socialist parties concerning the foreign policy of Bucharest. The
capital was alive with political discussion and the Western press had
arrived to capture some of the ambience. On more than one occasion,
reference was made to the "reopening" of the "little entente." Dubcek
and Tito had become political idols of a stature exceeded only by
Ceausescu. Inflated though the hopes of many Romanians may have
been, they were genuine. Things were moving in a favorable direction.
After two decades of kowtowing to Moscow, Romania, along with her
close allies, Czechoslovakia and Yugoslavia, might be able to do as
she "damn well pleased."—or so it might have seemed to many idealistic Romanians.

The students were especially enthusiastic. In spite of what
many Western analysts might have thought to the contrary, young
Romanians lent support, passive if not more, to the Bucharest administration in 1968. They could not easily remember the atrocities of
the Stalinist era, and, by nature of their youth, they tended not to
look in a backward direction. Ceausescu had done a great deal to
gain respect from students by showing a sincere concern for their
academic situation and for their role as future leaders of the country.
Student accommodations had been dramatically improved and, on the
cultural level, the student "class" was commonly regarded as privileged.

Still, the overall consensus in Bucharest in August, 1968, was that Ceausescu was doing his best, given the existing circumstances, to lead the country out of a difficult political position into a future that would see ever-expanding prosperity. In mid-August, when the president went to Prague for discussions with Dubcek, and, ostensibly, to lend his full moral support to the Czech leader, Ceausescu had earned the earnest admiration of even the most anti-Communist Romanian citizens.

Ceausescu returned to Baneasa airport on August 17, and was met by a wildly cheering throng, few of whom had been planted by Party officials. Optimism reigned supreme in Bucharest that day as the people enthusiastically accepted the official pronouncement that Alexander Dubcek was "A-OK." It would have been impossible to know then whether Ceausescu harbored any doubts about the future of Dubcek and that of the Czech brand of socialism. If so, he kept such thoughts to himself. Superficially satisfied, socialist Romania, the Latin renegade of the socialist world, prepared for the Independence Day celebration that was to take place the following week. The nation went through its routine somewhat more eagerly now, thoroughly unaware of the events the next several days would bring.

Bucharest was filled with foreigners those days. The press had come from all parts of the world to report on Romania's stand in the Czechoslovak crisis, and, especially, to catch Ceausescu's crucial statement upon his return from Prague. None of the journalists then assembled in Bucharest realized that a much more sensational story was in the immediate offing. Romania had never before played host to so many foreign tourists. There were visitors from every part of Western Europe, most of them heading towards Mamaia and the other Black Sea resorts. The country also received a large influx of Czech tourists. As a result of Dubcek's new program, Czech citizens were permitted for the first time since the close of World War II to travel freely in Western Europe. They were also taking advantage of the opportunity to see more of certain Bloc countries. For political curiosity as well as reasons of adventure Czech tourists flocked to Romania. At the time of the invasion, some Romanian sources estimated the number of Czech tourists in Romania to be about 40,000. Just one day later, many of these unsuspecting visitors became temporary exiles.

AUTHOR'S DIARY: AUGUST 21, 1968

Wednesday morning, August 21, I awoke to the longest day of my life. At about seven o' clock I was jarred from sleep by the

frightened sounds of crowds screaming below my apartment window.
I looked out to see hundreds of people parading through Brezoianu
Street below me, shouting slogans and creating a general clamor:
"P.C.R.! P.C.R.!" (a chant to the Romanian Communist Party), and
"Ceausescu, Tito, Dubcek, urah!" From all points of the city people
were converging on the huge Palace Square in Calea Victoriei. The
activity needed no explanation. It was obvious that the events of the
spring and summer had culminated in a disaster for the Czechs. The
Soviet Union and its allies—minus Romania—had invaded Czechoslovakia by military force. But on the morning of August 21, 1968, judging
by the pandemonium in the streets of Bucharest, one would have thought
that Romania, too, was in military conflict.

I rushed out as soon as possible to join the masses. It was an
experience such as I never could have imagined. Thousands of people
were pouring into the center of the capital, where Ceausescu was
about to deliver his now historic speech. The faces around me registered every human emotion, every passion. There was an electricity
in the air that permeated every individual present and, somehow,
bound us in spirit. I was a Romanian that morning. I felt and understood all that it meant for these people to be a small, threatened
nation that had been sacrificed just once too often.

In the distance, beyond the vast congregation, I could see a
Party-organized demonstration. Bearing enormous placards, a chorus
of young men was chanting party and patriotic slogans. At one point,
a lady near me, hysterical with emotion, screamed along with them:
"Traiasca Ceausescu! Traiasca Romania!" ("Long live Ceausescu!
Hail Romania!"). Even she seemed surprised by her spontaneous
outburst. I had no doubt that she was not a member of the Party; her
outcry, though, was most sincere.

When Ceausescu made his appearance at the outside podium of
the Central Committee headquarters, the crowds that packed the
square greeted him with a tumultuous orgy of cheers and applause.
Even the elements seemed to participate in that morning. As if inspired by a Verlaine poem, a melancholic drizzle was falling on
Bucharest. Dousing the feverish passions of the day, the rain seemed
a prelude to the heated days to come. There was a quick wave of
silence as the president began to speak. Here and there a woman
could be heard sobbing or a child crying in fright. Ceausescu spoke
to an attentive nation. His declaration was more impressive, that
day in the square, than the world press could ever have made it
appear. Nicolae Ceausescu spoke not as the president of a small
Balkan country, but as a great world statesman when he denounced
the Soviet invasion of Czechoslovakia and warned his countrymen that
Romania would have difficult days ahead.

The developments of the next several days are well documented.
As the free Czechoslovak radio stations went out of existence one by
one and the last pockets of physical resistance were snuffed out by
brute Soviet force, the complete occupation of a prostrate Czechoslovakia was "accomplished." The overlords in Moscow had again had
their way—but not entirely. Radio Bucharest and Radio Belgrade
took over when Prague was silenced. News of the events poured out
from the socialist bloc, giving the lie to the "facts" as Moscow invented them. The ethics of the Russian Bear were exposed not only
by an indignant West, but, more importantly, by socialist "comrades."
As Ceausescu continued his attacks, Bucharest took the spotlight
away from Prague.

Rumors ran wild throughout Bucharest. After Ceausescu had
alerted the nation to the need for military preparedness, he institutionalized the new "patriotic guards." As fears of an armed Soviet attack
mounted, local imaginations worked feverishly. By the evening of
August 21, the city was already alive with ominous "reports" that the
Soviet Union had massed troops along the Pruth River for an overnight invasion. Unverified accounts were coming in from the provinces
that Hungarian and Bulgarian troops had begun to move against Romanian posts. On a garden wall near the Party headquarters passers-by
could, for a brief time, read the chalked inscription "Vrem Basarabia!"
("We want Bessarabia!"), hastily scrawled by an anonymous patriot.
One elderly gentleman with whom I discussed the crisis told me: "I
haven't felt this excited since I shot down my first Russian pilot over
Iasi during the War!" In an awesome way the prevailing anti-Soviet
sentiment seemed to bring even dissident groups of Romanians together
in a united cause: Romania first and always.

In an effort to curtail general panic, the Party urged Radio Bucharest to issue repeated communiques throughout the night informing
the public of the state's efforts to stabilize the unusual situation. The
political representatives were doing all they could to assure both the
nation and the outside world of the country's benign position. Romania
remained opposed to the military occupation of Czechoslovakia, but the
country's leadership wanted to make it explicitly clear that Romania
posed no threat to the "security" of the Soviet Union. Nonetheless,
Ceausescu prepared the country's armed forces for any eventuality.

ROMANIA RETAINS ITS INDEPENDENCE

For a week Ceausescu reiterated his determination to maintain
Romania's independence as a socialist state. It was not until he

delivered his speech at Brasov the following week that some indications
of Soviet pressure became noticeable. Word leaked out early that
Soviet Ambassador Bashov had used pressure tactics in his meetings
with Ceausescu. Rumored accounts of "table-pounding" and vociferous
threats have yet to be publicly verified. Likewise, however, they
have yet to be officially denied. Still, in making allusions to "the inviolable solidarity of the fraternal socialist parties" and to the "importance of the Soviet Union's role in the struggle against imperialism,"
Ceausescu at Brasov was clearly softening his stand. The Romanian
people immediately recognized the tone of strained conciliation.

By mid-September it was certain that the Czechoslovak case
could only end as Moscow desired. It was now ridiculous to continue
talking of a Soviet invasion of Romania. Ceausescu had done a master-
ful job of holding his country's position without submitting to the will
of his Russian neighbors. The country found itself in a very delicate
political state of affairs, but continued to pursue its heavily nationalistic goal of self-industrialization. An important question was now
on everyone's mind: If the Soviet Union decided to put pressure on
Romania, in what form would it come? The most logical answer was
economic quarantine.

Since Ceausescu was in the unique position of having almost
complete control within the state and Party hierarchy (there exists
no pro-Moscow element within the Romanian Communist Party that
might be exploited by the Soviets), any Soviet political manipulation
in Bucharest could only result in a resurgence of Romanian nationalism
fiercely hostile toward Moscow. But the Romanian economy was still
largely dependent upon Soviet imports, especially for industrial produce and some raw materials. For reasons of their own, however,
the Soviets did not choose to exert the expected economic pressures.
True to its ideals, the Romanian leadership continued to expand its
trade with the West, possibly intending to diminish its trade with and
dependence on the Soviet Union.

As the new year approached, the events of August became less
important to Romanians, although the mere mention of those days
would still evoke an occasional scowl. What did remain was a sense
of unity. By early 1969, few Romanians considered that an armed
showdown with the Soviet Union would have brought anything short of
total disaster for them. However, there was now a national solidarity
that had perhaps been only of a racial and cultural nature the year
before. Ceausescu had won an overwhelming expression of support
in August. He was a unifying and stabilizing force at home, and had
also become a political figure of international prestige. His gutsy

insolence in the shadow of the Soviet goliath had tied his name to Dubcek's "new socialism," which was, after all, revered in the West. If the Romanian President had not intended at the outset to gain personal influence for himself, the international drama of 1968 had done so for him.

At the close of 1969, Romania was generally acknowledged to be an "independent" socialist state, superficially tied to the Warsaw Pact, and a nation with peaceful national goals. The Romanian chief of state had been an honored guest in Ankara, Teheran, Rawalpindi, and New Delhi. Bucharest had been host to the heads of state of France, Sweden, Austria, and the United States. A socialist Romania had preserved its fragile sovereignty and had survived to become a recognized champion of diplomacy and East-West detente.

THE FUTURE

The continuation of Romania's political stability in the 1970's is dependent on a number of axioms of the nation's own character. The Romanian people are Latin and they are extremely proud of their national heritage. No leadership in Bucharest can succeed without incorporating those nationalistic tendencies. The fact must also be categorically accepted by Westerners that Romania is a socialist state and will continue to be so into the foreseeable future. For geopolitical reasons, the country cannot go in any direction but forward. The Bucharest regime must continue its present policies in order to reap the benefits of any existing gains it has made. Also, Ceausescu, for reasons probably known best to him, cannot yet afford to gamble with drastic, deep-reaching programs of domestic liberalization. He is still watched contemptuously by Moscow, and, equally important, he cannot be sure how reliable internal factors would be if he granted lavish freedoms. Then again, perhaps it is possible that he is more of a "hard-liner" than he is often pictured. In any event, it is certain that he will continue his pragmatic policy of cautiously walking the ideological tightrope until he reaches the safety point. Although it is ultimately anyone's guess what the 1970's will bring for Eastern Europe, it is not altogether preposterous to wonder if, perhaps, Romania will become the first beneficiary of Alexander Dubcek's legacy.

10

THE
ECONOMIC EFFECTS
ON YUGOSLAVIA
OF THE INVASION
OF CZECHOSLOVAKIA

Werner Sichel

The purpose of this essay is to discuss in as scholarly a manner as possible some results of an event the full results of which will only be unfolded during the next decade or more. To be more specific, an attempt will be made to offer some partial analysis with respect to the economic effects on Yugoslavia of the five Warsaw Pact countries' invasion of Czechoslovakia during the night of August 20-21, 1968.

While this is a fascinating and intriguing subject, certain caveats, other than the time span that has elapsed since the invasion, must be offered. Not enough facts are available and all too often impressions, opinions, and speculation have to be substituted. Among the many qualifications necessary for the writing of this essay, this analyst can only claim that he is an economist who has an interest in the Yugoslav economic system and that he "was there," in Yugoslavia during the ten months immediately following the invasion.*

The questions raised in this essay often concern politics more than economics and both aspects must be understood in the context of changing socialist theory and the ensuing developments that have oc- curred in Eastern Europe over the past several decades.

---

*The author was a Fulbright-Hays lecturer at the University of Belgrade, Yugoslavia, for the academic year 1968-69.

POLITICAL AND ECONOMIC
BACKGROUND

Socialist theory originally appeared as a critique of capitalist society. After the 1917 October Revolution in Russia, it followed that capitalist economic and social relations had to be replaced by socialist ones and that in concrete terms private ownership of the means of production had to be replaced by social ownership and that the market economy had to be replaced by a planned economy. However, the period from the October Revolution to the enactment of the First Five-Year Plan in 1929 was a time during which much discussion took place in the Soviet Union and a great variety of methodological approaches, views, and interpretations of the basic principles of socialist theory and their implementation were considered. Once Stalin acquired the dominant role in the Party, the discussion ended and his model became "socialist theory." Stalin's interpretation was accepted not only for the building of Soviet society, but also as the theoretical solution for all other socialist countries. The construction of socialist societies in East European countries after World War II was based on this same theory and all other approaches were politically, socially, and ideologically excluded. Yugoslavia was no exception. The Yugoslav economic system in 1945 was based on complete centralization of management by the state, and on government planning as the basic method of resource allocation. As late as 1948, new measures were introduced that collectivized much of the agricultural sector and nationalized many enterprises that had been considered too small to nationalize earlier. In that same year, however, the Yugoslavs decided to embark on the construction of a new type of socialist system. Normal relations with the Soviet bloc were severed and open criticism of Stalinist doctrines of socialism were launched. It was not until 1950, however, that Yugoslav institutions began to change. By that time the concept that a viable socialist state cannot be achieved by the development and strengthening of state bodies and organizations was well entrenched in Yugoslav thought.

In contrast to the Soviet bloc countries, the Yugoslavs perceived the building of socialism as a decrease of state influence and as a free association of self-determining producers. The basic question became one of how to implement a system where the "working people" (the producers) became the leading social force. The answer started at the level of the enterprise, the basic unit of association of working people, with the introduction of workers' self-management in 1950. Workers' self-management is the system whereby the workers of an enterprise as a whole or their elected representatives—a workers'

council—determine the policies of their enterprise. Social ownership
has a very different meaning under workers' self-management than
it does under the Stalinist conception. The Yugoslavs argue that the
separation between the producer and the means of production is just
as serious in state socialism as it is in capitalism and that social
ownership must remain social in the sense that the owner is society
and not the state. Ideally, workers' self-management allows the working people to decide on the use of the means of production, to manage
production processes, and to allocate material goods—all on the basis
of their participation in production. In actuality, a great deal of state
intervention (local, Republic, and Federal) has taken place in Yugoslavia, and while the principle of workers' self-management has never
been abandoned, important economic variables such as prices, investment funds, foreign trade, and enterprise management personnel
have often been controlled by the state coordinators. The results of
workers' self-management tempered by state intervention have been
very good. The United Nations Statistical Yearbook shows that from
1952 to 1962 Yugoslavia occupied second place in overall economic
growth in the world (only Japan grew more rapidly) with an average
rate of 7.6 percent. Per capita real income rose from $140 shortly
before World War II to over $500 in 1964. Since these results were
most satisfying, growth per se was given lower priority by the mid-
1960's. Structural problems that had long been largely ignored were
now confronted. Most disturbing were the shortages that appeared in
the raw materials, capital goods, and energy industries; the existence
of extensive excess capacity in many manufacturing industries; and
the growing deficit in the balance of payments. There was relatively
little pressure to revert back to more centralized planning and there
was general agreement that state intervention had hampered workers'
self-management. Therefore, it was decided to introduce some major
economic reforms that would further restrict the role of the state and
thus give more responsibility to working organizations. The most
outstanding features of the 1965 economic reforms included the freeing
of a great many prices that had previously been set by the Federal
Price Office, tax law alterations that increased the share of economic
organizations in the distribution of net product from 51 to 71 percent,
and significant decreases in tariff rates that challenged Yugoslav
enterprises to compete with foreign competitors. Adjustments to
changes brought about by the reforms, which exhibited themselves in
slower growth in some sectors, growing structural unemployment,
and mounting trade deficits, were evident at the time of the invasion.
It was a period of some vulnerability and no serious blow to the economy
could be tolerated.

YUGOSLAV-CZECH RELATIONS

In the time immediately preceding the invasion when the new Czech oslovak leadership was being severely challenged by the U.S.S.R., the Yugoslavs had a decision to make. Should they remain neutral in the debate or should they speak out against the pressures being applied by the U.S.S.R. on the Czechs to abandon the new Dubcek democratiza- tion policy? The decision seemed to have been an easy one for the Yugoslavs to make. They had only to think back to 1948 when they denounced Stalinism and chose their own path to socialism. In fact, a return to Stalinism in no small measure threatened Yugoslavia even in 1968. So the Yugoslavs forcefully and courageously spoke out against "those leaderships of Communist parties of certain European socialist countries." One editorial printed in a Yugoslav periodical about three weeks before the invasion spoke of the events and reactions relating to Czechoslovakia as causing "painful apprehensions about the revival of concepts concerning 'uniform socialism' which knows nothing about the rights and requirements of the working class in this or that coun- try but only about the impeccability of the dogma."[1] The editorial went on to say that there was no doubt that the leaders who represented the policy of "democratic revival" of socialist relations in Czechoslo- vakia had won in the Presidium, the Central Committee, the National Front, the entire Party, and in society in general through "legitimate means of political confrontation" and that this fact was being deliber- ately disregarded by those socialist countries that criticized it.

The Yugoslavs lent their support to the Czech people in any way they could. During those very tense days before the invasion the bonds between the two nations grew very strong. During a public meeting held in Prague on August 2, just after Czech-U.S.S.R. talks in Cierna and just before the talks in Bratislava, slogans were chanted: "We want a free republic"; "Independence, sovereignty, freedom"; "Yugo- slavia and Romania to Bratislava"; "Long live Comrade Tito"; and "We trust Dubcek."[2] A week later Tito showed Yugoslavia's support by visiting Prague. On the eve of his departure Borba wrote that

> Yugoslavia and its league of Communists have lent—since
> the very beginning of new trends in Czechoslovakia—full sup-
> port to the strivings which mean an important contribution
> to the richness of socialist paths, to the democratization and
> full equality of all nations. Our unanimous, unreserved sup-
> port to all aspirations of the friendly country has been in-
> spired not only by the traditional sympathy and confidence
> which we have always displayed for the people and working-
> men of Czechoslovakia, but also by our own experience from

the struggle for the just principles of socialist and inter-
socialist relations.[3]

Tito was very warmly received in Czechoslovakia. He spoke of
the Yugoslav experience and its defense and development of the Yugoslav independent road to socialism. He stressed that Czechoslovakia
and Yugoslavia had much in common, that the two countries both wanted
to build socialism, and that the mutual support and backing they offered
each other was useful to world socialism.

Czechoslovakia and Yugoslavia have had good economic relations
for a long time. They have been traditional trading partners. During
the period between World Wars I and II, standard commodity lists
were drawn up on a year-to-year basis, but after World War II, long-
term agreements were used which considerably increased trade.
Both as a buyer and a supplier Czechoslovakia has become a very
important trading partner for Yugoslavia. In 1967, commodity exchange between the two countries amounted to $178 million. Other
forms of economic cooperation have also developed in recent years.
The two countries have found greater and greater mutual interest in
industrial cooperation, which often involves the sale of goods in third
markets. Also, scientific and technical cooperation has increased
over the past several years. Future economic relations between the
two countries looked very bright and the Yugoslavs were quite eager
to take advantage of this economic potential.

After the Czech-U.S.S.R. meeting in Bratislava, which took place
during the first week in August, a declaration was signed that relaxed
tensions and found Czechs speaking of "victory in peace."[4] However,
during the night between August 20 and 21, an army a half-million strong
of five socialist countries crossed the borders of Czechoslovakia. They
were well equipped with modern weapons, under a single command,
and they overwhelmed and occupied the country within a matter of a
few hours. While from a military point of view the invasion was a
complete success, it met with the resistance and condemnation of the
Czechs, and more important, of practically every nation in the world.
World public opinion, with the exception of Fidel Castro, strongly disapproved the action of the Warsaw Pact countries. In order to justify
the invasion, it was alleged that Czechoslovak independence had been
threatened by an imperialist plot; later this was switched to an assertion that Czechoslovak socialism was endangered by internal
counterrevolution. It was contended that the invasion had been carried
out at the request of the Czech Communist Party and of Czech state
officials. All these arguments were completely unfounded and they
did not conceal the fact that a socialist country had been militarily
overrun and occupied by a group of other socialist countries and this

completely against the will of its government and people.

YUGOSLAV CONDEMNATION OF THE
SOVIET INVASION

The outcry by the Yugoslavs against the invasion was loud and clear. The initial statement by President Tito was:

The entrance of foreign military units into Czechoslovakia, without an invitation, or without the approval on the part of the legal government, has worried us deeply. The sovereignty of a socialist country was thus violated, and a serious blow has been inflicted on the socialist and progressive forces in the world.

During my visit to Prague and during my talks with the Czechoslovak leaders, and with Comrade Dubcek, I became convinced that they are determined to frustrate any attempt of anti-socialist elements to hamper a normal development of the democracy and socialist progress in Czechoslovakia.

The joint document which was signed on that occasion, is a confirmation of this.

However, with the latest events, the jointly accepted decisions of "the Six" in Bratislava have been unilaterally annulled, and measures have been undertaken which will have far-reaching and extremely negative consequences for the whole revolutionary movement in the world.[5]

A hurriedly called session of the Presidium and the Executive Committee of the Central Committee of the League of Communists of Yugoslavia (LCY) was held at Brioni on August 21 to discuss the invasion. The following quote from Borba expresses the unreserved support that the top policy-making organ of Yugoslavia gave to Czechoslovakia during these first difficult hours. It should be understood that at this very time there were many Yugoslavs who believed that "they would be next."

Expressing the feelings, the deep anxiety and indignation of all peoples of Yugoslavia, and of all members of the League of Communists, because of the violation of the sovereignty of an independent socialist country, which is in deep contradiction with the elementary rights of every nation to determine and decide on its own fate—the Presidium and Executive Committee of the Central Committee of the League

of Communists of Yugoslavia have unanimously expressed
full solidarity with the peoples of Czechoslovakia, with
the working class, government, and leading organs of the
Communist Party of Czechoslovakia with Dubcek at its
head. In conformity with the League of Communists assumed to date, and approving Comrade Tito's statement
today in full, the Presidium and Executive Committee are
extending all-out support to the justified demands of the
legitimate representatives of the Socialist Republic of
Czechoslovakia for the withdrawal of the occupation forces,
for the respect of the principles of sovereignty and independence, for allowing the normal activity of the democratically elected state and party forums, and for the release of
the representatives of the people and party.[6]

Borba next pointed out the international implications and then
in a closing paragraph made a plea for solidarity of the Yugoslav
people at that crucial time:

The latest development of events shows that it is not only
the question of an attack on Czechoslovakia, but also of an
important turning-point in history, of relations between socialism in the world, of the international workers' movement, and of the fate of peace in Europe and in the world.
This intervention is a serious blow to the socialist and all
progressive forces in the world, which encourages the most
reactionary forces, leads to the sharpening of the cold war,
and has far-reaching negative consequences for the whole
development of international relations.
     . . . Simultaneously, they [the Presidium and Execu-
tive Committee] are calling upon all working people of Yugoslavia to gather even more closely around the League of
Communists of Yugoslavia, its policy of defense of independence and equalitarian relations between nations, to fight
with even greater determination for a general progress of
socialist relations on the basis of self-management and
direct democracy, to oppose energetically attacks against
the basic achievements of socialism, no matter from what
side they may come, and to prevent any provocations and
attempts at exploiting these events, which would weaken
the unity of our peoples.[7]

Other national groups to make public statements concerning the
invasion included the Yugoslav Trade Union Federation, the Yugoslav's

Peoples Army, the Federation of Associations of Veterans of the
National Liberation War, the Yugoslav Youth Federation, and the
Yugoslav Federation of Authors. The Yugoslav Trade Union Federation
stated that they "most severely condemn the brutal use of armed force
and consider that in this way a heavy blow has been inflicted to socialist
development in Czechoslovakia and immense damage caused to socialis'
and progress the world over."[8] The Army and the Veterans Federation pledged to support Tito, termed the invasion a "flagrant violation
of the most essential norms of international law" and, in reference to
the "aggression," stated that they were "deeply embittered." The
Yugoslav Youth Federation issued a long statement denouncing the
occupation and stating that it

> lends unreserved support to the peoples of the Czechoslovak
> Socialist Republic, to the working class and the Communist
> Party with Comrade Alexander Dubcek as leader, to the
> youth and its political organization, to the Czechoslovak
> Youth Federation and its struggle for preservation of inde-
> pendence and national sovereignty, as well as the right to
> decide about their own road of socialist development.[9]

The Yugoslav Federation of Authors wrote an open letter to
Czech "intellectuals" stating that they received the news of the occupation "with horror and condemnation" and offering hope that the
"great ideas" for which the Czechs are fighting will beat the "force
of aggression and violence."

The outspoken condemnation of the invasion expressed in the
above statements was echoed by countless statements from local communities, from regional groups, from the level of the Republic, and
from prominent individuals. In Belgrade, for example, a very strong
open letter denouncing the invasion and demanding immediate withdrawal was issued; a joint session of forums of political organizations
in Belgrade was held which in addition to denouncing the Warsaw Pact
action announced that reception centers had been organized in Belgrade
for Czechoslovak tourists who could not get back to their country; and
over 250,000 inhabitants of Belgrade attended a massive rally at Marx
and Engels Square at which they energetically condemned the violation
of Czechoslovakia's sovereignty. Both individuals and enterprises
showed their deep feelings by providing accommodations, cash, food,
and other items. Many hotels and restaurants did not charge for lodg-
ings and food. A large petroleum enterprise (Jugopetrol) gave away
twenty liters of gasoline to every motorized Czech tourist. Citizens
in the outlying parts of Yugoslavia who are not usually very concerned
about international affairs were distressed to the point where thousands

of telegrams in support of the Party's and especially Tito's words condemning the Warsaw Pact action were received by President Tito.

Much more evidence could be offered to show the deep feelings of the Yugoslavs and the strong support that they offered the Czechs, but the above will suffice.

The Warsaw Pact countries, as would be expected, responded vigorously to the Yugoslav outcries with some bitter attacks of their own. Daily attacks against Yugoslavia were launched in Soviet newspapers, on the radio, and on television. Yugoslavia was said to have "joined the imperialist chorus." Polish, East German, and Bulgarian newspapers echoed these sentiments. They further insisted that the Yugoslav system had failed and that the Yugoslav path to socialism was a false one. The Yugoslav press responded to these assaults by pointing out the fallacious reasoning used and then again attacked Warsaw Pact policies in connection with Czechoslovakia. Six months later the U.S.S.R. was still attacking Yugoslavia. Under the guise of being critical of the theory of market socialism, economists in the Institute for Economics of the Academy of Sciences of the U.S.S.R. attacked the policy of Yugoslavia. They labeled the Yugoslav policy as "rightist revisionism" and as an eclectic mixture of bourgeois theories of "industrial society" and "convergence." The management of the Yugoslav economy was criticized for diminishing the economic role of the socialist state, for ignoring the role of economic instruments (central state planning), and for the lack of state investment. They also alluded to certain Czech economists who had adopted the ideas spread in Yugoslavia—"the program of revisionism."

"BUSINESS AS USUAL"
WITH WARSAW PACT COUNTRIES

The reader of this essay, which is purported to deal with the economic effects on Yugoslavia of the invasion of Czechoslovakia, may now expect to read about the momentous economic repercussions of this bitter rift. If any momentous economic repercussions took place, they have been well hidden. Of course, as indicated at the very beginning of the chapter, some important long-run effects may become evident. What has been most impressive, however, has been the strong verbal debate between Yugoslavia and the Warsaw Pact countries and the simultaneous "business as usual" atmosphere that prevailed. A few illustrations, all of which took place very shortly after the invasion, will help to demonstrate this point.

On August 30, 1968, an exhibition of Yugoslav light-products industries took place in Leningrad. It ran until September 15, during which time over 200 Yugoslav manufacturing enterprises participated. Opening ceremonies were attended by the Yugoslav ambassador to the U.S.S.R. and the deputy chief of administration of the Federal Chamber of the U.S.S.R. Hopes were expressed that the exhibition would contribute to the further development of trade between the two nations and to their mutual benefit.

On September 4, 1968, railcar producers in Yugoslavia sent their representatives to Moscow to negotiate deliveries of freight cars to the U.S.S.R. Yugoslav representatives simultaneously drew up lists of goods that the Soviet Union would export to Yugoslavia, equivalent to the value of freight cars.

On September 8, 1968, an agreement was signed in Moscow between representatives of a Yugoslav and a Russian enterprise that provided for an entire oxygen factory to be built by the Russian enterprise in Yugoslavia.

A last example involving the Soviet Union of "business as usual" while vicious Yugoslav and Soviet attacks against each other were going on was the meeting of the Executive Committee of the Council for Mutual Economic Cooperation that took place in Moscow during the last week of September. Attending this meeting were the deputy premieres of the U.S.S.R. and Yugoslavia together with their counterparts from Bulgaria, Hungary, the German Democratic Republic (East Germany), Mongolia, Poland, Romania, and Czechoslovakia.

Illustrations of this same phenomenon involving Yugoslavia and Warsaw Pact countries other than the U.S.S.R. were also evident. On September 3, 1968, the Yugoslav-East German Committee for Economi and Scientific-Technical Cooperation met in Belgrade. Two days later a protocol was signed on scientific-technical cooperation between the two countries that involved 115 Yugoslav experts' visiting East Germar for the purpose of acquainting themselves with manufacturing in that country, while 114 East German experts were to visit Yugoslav enterprises for the same purpose. They also dealt with the mutual ceding of technical documents, the using and training of each other's experts, and some direct scientific-technical cooperation agreements between enterprises of the two countries.

A few days later, twenty Yugoslav enterprises took part in the International Fair of Consumer Goods at Leipzig (East Germany), where they sold about $1 million worth of goods.

With the possible exception of Russia, the most forceful attacks on Yugoslav reaction to the invasion came from Poland. Yet, on September 9, 1968, a session of the Yugoslav-Polish Commission for Scientific-Technical Cooperation opened in Warsaw. They signed a protocol that not only continued but expanded cooperation in several spheres. On September 13 the two countries signed an agreement whereby Poland granted to Yugoslavia long-term credit totaling about $32 million that Yugoslavia was to return by delivering alumina to Poland over a period of time.

On September 12, 1968, President Tito opened the Zagreb Autumn Fair, the largest "economic show" offered by Yugoslavia. Business as usual prevailed. In fact, Kiro Gligorov, vice president of the Federal Executive Council, made it very clear when he said: "We do not want and will not give any reason for losing any business partner or any friend in the world, either in the West or in the East or in countries of Africa, Asia, and Latin America. Therefore any moves which introduce economic, political, or military tension in economic relations and in world trade are alien to us."[10] In attendance were 5,000 foreign and 1,250 Yugoslav exhibitors. Including the Soviet Union and Czechoslovakia, 52 countries were represented and 200,000 different products were displayed. Everyone was pleased with the results.

Yugoslavia has for a long time believed that its best strategy for economic growth was to adopt a policy of nonalignment. Since the invasion of Czechoslovakia and world condemnation of this action, Yugoslavia has sought to take advantage of this situation by making it very clear that it is following a policy of nonalignment. Yugoslavia has taken an active role as a leader of nonaligned countries. Conferences have been held and many statements issued that denounced bloc divisions and called for equal participation in international economic relations. In March, 1969, President Tito, in his report to the Ninth Congress of the League of Communists of Yugoslavia, said:

> The development of international relations has reaffirmed the significance of the policy of non-alignment which has played an exceedingly important role in easing tension, removing the danger of a world conflict, and solving major international problems.
>   At the Belgrade Conference of non-aligned countries, which was held under conditions of extreme exacerbation of international relations, the need to preserve peace was the focus of attention. The declaration adopted at this conference pointed out how imperative it was to transcend bloc divisions and consistently apply the principles of peaceful coexistence.

. . . it has emerged into a broad movement for peace,
independence and equal international cooperation, and
against all forms of artificial separation, economic, racial
and other kinds of discrimination and division of the world.
The acceptance of the principles and substance of the
policy of non-alignment by a growing number of countries
is proof of the growth of forces which consider this policy
the most adequate way of struggling for the preservation of
independence and consolidation of security.[11]

One may argue then, that the invasion offered Yugoslavia an
opportunity to more freely (at lower risk) and actively pursue economic
relations with the West and yet maintain economic relations with the
Soviet Union and the other East European countries. The evidence is
adequate that since the invasion economic relations with the West and
the East have increased, but what cannot be satisfactorally shown is
cause and effect. Possibly many of the dealings that will be discussed
here would have occurred anyhow and cannot be attributed to the invasion of Czechoslovakia and the world condemnation that followed.

ECONOMIC RELATIONS WITH THE WEST

In late September, 1968, a Yugoslav delegation led by the vice
president of the Federal Executive Council, Kiro Gligorov, attended
the annual conference in Washington, D.C., of the International Bank
for Reconstruction and Development, the International Monetary Fund,
the International Association for Development, and the International
Financial Corporation. Yugoslav government officials had attended
these before, but for the first time the delegation included representatives of several Yugoslav banks. These international financial institutions had, since their foundation, provided financial aid to Yugoslavia
in the amount of $340 million, primarily for construction of roads,
modernization of railroad systems, expansion of electric power, and
modernization of industry in general. Gligorov returned from Washington very optimistic that loans to Yugoslavia would be significantly
increased. He noted then in response to proposals for modern double-
lane highways and modernization of industry that Yugoslavia submitted
"We were met with understanding and support and we expect a mission
of the Bank to visit our country as soon as next month. . . ." He told
of meeting with President Johnson, influential cabinet members,
American bankers, and American businessmen. He stated the "the
main motive for all these talks was to secure expansion of economic
cooperation on the basis of partnership and equality, more room for
our trade on the markets of the U.S.A. and other Western countries,

financial and banking cooperation, cooperation of our industry with
the industries of the most developed countries, and so on."[12] He indicated that Yugoslavia has an excellent chance to strongly penetrate
the American as well as other Western markets, to export more industrial products and services, to build various projects in these
countries, and to cooperate in joint ventures for other markets.
Gligorov summed up his satisfaction by saying: "I was received in the
U.S.A. with friendly attentiveness and feelings manifested towards
our country, its efforts, and its future successful development."[13]

About two weeks after Vice President Gligorov's return to
Yugoslavia, Under Secretary of State Nicholas Katzenbach visited
Belgrade for talks. The following review of the talks in a prominent
Belgrade newspaper drew an implicit comparison between U.S.S.R. and
U.S. policy:

> Even though it is a question of a superpower and of a small
> country, the exchange of views between Yugoslav and
> American statesmen always took place upon an equal basis
> and with the respect of positions of the partners. It could
> not be otherwise when it is known that the relations between
> the United States and Yugoslavia in general are based upon
> the principles of peaceful and active coexistence and this
> means also upon the principles of equality, mutual respect,
> independence and non-interference, let alone the respect
> of national sovereignty and territorial integrity which stands
> to reason.[14]

Since Katzenbach's visit substantial progress has been made in
Yugoslav-American economic relations. One example is a 1969 agreement between a tractor enterprise in Osijek, Yugoslavia, and the Ford
Motor Company whereby the Osijek factory will become a "center for
the production, assembly, and sale of Ford products."[15] Some of the
most important business agreements have been between large U.S.
agricultural and food firms and food combines in Yugoslavia. A
Yugoslav food combine that is made up of many enterprises from all
over the country will provide single or a category of agricultural
products for the American firm and is thus able to penetrate well-
developed world markets. Separate agreements have been signed on
cooperation in production, processing, and sale of foodstuffs that have
included corn, peas, tomatoes, apples, and peaches. The American
firm obligates itself to secure production programs, know-how, and
the market. More recently a combine of Yugoslav wine producers
has been successful in making an agreement to sell large quantities
of wine in the U.S. market.

In March, 1969, ten American and West European banks and six Yugoslav banks announced that they were forming an international investment company for Yugoslavia. The Company had starting capital of $520 million, half of which was provided by the International Bank, 20 percent by the Yugoslav banks, and the remainder by the American and West European banks. The stated intention of the new company is "to affirm the Yugoslav economy in the international capital market and to supply its investors with the most modern technological media in development of projects that guarantee repayment of credits and some profit."[16]

Economic cooperation with Western Europe has been increasing. With the exception of satisfactory agreements being made with the European Economic Community (EEC), economic relations have been good with West European countries. In June, 1969, it was reported that of the sixty long-term industrial and technical cooperative deals that have been made by Yugoslav enterprises with foreign firms, more than 80 percent have been with West European countries.[17] Tito in his report to the LCY in March, 1969, stated:

> Our relations with European countries are acquiring even more substantive and richer forms of economic, cultural, and political cooperation. This also comes to the fore in increasing exchanges of views and in meetings both at the state and the socio-political level. Yugoslavia's relations with Western European countries are a case in point of successful collaboration between countries with differing social systems. At the same time, such relations are elements of stability and a useful contribution to broader European cooperation.
>
> In 1968, our trade with Western European countries achieved the sum of over 1,500 million dollars. Our imports account for 55 percent of this and exports by about 45 percent. True, this is a negative balance of trade which is, however, covered in large part by non-commodity flows.[18]

Tito went on in this report to complain bitterly about the "discriminatory policy" of the EEC. This had been the case since the 1961 Rome Agreement on tariffs, which were set for "other countries" by the EEC. In addition, other restrictive practices such as quotas, surcharges, and "antidumping" measures have been invoked from time to time. Two months after the invasion of Czechoslovakia negotiations were begun between EEC officials and Yugoslavia to draw up a trade agreement. No other socialist country had ever been given this opportunity and there was much cause for optimism. Lionello Levi Sandry, the vice president of the EEC Commission, spoke very highly of Yugoslavia after his October, 1968, visit with Yugoslav businessmen and officials. He said that Yugoslavia is a country that "will unavoidably, due to the structure which it has built and the objectives which it intends to realize, strengthen its relationship with the European Economic Community."[19] He also said that he was favorably impressed with the sincere European orientation that he found among political, trade union, and business leaders. "The Community for its part," Sandry said, "has a deeply friendly attitude towards Yugoslavia" and he stressed the interest of the Commission in "enabling Yugoslavia to develop its trade with the community in those sectors where resistances on the part of certain interested economic circles exist."[20] Yugoslavia appointed a special ambassador to the European Common Market headquarters in Brussels but the trade agreement did not follow. The talks with Yugoslavia were served and the EEC deferred its decision to authorize the Commission to resume talks on both May 13 and July 23, 1969. The important stumbling block was Yugoslav agricultural exports, especially beef, corn, and tobacco, which involve about 40 percent of Yugoslavia's agricultural exports and which are being "discriminated" against by high surcharges on "other countries" exporting to EEC countries. All the EEC countries except France want to resume talks leading to a trade agreement with Yugoslavia. Only France is a serious competitor with Yugoslavia in regard to the agricultural products mentioned. The other EEC countries stand to gain from a trade agreement with Yugoslavia. During the first six months of 1969 trade between Yugoslavia and the EEC countries increased by 23 percent (both exports and imports) over the first six months of 1968.[21] However, since a substantial deficit existed before, the 1969 like percentage increases only widened the deficit.

Very good economic relations have been experienced between Yugoslavia and the EFTA (European Free Trade Association) plus Finland. About 12 percent of Yugoslav exports go to these seven European countries ($160 million in 1968) and in the first few months of 1969, year-to-year increases amounted to 15 percent. Yugoslavia is with EFTA, as with EEC, experiencing a substantial trade balance deficit. However, the Yugoslavs are optimistic that this deficit will be narrowed as cooperation intensifies in the form of closer mutual contracts of individual bodies of the EFTA organization. At the conclusion of talks held in June, 1969, between the secretary general of EFTA and Yugoslav officials, Politika wrote that the deficit in the balance of trade between Yugoslavia and EFTA is expected to be eliminated.[22]

ECONOMIC RELATIONS WITH
EASTERN EUROPE

Numerous examples of intensified economic relations between
Yugoslavia and the developed countries of the West during the period
since the Warsaw Pact invasion of Czechoslovakia have been presented
It has been speculated that the invasion may have given some impetus
to this better relationship. However, what must be emphasized is
that this increase has not been at the expense of economic relations
with the socialist countries. It is very clear that an atmosphere of
"business as usual" prevailed during the months right after the invasion when the bitterest vocal outbursts condemning the Warsaw Pact
countries were taking place. After that the nonaligned policy, which
was given maximum exposure, was translated into an economic policy
of "all-around economic cooperation." In March, 1969, Tito had already considerably "lowered his voice" with respect to the Warsaw
Pact countries when he said:

> we wish to underscore that Yugoslavia, regardless of the
> existing differences in views, supports the surmounting of
> the resulting difficulties and the further development of
> relations with all socialist countries, as that is in the com-
> mon interest of our peoples, of peace and of socialism.
>   . . . as a socialist and non-aligned country, Yugoslavia
> will develop comprehensive cooperation with all countries
> on principles of equality, independence, sovereignty and
> respect for the territorial integrity of all countries.[23]

A good example of the translation of this policy into economic
policy is the following quote from a Federal Institute planning report:

> Yugoslavia as a relatively small country must pave its way
> and find its place within the world economy and the world
> market. To this end it will orient itself towards broad eco-
> nomic cooperation with other countries in the interests of
> all, which on a long-term basis means its inclusion and
> real integration within world economic trends and broader
> economic cooperation with all nations to the interests of
> both sides.
>   . . . cooperation should become intensive with almost
> all countries in three large regions of international trade:
> with countries of the developed West, socialist countries,
> and developing countries. A rational distribution of our
> exchanges, among other things, decreases the risk to which

our relatively small country, with her independent economic policy, may be exposed in complicated international
situations, in possibly revived conditions of pressure, block-
ades, like those occurring in the past.

    . . . as far as the dispersion of our trade is concerned,
it is necessary to maintain economic relations with a large
number of countries and if possible to increase the volume
of trade.[24]

On the basis of this policy and in spite of, rather than as a reaction to, the invasion, good economic relations with the Eastern European
countries including the U.S.S.R. have been actively pursued by Yugoslavia. Very shortly after the invasion, Ekonomska Politika, in an
article dealing with upcoming trade negotiations with East European
countries, expressed the concern in the following paragraph:

The newest events in Czechoslovakia and all the implications which might result from them in the economic sphere
will certainly disturb the already worsened atmosphere for
such negotiations, as our experience teaches us that non-
economic elements have often prevailed in our relations
with the East European countries.[25]

Yugoslav trade with Eastern Europe is a significant proportion
of her total trade. For the first six months of 1968, Yugoslav exports
to the seven East European countries (Bulgaria, Czechoslovakia,
Hungary, East Germany, Poland, Romania, the U.S.S.R.) amounted to
38 percent of total Yugoslav exports while imports from these countries
accounted for 29 percent of total Yugoslav imports. Even with this
percentage differential, a deficit of about $120 million on an annual
basis was evidenced during this period, about one third of which was
a result of an unfavorable trade balance with the U.S.S.R. Even larger
deficits were expected for 1969, but substantial increases in exports
were also forecast. For the first six months of 1969, exports to Eastern Europe increased by 13 percent and to the U.S.S.R., by 28 percent
relative to the like 1968 period. Yugoslavia's trade with the U.S.S.R.
had moderately increased over the previous few years (from $296
million in 1965 to $347 million in 1966 to $383 million in 1967 to $394
million in 1968). However, an increase to well over $500 million was
anticipated for 1969 and the 28-percent rise during the first six months
offers credence to that prediction.

The improved economic relations between Yugoslavia and the
Soviet Union since the invasion are not only manifested in the amount
of international trade between the two countries but also in their credit

arrangements and their scientific-technical cooperation. Yugoslavia
has obtained credit from the Soviet Union for construction and equipment of several electric power and metallurgical projects in Yugoslavia.[26] These projects have brought about a degree of cooperation in
production between enterprises of the two nations which may be expanded upon in the future.

At the beginning of 1969, an agreement between the two countries
was signed dealing with cooperation in the passenger automobile industry for the 1969-75 period. Under this agreement, the Yugoslav
automobile industry and its partners, which are to carry out deals in
Yugoslavia, will deliver parts to Togliati, a Soviet automobile enterprise, for a new Soviet passenger car that the U.S.S.R. will manufac-
ture under a Fiat license. It is estimated that over the length of the
agreement the value of these shipments will be about $666 million.
The Soviet auto industry will in the same value and during the same
time period deliver manufactured passenger cars, spare parts for
them, and certain machines to Yugoslavia.

In the ship-building industry, another such agreement was expected to be concluded very soon. This one calls for Yugoslav ship
building enterprises to deliver ships to the U.S.S.R. in the amount
of about $200 million during the 1971-75 period. Negotiations are
also being held on similar arrangements in the machine-building industry and in the pharmaceutical industry. More cooperation is also
evident in the scientific-technical sphere. Negotiations have been held
throughout 1969 within the Mixed Yugoslav-Soviet Committee for
Economic Cooperation, which is composed of representatives from
both Yugoslav and Soviet enterprises. It may be concluded from these
illustrations that Yugoslavia has not been ignoring its third most
important trading partner and that the new political climate brought
about by the invasion of Czechoslovakia may have aided rather than
harmed Yugoslav-Soviet economic relations.

CONCLUSIONS

This essay began by offering certain caveats. The time has
been relatively short since the invasion occurred, the amount of factual material available is not abundant, and impressions and opinions
must often be relied upon. The factual material that has been presented here is quite revealing and has given rise to a certain amount
of speculation on the part of the writer, but it is not sufficient evidence
to clearly show "cause and effect." Maybe that is expecting too much.
One must be satisfied with learning that Yugoslavia's economic

relationship with the West has significantly improved since the invasion, rather than that the opposite has occurred; that Yugoslavia has found the U.S.S.R. a more cooperative business partner since the invasion; and that Yugoslavia's economic relations with other Warsaw Pact countries have also improved rather than deteriorated.

While the U.S.S.R. may have achieved its limited objective of temporarily "normalizing" Czechoslovakia via the invasion, its broader objective of compelling the increasingly independent satellites, particularly Yugoslavia, to accept the concept of limited sovereignty was not realized. World condemnation of the Warsaw Pact action freed Yugoslavia to seek closer economic ties with the West while yet espousing a nonalignment policy intended to prevent an erosion of Eastern ties and, in fact, to force greater economic cooperation with the U.S.S.R.

NOTES

1. Komunist, August 1, 1968, p. 3. Translated in Joint Translation Service, Belgrade, No. 5084, August 1, 1968, p. 36.

2. Borba, August 3, 1968, p. 2. Translated in Joint Translation Service, Belgrade, No. 5086, August 3, 1968, p. 30.

3. Borba, August 9, 1968. Translated in Joint Translation Service, Belgrade, No. 5091, August 9, 1968, p. 22.

4. At Bratislava the six parties (U.S.S.R., Poland, Bulgaria, Hungary, East Germany and Czechoslovakia) that participated signed a Declaration of Friendship that expressed their firm determination to do their utmost in order to promote all-round cooperation between their countries on the basis of equality, respect for sovereignty and national independence, territorial integrity, mutual brotherly aid and solidarity.

5. Borba, August 22, 1968, p. 1. Translated in Joint Translation Service, Belgrade, No. 5102, August 22, 1968, p. 20.

6. Ibid., pp. 2, 22.

7. Ibid.

8. Ibid., pp. 17, 18.

9. Borba, August 23, 1968, p. 4. Translated in Joint Translation Service, Belgrade, No. 5103, p. 39.

10. Borba, September 13, 1968, p. 1. Translated in Joint Translation Service, Belgrade, No. 5121, September 13, 1968, p. 45.

11. Josip Broz Tito, "Current Internal and International Problems and the Role of the League of Communists of Yugoslavia [LCY] in the Socialist System of Self-Management." Report by the President of the LCY submitted to the Ninth Congress of the LCY. Belgrade, March 11, 1969, pp. 97-98.

12. Borba, October 8, 1969, p. 1. Translated in Joint Translation Service, Belgrade, No. 5142, October 8, 1968, pp. 37, 38.

13. Ibid.

14. Politika, October 20, 1968, p. 3. Translated in Joint Translation Service, Belgrade, No. 5153, October 20-21, 1968, p. 41.

15. Politika, June 8, 1969, p. 8. Translated in Joint Translation Service, Belgrade, No. 5345, June 8-9, 1969, p. 42.

16. Vjesnik, March 19, 1969, p. 13. Translated in Joint Translation Service, Belgrade, No. 5303, April 18, 1969, p. 63.

17. Politika, June 8, 1969, p. 8. Translated in Joint Translation Service, Belgrade, No. 5345, June 8-9, 1969, p. 40.

18. Tito, op. cit., p. 105.

19. Politika, October 25, 1968, p. 3. Translated in Joint Translation Service, Belgrade, No. 5157, October 25, 1968, p. 47.

20. Ibid., pp. 47, 48.

21. Borba, August 12, 1969, p. 2. Translated in Joint Translation Service, Belgrade, No. 5400, August 12, 1969, pp. 16, 17.

22. Politika, June 8, 1969, p. 5. Translated in Joint Translation Service, Belgrade, No. 5345, June 8-9, 1969, pp. 20, 21.

23. Tito, op cit., p. 109.

24. Privredni Pregled, July 28, 1969, p. 3. Translated in Joint Translation Service, Belgrade, No. 5401, August 13, 1969, p. 52.

25. Ekonomska Politika, August 26-September 1, 1968, p. 1119. Translated in Joint Translation Service, Belgrade, August,29, 1968, pp. 28, 29.

26. These include the Hydro-Electric Power Station (Djerdap), and the Thermo Electric Power Station Kosovo (Obrenovac).

**THE INVASION:
EFFECTS
ON THEATER
AND DRAMA
IN EASTERN EUROPE**

E. J. Czerwinski

An event such as the Soviet invasion of Czechoslovakia could be
expected to affect literary and cultural affairs in other parts of Eastern
Europe. Shortly after August, 1968, a definite profile, especially in
the theater, began to take shape. Dialog, the Polish theater monthly,
lost its editor, Adam Tarn, and the Theater of the Absurd, together
with experimentation in theater and drama, ceased to exist in Poland.
Censorship, dormant or almost dead since the mid-1950's, began to
appear in Yugoslavia, especially in Belgrade and Zagreb. In the Soviet
Union writers such as Victor Rozov and Alexey Arbuzov, who had
for the past ten years flirted with experimentation in their dramas,
have, in their latest works, adhered to standard themes—unrequited
love, sacrifice of the male's ego, criticism of past mistakes in the
light of today's optimism, and old war stories. Producers, directors,
and writers in Hungary and Romania have managed to avoid contro-
versy in the hope that the slight gains made in the past five years
will not be suddenly nullified. In the theaters of Czechoslovakia political comment has been silenced since September, 1969.

There is little doubt that the invasion precipitated the above
changes in East European theater, but one must not be too quick to
place the blame wholly on the Soviet Union and the Warsaw Pact nations. Nothing ever happens "just so" in Eastern Europe. The situation in Poland was brought about as much by the persecution of
"Zionists" as by the invasion. Undoubtedly, both these events were
tied in with Czechoslovakia's determination to give socialism a human
face, which in itself was a reaction to the Stalinist tactics of the
Novotny era. As for Yugoslavia, the Soviet invasion and the Brezhnev

doctrine ironically helped divert public criticism of economic problems
that were then plaguing Yugoslavia. Regardless of the reasons, censorship has already been imposed in Yugoslavia, the former bastion
of freedom in the arts, and no one (at least not among the 500 intellectuals who participated in the two forums in Belgrade called to discuss
the state of the arts) is willing to predict how far the censor will go
to silence criticism, nor is anyone certain of precisely what ideas and
themes are subject to censorship. The purpose of this study is to
compare various themes that have emerged in plays written since
August, 1968, with those that existed prior to the invasion. The theatrical scene in Yugoslavia and Czechoslovakia during 1968-69 will
also be discussed in relation to the changes that have occurred during
this period.

WAITING AND NOTWAITING

When the history of Czech and Slovak drama and theater is
written at some future date, the period dating from 1968 will be extremely difficult to evaluate if tapes of performances are not taken
into account. For it is no secret to anyone that texts of plays have
been rewritten, expurgated, and injected with satirical elements that
comment on political events since August, 1968. Kat a blazen (The
Executioner and the Jester), written by Jiri Voskovec and Jan Werich
in 1934, was resurrected as something of a popular antioccupation
piece. The Jester symbolized the Czech nation; the Executioner,
the occupiers—especially the Russians.

Like the Jester-Priest metaphor in Polish literature since
1959, the Jester-Executioner metaphor was injected into almost every
play (and even musical, e.g., Pan Alcron vdava dceru [Mr. Alcron
Marries Off His Daughter] at the Karlin Music Theater in Prague)
that was produced in Czechoslovakia after August, 1968. A great
deal of material was incorporated into the stage-business improvised
in plays that were in repertory prior to that time. But unlike the
Polish use of the Jester-Priest metaphor, the Czechs chose to make
the Jester-Executioner metaphor a form of civil protest in the arts.
The metaphor was not thematically developed as in many of the Polish
plays, but often simply interjected as a comment in the original text.
Used in such a way, it was never a part of the actual theme.

In fact the worth and value of a performance up to September 1,
1969 (the date when strict censorship was introduced in the theaters
of Czechoslovakia), was measured by the number of times a political
message was recognized by the audience and applauded. Even the

revival of Karel Capek's plays came under the influence of the Jester-Executioner metaphor. At performances in Prague of The Insect Play and The White Illness the audiences seemed to extract new meaning from Capek's works, which were written shortly after World War I. Because of the political situation that existed then (and now), Capek's plays as staged in Prague (few were staged elsewhere) seemed even more contemporary than the issue-involvement-political plays of Peter Weiss, Rolf Hochhuth, etc. Viewing Capek's (and his brother's) works against the background of present-day Czechoslovakia, one realizes that Capek more than any other one writer is the precursor to and a great influence on the modern theater of political involvement.

Czechoslovakia during 1968 and up to September, 1969, was a political battleground and its theater of political comment (as distinguished from a theater presenting political plays) placed the emphasis of theater where it belonged, that is, squarely in the middle of the nation's daily life. The political "comment" was usually a bit of business, e.g., a bear hug, Russian-style, sometime with knife in one hand (as in Kat a blazen at the Evening Theater of Satire in Brno), or a pointed remark concerning the guest who has overstayed his welcome.

For the theater critic such an approach to theater presents an obvious danger: Political significance can easily overshadow artistic merit. This inevitably happened during the period under discussion. Maxwell Anderson's Barefoot in Athens, produced at the Vinohrady Theater, for example, was considered by many critics and theater-goers as the most important and "significant" play of the year. Audiences expressed their approval of a stubborn man who refused to compromise truth by continual bursts of applause. This enthusiasm which sprang from patriotic hearts was commendable, but it undeniably tended to make of a play and the theater an arena of public opinion.

On the other hand, a critic who dismisses every play with political overtones as being merely of local interest may be committing an even greater blunder. The Theater of Political Issues and Involvement is very much today's theater, as the Theater of the Absurd was ten or fifteen years ago. Czechoslovakia may be in the same position that Poland found itself when the Theater of the Absurd was inaugurated in France almost two decades ago. Poland, almost alone of all the East European countries, was in the mainstream of that movement. Even the film thrived during that artistically fertile period. When artistic freedom was silenced in Poland in 1956, Czechoslovakia became the center of artistic activity. The country stood, as Poland did in 1957, like a defiant child—punished for disobedience but stubbornly refusing to be subdued. It may be that had Czechoslovakia been given an opportunity it would have taken a leading part in the international world of letters and could have become the voice of all intellectuals in the Slavic countries.

Censorship was almost nonexistent in the country's theaters up to September, 1969. Only one production (as far as is known), a ballet entitled "Ponekud cerna kolaz" ("A Slightly Black Collage"), was ordered to soften its political message. The Prague Studio Ballet, though acknowledging the censor's admonition, nevertheless chose to keep the ballet in its original form and presented it on their tour.

Several popular songs, however, were forbidden to be played on the radio or performed on television. Most of these musical pieces were popular during the first months of the Soviet occupation and helped keep the morale of the nation high and its spirit defiant. Among these songs were "Martha's Prayer" ("Modlitba") as sung by Marta Kubisova and "Our Daily Prayer" ("Zpev nas vezdejsi") as performed by Helena Vondrackova. The two young singers were part of the ensemble known as The Golden Kids, which also featured the star of the movie, Closely Watched Trains, Vaclav Neckar. The songs mentioned were defiantly included in almost every program given by the group in theaters and concert halls. Several films were also slated to be censored and were forbidden to be shown in Czechoslovakia, among them Vojtech Jasny's brilliant Vsechni dobri rodaci (All Good Countrymen).

The Semafor Theater and the Cinoherni Club in Prague were the first to be singled out as examples of decadent art and were forced to change their artistic policies after September. Prague's theaters are among the finest in the world and the above two offered some of the most exciting theater to be found anywhere. Semafor's director, Ivan Englich, and the Cinoherni (Dramatic) Club's husband and wife team, Alena Vostra and Jaroslav Vostry, kept up the morale of the nation by uncompromisingly producing artistically motivated works at their theaters.

But theatrical activities in Czechoslovakia are not only limited to Prague. In Bratislava (Slovakia) Divadlo na korze (The Theater on the Promenade) compares quite favorably with any operating in that country.[1] Playing nightly to an audience of some eighty people, this theater in the cellar of an ancient building on a side street has made a reputation for itself as one of the most original and entertaining satirical theaters in Europe. The success of this chamber theater is largely due to its young outspoken actors, writers, and directors, and to the comic and dramatic talents of Milan Lasica and Julius Satinsky.

It is difficult to classify these two young men. Working under
the formula name of L+S, they write their own material, act in their
own productions, and help direct theater operations, which include
the publication of an eight-page monthly broadside called Infarkt (Heart
Attack).

The administrative director of the Promenade is Kornel Foldvari,
who was described in the first issue of Infarkt (January, 1969) as
" 'cruel Kornie,' editor-in-chief [all members of the staff are given
this title in Infarkt]—a representative of Zionism and racial intolerance,
the long arm of South African colonialism in the West Slovakia area."[2]
Lasica was also introduced as editor-in-chief and author of "peripheral
works without any artistic merit whatsoever." Editor-in-chief
Satinsky was quite accurately characterized as "cynically [making]
light of everything that to us is sacred."

The policy of Infarkt and Promenade was enunciated in poetic
form by another editor-in-chief, Marian Labuda, in the following poem
whose bite is derived from a play on the word vie. In Slovak vediet
means "to know" (viem-I know, vies-you know, etc); in French, la vie
means life:

> Co ja viem.
> Co ty vies.
> Co on vie.
>
> C'est la viem.
> C'est la vies.
> C'est la vie.[3]

Thus far Lasica and Satinsky have written material for two
productions, Soiree and Radostna sprava (A Joyful Management).
The programs for both productions are further extensions of Infarkt
and will probably become collectors' items when the theater is forced
to change its policy. The opening page of the program for A Joyful
Management, for example, includes a photograph of a huge man's
buttocks. The caption reads: "I'll give you Socialism with a human
face!" The program for Soiree contains the poem quoted above, entitled, "Co je zivot?" ("What Is Life?").

As something of a reward for Promenade's uncompromising
world-view and its battle against the unseen but ubiquitous Great Bear,
Lasica and Satinsky were invited to present their two productions at
the Semafor Theater in Prague in 1969. In a country where Czechs
and Slovaks seldom see eye-to-eye on any issue, the invitation extended

to the Promenade may yet go down as a theatrical landmark. In fact
this Slovak group has become so popular that, according to Jovan
Cirilov, artistic director of Atelier 212, it was invited to represent
Czechoslovakia's contribution to the avant-garde at Belgrade's Festival
of Modern Trends in Theater (Bitef) in 1970. However, the group
could not accept the invitation.

Some of the satirical pieces written by Lasica and Satinsky were
recently published in Necakanie na Godota (Notwaiting for Godot).
Most of the sketches are short, consisting of only five or six pages
("In the Train," "Such a Strange Dream," and "The Telephone"). The
satire, although pertinent to political conditions in Czechoslovakia
today, is of a more universal nature: Cruelty, stupidity, violence,
sex, and institutions that proscribe freedom are favorite targets. In
the playlet "Miru mir" ("Peace of Peace"), two soldiers (Friendly and
Unfriendly) are discussing the purpose of war. During the telling of
an anecdote, Friendly Soldier is shot, just as he is about to inform
Unfriendly Soldier what war is for:

> Friendly:　　(Laughing heartily) War is for . . .
> (Suddenly he is shot by mistake).
>
> Unfriendly:　(Not comprehending what has happened)
> So, what did he say? (Examining the dead
> body) Hello. Why you're dead! (Shouting
> toward the wings) You naughty things!
> Shooting a man during a conversation. And
> now who's going to tell me that anecdote?[4]

According to Lasica, the material for these sketches is written
specifically for the Promenade, where the small size of the audience
dictates subject matter and manner of presentation. The audience
expects to be treated as part of a large family and often acts like one,
sometimes contributing its own quips, more often expressing approval
by prolonged applause. Both actors and viewers are repaid for their
colloboration in terms of a theatrical experience that is at once
entertaining, uplifting, and educational.

Lasica and Satinsky admit their debt to Stawomir Mrozek and
the Theater of the Absurd. But judging from their journal Infarkt,
and their two productions at the Promenade, if a debt ever existed,
it has been paid in full; and writers in the future may very well
owe much to them. Unfortunately, since early 1970 Infarkt has
ceased to exist and the theater has had to make drastic changes in
its policy.

CONSCIENCE OF A COUNTRY

Perhaps the best known and most representative Czech dramatists today are Ivan Klima and Vaclav Havel. Both have produced a
body of works in the past five years that illustrate the artist's particular concern in that society. Although they employ different idioms
and approaches, their preoccupation with present-day reality is similar.

Speaking with Havel, one is impressed by his low-key delivery,
his gentle nature, his simple words that neither startle nor bore, his
mannerisms that include a hesitation in speaking and an alveolar
purring "r." Born in 1936, son of wealthy parents whose riches were
confiscated after the war, victim of prejudice that prevented him from
enrolling in any school, Havel knows quite well the ironic limitations
of wealth on one hand and the beneficial aspects of penury and deprivation on the other. Only the experiences of his unfortunate family
and the lessons that life has taught him have aided him in saving his
artistic integrity in his battle both with well-meaning critics of the
West and devoted Marxists of the East. His dilemma is similar to
Mrozek's, except for one important element: Mrozek is no longer
a Polish citizen and the threat to his survival may be too great to
overcome the forces of destruction that haunt the artist. On the other
hand, Havel is determined to remain a part of the Czech community
and to be its spokesman, and in this way may evade the pursuing
Furies and, like Solzhenitsyn in the Soviet Union, continue his quest
for national and personal identity.

Havel, by his own admission, is an optimist and does not care
for the works of his countryman, Karel Capek, nor does he conceal his
agitation when one suggests that his own plays are an extension of
Capek's works written shortly after World War I. Perhaps the reason
for Havel's discontent with such comparisons lies in the fact that he
does not agree with Capek's pessimistic appraisal of the human lot.
In a way, Havel continues to negate Capek's philosophy in each of his
plays and has tried to destroy the myth that man is merely an insect.
His plays are really a hymn to man: In Havel's world man is far from
being a machine and actually acts badly the role forced on him by
technology, that double-edged sword that mirrors at once man's
achievement and possible destiny.

Havel's war on machines and computerized society forms the
basis of all his works. He admits that he is concerned with man's
loss of identity, a simplistic way of saying that he dreads the possibility that man will more and more depend on machines and computers

to rule his life. Havel is fascinated by machines that refuse to stop thinking.[5] His three full-length plays have probed that area of man's existence that depends on motorism for survival—an artificial language, a computerized system of social behavior, and a mechanized answer to the question that has puzzled many Hamlets: "To be or not to be?"

His first full-length play, The Garden Party (1963), is also Havel's most subjective work. Peter Pludek, "the black sheep of the family," who "looks like a bourgeois intellectual," could very well be a self-portrait of Havel. Because Havel, unlike Father Pludek who had "five proletarian great-uncles," was the heir of a family fortune that included ownership of the Barrandov Film Studio and Prague's Lucerna Restaurant, he was not allowed the benefits bestowed on the more unfortunate sons of the working class: an apartment, a decent living wage, and an education. Havel has had to struggle against ferocious attempts to literally liquidate him. The Garden Party is a type of absurd ritual in which the act of being and not-being is commemorated.

Hugo, the Pludeks' "darling little dope" is also a symbol of the working class, the pampered darlings of a system that has championed the former underdogs and in turn has persecuted the innocent children of former wealthy magnates. Hugo is as much divorced from the system as he is from his parents. In his solitary game of chess, he is always the loser.

So is the bureaucratic system, with its impossible jargon. Although the babble of words produces hearty laughter from the audience, it also provides poignant memories for those familiar with just such a system. Even the term Liquidation Office is associated with recent history: The Director's game of "hitting the sack" conjures up the futility of a people caught up for almost two decades in a meaningless struggle of "liquidating the liquidation," that is, eradicating the remnants of an almost nonexistent past.

The world in which the Pludeks live is a nonsense world, and it is ironical that it is not Peter the intellectual but Hugo of the system who can derive sense from it, even when the latter is forced to depend on the obfuscated language of that system to express his thoughts. Hugo enunciates Havel's own point of view concerning the battle for survival in a dehumanized society: "I know I want to be all the time and that's why all the time I must a little bit not-be."[6] One hesitates to lean too heavily on biographical data, but Havel's play seems rather like an unedited, personal Notes from the Underground (conversations taped during one normal working day). As such it contains both the

virtue of spontaneity and the dullness of repetition. But what is far
more important, it has an ominous ring of truth.

Havel's second play reflects a system that has dehumanized
man: In The Memorandum, notwithstanding the blind activity of all
the characters (Ballas' menacing plots aimed first at usurping Gross'
authority than at undermining the system in general; Pillar's nodding
head that makes of him and Ballas a modern version of Gogol's Dob-
cinskij and Bobcinskij; Hena's mechanical movements in combing
her hair and running errands; the staff's preoccupation with lunch
breaks) there is no real progress, no attainment of any desired goal.
In the opening speech Havel sets the scene for the chaos that is to
follow: "Ra ko hutu d dekotu. . . ." (nonsense language).[7] The attempt
to mechanize communication and to make of man an RUR* is resisted
by only one man, Gross, who sees Ptydepe** for what it is—a means
of victimizing man and making imagination and thinking obsolete.
Gross, the humanist, who believes in the concept "that every single
member of the staff is human and must become more and more human,"
fears that Ptydepe will lead man to "self-alienation."

It is interesting to note that Gross' ideas are often expressed
by Havel in his interviews. "I write about alienation and dehumani-
zation because these are elements in man's development that must
be destroyed before they destroy man," Havel remarks simply. Having
been victimized himself by a system that was meant to "help everyone,"
Havel's own tragedy seems to be encompassed in Gross' pathetic
words: "Why can't I be a little boy again? I'd do everything differently
from the beginning."[8] Ballas' reply to Gross seems also an answer
to Havel's predicament: "You might begin differently, but you'd end
up exactly the same—so relax!"[9] If Ballas' observation is correct,
what sense is there in trying to change or improve a system? If his
comment is also Havel's own point of view (and it would appear to
be so, judging from the denouement of the play and his own comments),
then the most one can expect from such a game is that things will
remain virtually the same; only the players will change places.

One questions Vera Blackwell's criticism of Gross that "cowardice is the 'force' behind Gross's actions, no matter how well

---

*Rossum's Universal Robot—from a 1920 Capek play of the
same name.

**The newly imposed language of efficiency.

disguised by his pleasant, sympathetic manner. Cowardice is the arch-villain of the play, because, together with the indifference of the more or less passive onlookers, it has made possible the introduction of Ptydepe."[10] It is not cowardice but blind obedience to authority that is the arch-villain in the play, obedience that can make a nation follow its leaders to inevitable doom and destruction. Recent events in history have served Havel well.

The jesters are already present in The Memorandum, written four years before the invasion (1964-65). The executioners, however, are far less defined. They remain invisible, but their presence is always felt. Like Gian Carlo Menotti's The Consul and Arthur Koestler's Darkness at Noon, Havel's Memorandum, has as its villain both a "paper" monster and a psychological one. But unlike the two mentioned works, this Czech play is a black comedy. For Czech audiences it is a journey through the worn-out and well known. Ballas' disillusionment with the "system" is almost a parody of the sentiments of old Party-members: "Where's the enthusiasm we all felt when we were launching Ptydepe! I worked at it as stubbornly as a mule! You know, drank only water, ate only purple hearts, went without sleep, just slaved and organized; when the cause was at stake, I was quite ruthless. . . . That was the best time of my life! and now see how it's all turned out! This isn't what we wanted, was it?"[11]

Even the office routine is simply a transplant of any Czech office. The allusions to food that abound in the text are a reference to a normal preoccupation in a country where shortages of all kinds are quite common. And the bizarre procedure in which victim becomes victor is also an example from real life and an aspect of the political and social structure. That Gross joins the victimizers in order to "salvage the last remains of man's humanity"[12] and in so doing must sacrifice Maria's well-being is an irony that a Czech audience can easily grasp.

Notwithstanding the events of 1968-69, at least one line in Havel's play has become obsolete. Gross explains to Maria: "We're reaching for the moon and yet it's increasingly hard for us to reach our-selves."[13] It remains to be seen if man will someday achieve the greater of the two feats.

Havel's latest play, The Increased Difficulty of Concentration (more accurately, The Impeded Possibility of Concentrating), could easily be subtitled: A Life in the Day of a Czech Intellectual. Its originality lies in its destruction of time boundaries: The action of the play is sequential only as it touches upon Dr. Huml's love affairs and his encounter with Puzuk, the computer with all the questions and no answers.

Puzuk is controlled by a team under the guidance of Dr. Balcar. Miss Balcar, a latent woman under her research garb, admits that they "are trying to learn from foreign experiments, although in principle [they] don't intend to accept their results mechanically."[14] Huml is fascinated by the possibility that Miss Balcar and her colleagues may manage "to shape human individuality scientifically," which in turn would limit "such phenomena as, for example, alienation"—a favorite Havelian theme. But Puzuk the computer proves to be only too human. After being placed alternatingly into a refrigerator and an oven, Puzuk asks his tormentors: "May I have a little rest?"

In the end Huml adds another problem to his already complicated love-life: Dr. Anna Balcar, the social scientist, throws herself at Huml and like the man with a heart that he is, he accepts her advances. Unable to break off with his mistress, Renata, foiled in his attempt to seduce Blanka, his secretary, and still attached to his long-suffering wife, Huml finally pinpoints the reason he is what he is: "The basic key to man does not lie in his brain but in his heart." This precept also forms the basis of Dubcek's "socialism with a human face."

And this is what Havel has been saying since he began writing. Even though his latest play comes close to being farce and leans heavily on Mrozekian-type humor, it is in keeping with Havel's simple dictum that matters of the heart cannot be arranged by machines, science, technology, or political systems. The heart has no master— not even man.

But there is danger in categorizing and oversimplifying Havel's works. One critic recently noted, for example, that "the ultimate aim of Havel's plays, for instance, is the improvement of man's lot through the improvement of man's institutions."[15] This appraisal was made prior to Concentration, which certainly hardly hints at the "improvement of man's institutions," unless one is to accept the banal exchange between Balcar and Huml concerning scientific individuality to be dialectical arguments for the improvement of man's condition.

Nor can one say that Havel's plays do not fit into "the compartment marked 'Absurd,'" because they are "socially committed" and do "not reflect any metaphysical despair."[16] Such logic would also rule out Edward Albee, Harold Pinter, Arthur Kopit, Mrozek, and dozens of other dramatists of the Absurd. Metaphysical problems must be dramatized and the school of the Absurd has merely revolutionalized ways of presenting "metaphysical despair," alienation, problems of communication, and other ailments and symptoms of our age on the stage. Havel belongs to the tradition of the Absurd by contiguity if for no other reason. But there are other reasons: The devices he employs belong to the idiom of the Absurd—destruction of time-space boundaries, audience-involvement, and, above all, themes that he develops, themes that Mrozek, Padeusz Rozewicz, Tymoteusz Karpowicz, Ireneusz Iredynski, Aleksandar Popovic, Midorag Bulatovic, Jerzy Broszkiewicz, and Stanislaw Grochowiak have also developed.

Then, too, as with the works of the Absurdists, Havel's plays call for a special kind of acting. Unlike Brecht, who insisted on Verfremdungseffekt, a type of super-honesty on the part of the actor who was asked to mimic rather than be a person in a play, Havel has gone to the other extreme: The actors must at all times concentrate on the business at hand, forget that they are actors, forget that they are people in a play, forget that the world in which they find themselves is floating in a fragile bubble. His plays call for a style of acting that is at once antipsychological, antirealistic, antiromantic; yet, because of the stress on complete actor-involvement in regard to business at hand—in spite of the absurdity, banality, idiocy, or sense of the situation—Havel's plays affect the audience both personally and psychologically, evoking a type of participation that Brecht dreamed about. Whether the business includes promoting a new super-complicated language, or involves the question whether "to be or not," or merely projects a day in the hectic life of a Swejk with sex appeal, the actor is asked to forget all else and project the very essence of the dramatic moment and situation. The key to Havel's plays lies in the actor. The success of a performance is directly proportional to the degree of verisimilitude that the actors can register with the audience. Judging from the number of productions of his works all over the world, one need not be afraid to say that the key to his plays has been found.

KAFKA'S CASTLE
DURING THE PRAGUE SPRING

The same cannot be said of the works of Ivan Klima. Unlike Havel, who dramatizes contemporary man's agony in terms of technological sterility, Klima expounds his themes through mock-allegory. His plays have a political orientation, but because of their Aesopian language and vague allusions, they are somewhat difficult to grasp by

Western audiences who are not entirely familiar with the cultural and
political scene in Czechoslovakia. The Castle, for example, could be
interpreted as a comment on the changes that must occur in any political system, but the oblique references to the "Old Order" and patterns
of behavior of the inmates of the Castle seem to suggest an Eastern
country. Josef, the latest member to join the group of famous old
people (the Old Order) in the castle, replaces Ilya, who has presumably
suffered a coronary.

As in any establishment, the old members are afraid of the new
ones, in this case, Josef Kan, whom they see as a threat to their well-
being. His youth, coupled with his strange habit of carrying an um-
brella and whistling "The Wedding March" from Lohengrin, unnerves
them. The Castle is a symbol of an abortive society. Populated by
would-be-artists, philosophers, and scientists, it is a bastion of fear,
hate, jealousy, and studied failure, Interpreted in these terms, the
Castle becomes the symbol of any society and can be understood by
citizens in any country.

But it is only when Josef realizes that the Castle is a place of
no exit that the play becomes localized. He becomes violent, insisting
on an investigation into the causes of Ilya's death. Haba, the investigator, arrives and proceeds with the investigation. In employing the
Castle as symbol of present-day society, Klima leans heavily on both
Kafka and the idiom of the Absurd. Josef's anguish has metaphysical
roots. The members of the Castle seem to be mock-allegorical
figures who represent a sterile world that is just as metaphysically
stillborn as that created by Samuel Beckett, Fernando Arrabal,
Rozewicz, or Mrozek. These jesters are looking for no absolutes
because in their world there is no such thing. Only the brooding
presence of an absolute executioner is real.

Klima's point is well made and could be viewed as his own
feelings concerning the liberating spirit that cleansed Czechoslovakia
after 1965: The Investigator (Haba) exits and the members of the
Old Order resume their non-activities. Life goes on again as for-
merly, and the first order of business is to strangle Josef—just as
Ilya was strangled at the beginning of the play. Viewed in the early
1970's, The Castle seems even more prophetic than when it was written
in 1966. The more things change, the more they remain the same.

The Master, Klima's next play, is also somewhat allegorical,
and seems almost to be an extension of The Castle. In both plays
the plot revolves around a murder, in this case the poisoning of Anna
and the murder or suicide of the father. In both plays neither the

murderer nor the motive is revealed. The Master Coffinmaker is
employed in much the same way as the Castle in Klima's earlier play.
The Master is both a hope for a better future and a reminder of the
past, a past that included fear, infamy, suffering, and duplicity. As a
symbol of hope, the Master is also a voice for the present and a proph-
ecy of things to come. The Master was all things to the members of
the family: a savior, a murderer, a friend, a stranger, a nemesis,
and an innocent bystander. His words that described a peaceful beauti-
ful desert both aggravated and consoled. As a spokesman for a nation
the Master has his own excuse for being: Had he not appeared, the
people would, in all probability, have invented him—so great was the
need of a simple explanation for the tragedy that had befallen the
nation during the past thirty years. Klima's reasons for the suffering
endured by the people are as good as any, but his statement (made by
Leon) that the desert is anywhere, "wherever you will it to be,"[17]
seems somehow rather arbitrary. Perhaps Klima is saying that the
desert is that limbo-like time and place that preceded the time of
liberalization. The Master, during the course of the play, offers
Francesca solace in the desert, although he readily admits that it
is far from an ideal place, and at best, merely bearable. Judged in
this light, the events since September, 1969, would portend a return
to that desert of the mind.

Klima's latest play, written shortly after the invasion, is the
only play written during this period that deals with the problems con-
fronting the nation.[18] The main action of the play, The Jury, seems
to be a pretext for other more relevant matters—comments on events
and attitudes in contemporary Czechoslovakia. Klima states his
prejudice in the opening scene, ironically, in the mouth of the Prose-
cutor: "1968 [is] a year we should indeed be proud of."[19]

Again, in the argument of the Counsel for Defense, Klima shat-
ters the fictional moment of disbelief:

Counsel for Defense: I have seen only one instance where
the defendant was not present during the final day of
the trial . . . . Your Honor, I have reason to fear
that this case might be related to—

Judge: The court does not share your fear![20]

The world onstage becomes an extension of the real world. The actors
and the audience have similar roles to play, roles assumed by a whole
nation for more years than memory cares to remember. The play,
then, is more an injunction against past offenses and distortions of

the law than a court trial in which a mere murder is discussed. The Judge's instructions to the jury seem better suited for a Gogolean world than for contemporary Czechoslovakia; "But most important, you and you alone hold in your hands the fate of our system of justice, our pure, incorruptible justice."[21]

The Jury is a cri de coeur. Klima's words jab consciences and open old wounds. The Historian's speech, for example, echoes the newspaper and journal accounts printed in 1968 and 1969 that opened debate on Masaryk's alleged suicide and the crimes of the fifties:

> Ladies and Gentlemen: Did you know that history has proven that most people who had been executed had later been found to be innocent? Particularly when judging their crimes from our present point of view. People were stretched on racks, strapped to wheels, buried alive. For what? For infidelity, for stealing a few cups and saucers, for walking through a cornfield, for being accused of witchcraft. Weren't they really innocent when viewed by common sense? Suppose the men we condemn today might at some future time seem just as innocent to our own descendents? Merely sick and unhappy. Suppose our own conduct might one day be found equally cruel, equally unjust and criminal?[22]

The Historian's rebuttal to the Captain's question is an explicit statement of the play's theme: "We are surrounded by laws which are not of our creation."[23] In a country of jesters only the executioners dictate standards of conduct. Jesters can merely stand and wait. But even assuming this stance, Klima seems to argue, they also serve and are a part of the grand tragedy of a nation.

In effect, the trial, the deliberation, the verdict, and the mock show of justice end in absurdity: The defendant is guillotined "while trying to escape." What pretense for deliberation there was before is now obviated by the defendant's death; but the Judge and authorities still insist on a verdict. The five jurors—the Barber, Civil Engineer, Historian, Grocery Woman, and Captain—must play out the absurd trial to its alogical conclusion.

In the end nothing has changed. Those whom the state considers guilty are declared guilty. Coercion is subtly and unobtrusively inflicted. The innocent dead man must be adjudged guilty so that he cannot harm the state. Justice must triumph, even though unjustly arrived at. It is the wise man who understands this paradox: It is the circumspect and prudent man who accepts this formula and pronounces the sentence on the dead—"Guilty!"[24] And it is a kind of tragic irony that those who collaborate with the Judge and state leave the courtroom without a trace of guilt, satisfied in their belief that nothing else could have been done. Only the Historian suffers mental anguish—only he has had the courage to renounce injustice: "The real murderers are still walking among us!"[25] The former jester begins to speak like a priest.

Klima's play is a witness to that moment in Czech-Slovak history when people were unafraid and had the courage to ask their own questions. It may be that history will someday record the fact that during its most trying hour Czechoslovakia had writer-spokesmen who were also consciences of their nation. Depicting their people as jesters and their enemies as executioners, these writers have merely fallen back on a literary tradition that goes back to Jaroslav Hasek's novel, The Good Soldier Schweik. The question is how long will a nation accept the mantle of the jester?

THE ANXIOUS NEIGHBOR

The present situation in Czechoslovakia, with its censorship and other repressions, although highly deplorable, is understandable. The Soviet-backed conservatists feel that they must have complete control in order to have any control at all. But recent events in Yugoslavia are more difficult to evaluate. They have given intellectuals and artists in that country some very anxious moments.

Before and immediately after the invasion the theaters in Yugoslavia had carte blanche over selection and production of plays. Even Jovan Hristic's play, Sedmorica: Danas (The Seven: Today), which could be interpreted as a criticism of the Warsaw Pact invasion, was successfully produced in Zagreb. Except for Aleksandar Popovic's Kape dole (Hats Off), which was removed from Atelier 212's repertory after only three performances, no play had been censored in 1968.[26] Since September, 1969, however, a number of incidents have occurred that suggest further repressions are imminent. Popovic's latest plays, Druga vrata levo (Second Door Left) and Pala karta (A Dead Card), which were scheduled for production by Atelier 212 and the Yugoslav Theater of Drama respectively, were suddenly cancelled.[27] A dramatization of Dragoslav Mihailovic's Kad su cvetale tikve (When the Pumpkins Were in Bloom), scheduled for production at the Yugoslav Theater of Drama, suffered the same fate.

Other examples of censorship can be cited. Many intellectuals in Yugoslavia, it must be stated in fairness, feel that the latest rash of literary repressions is merely coincidental with the transfer of power from Tito to a committee of political potentates selected from each republic. Few view these infractions of freedom as a return to repressive measures. But for artists and intellectuals who have enjoyed almost complete freedom during the past decade or so, the latest incidents bear watching. To them recent censorship seems the more ominous because unexpected.

To understand the targets of repression it may prove valuable to evaluate the current state of censorship in Belgrade—in particular, to discuss the themes in the two plays previously mentioned, Second Door Left and The Seven: Today. In Second Door Left the jesters are children, offspring of Father and Heavenly, who wish to keep their children forever-docile by forcing them to be forever-ignorant. The mini-jesters rebel, however, and begin to ask embarrassing questions:

Dove: How were we born?

Bestman: Is this finally our freedom?

Father, in turn, is forced to ask himself a question that destroys his false Eden: "How on earth can they be ours if we're not theirs?"[28] The children decide to give birth to "one new life," which Heavenly and Father destroy with noise and pollution. In the end, however, the parents' hopes to restore the false Eden are nullified by the youngest child, Tantuz Lilliput, who wakes up his brothers and sisters from their stupor: "Has one defeat disenchanted you so much! But we're still young! We'll give birth to one more new child!" As if insisting on his new-found freedom, the mini-jester doffs the cap of the fool and awakens the stunned audience: "The performance is over, and now you can all go quietly to your own homes.[29]

The children-jesters in Popovic's play battle a visible executioner—their own parents. And since authority by any name (even parental) can suggest governmental authority, it is not surprising that Second Door Left was singled out for censorship.

It may be that the play's references to restriction and slavery were too blatantly stated. Hristic's play in this respect is much safer, since his study of power-politics makes only covert and oblique references to present-day reality. Basing his play on Aeschylus'

<u>Seven Against Thebes</u>, Hristic retains the main characters, the brothers Eteocles and Polynices. The plot, too, remains somewhat intact: Polynices has come to replace Eteocles as ruler of Thebes. The arguments that both use, however, in gaining their ends make of the play a forum for the discussion of the Brezhnev "Doctrine of Interference." In the end, unlike the turn of events in Czechoslovakia, Polynices chooses to fight Eteocles for what he considers his right to rule Thebes. He no longer trusts in the jester's commodity— words and guile—and decides to battle the forces of evil. The executioner—Eteocles—stands opposite his opponent—Polynices—dressed only in battle attire. Hristic, in this last tableau, seems to suggest that the role of the jester is an ephemeral one and that in time the executioner must be faced on his own terms.

The role of the jester is always a dangerous one because it involves "a negative vigilance in the face of any absolute."[30] Seen in this light the absolute is always an enemy that must be attacked. In Eastern Europe the jesters have not yet donned battle attire, nor does it seem probable that they ever will. But the executioners are taking no chances.

NOTES

1. The Promenade also consists of a repertory acting company. This group has produced a number of avant-garde works, such as Mrozek's <u>Charlie, Striptease</u>, and <u>On the Open Sea</u>, and Beckett's <u>Waiting for Godot</u>. Lasica's wife, Sora Kolinska, an excellent actress and singer, is also a member of the acting group.

2. Insert of <u>Infarkt</u> in <u>Mlada Tvorba</u> <u>(Young Creative Works)</u> XIV, No. 1 (1969), 29-36.

3. <u>Infarkt</u> I, No. 3 (March, 1969).

4. Milan Lasica and Julius Satinsky, <u>Notwaiting for Godot</u> (Bratislava: Tatran, 1969), p. 99.

5. Havel's works consist of the following: <u>Autostop</u> (with Ivan Vyskocil), 1961; <u>Nejlepsi roky pani Hermanove</u> (The Best Years of Mrs. Herman), written in collaboration with Milos Macourek, 1962; <u>Zahradni slavnost</u> (The Garden Party), English translation, 1963; <u>Vyrozumeni</u> (The Memorandum), English translation, 1965; and

Ztizena moznost soustredeni (The Increased Difficulty of Concentration), 1968. His latest work, a scenario written in collaboration with
Jan Nemec, also probes the subject of man and his relation to machines. Entitled Heartbeat, the plot deals with a heart-transplant
patient and the complications that arise from man's unconscious striving to become more machine-like and to depend entirely on the kind-
ness and goodness of computerized motorism. Havel has also written
poetry, plays for radio and television, and essays. Former resident
dramatist of the Balustrade Theater, he now lives in Prague and de-
votes most of his time to writing.

6. Vaclav Havel, The Garden Party, trans. Vera Blackwell
(Dilia, Prague, 1967), p. 69.

7. Vaclav Havel, The Memorandum (London, 1967), trans. Vera
Blackwell, p. 9.

8. Ibid., p. 47.

9. Ibid., p. 101.

10. Vera Blackwell, "The New Czech Drama," The Listener,
January 5, 1967, p. 10.

11. The Memorandum, p. 81.

12. Ibid., p. 108

13. Ibid., p. 107.

14. Manuscript of Concentration, unpaginated, translated by
Vera Blackwell. Mrs. Blackwell is Havel's English translator, and
he prefers that her translations be cited.

15. Blackwell, "The New Czech Drama," p. 10.

16. Ibid., p. 10.

17. Ivan Klima, The Master, trans. Ruth Willard (Xerox copy,
1967), p. 65. Subsequent quotations from Klima's plays are taken
from translations by Ruth Willard.

18. It is interesting to note that neither Havel nor Milan Kundera
dealt with any of the problems brought about by the invasion. The
latest works by both writers are saturated with sex. Klima's latest

two one-act plays (A Bridegroom for Marcella Klara) are also less weighty than his earlier works.

19. Ivan Klima, The Jury, trans. Ruth Willard (Xerox copy, 1969), p. 1.

20. The Jury, p. 3.

21. Ibid., p. 5.

22. Ibid., pp. 15-16.

23. Ibid., p. 16.

24. Ibid., p. 55.

25. Ibid., p. 60

26. Popovic's play was banned, according to reliable sources, because the two leading characters seemed a parody of the president of the republic and his wife. His latest plays, Ljubi, ljubi (Kiss, Kiss), and Sitna ljubicica (Tiny Little Violet) have yet to be premiered.

27. For a discussion of Popovic's works see E. J. Czerwinski, "Aleksandar Popovic: Belgrade's Poet of the Streets," Books Abroad, Summer, 1969; also, E. J. Czerwinski, "Aleksandar Popovic and Pop-Theater: Beyond the Absurd," Comparative Drama, Fall, 1969, pp. 168-75.

28. Second Door Left, translated by E. J. Czerwinski, Drama and Theatre, Winter, 1969-70, 102-17. The play was premiered at Theater La Mama on April 1, 1970, directed by Popovic.

29. Ibid., p. 117.

30. Leszek Kolakowski, "The Priest and the Jester," in The Modern Polish Mind, trans. Pawel Mayewski (New York: 1963), p. 326.

E. J. CZERWINSKI is Professor of Slavic Languages and Literature at the State University of New York at Stony Brook. Prior to coming to Stony Brook Professor Czerwinski taught at Kansas University from 1967 to 1970, at the University of Buffalo from 1966 to 1967, and at the University of Pittsburgh from 1965 to 1966. He received his doctorate from the University of Wisconsin.

Professor Czerwinski's area of specialization is drama and theater and comparative Slavic literature. He has published widely on the drama and theater of Poland, Czechoslovakia, Yugoslavia, and the Soviet Union. He has recently opened a Slavic Center in Port Jefferson, N.Y. As artistic director he plans to develop a Slavic theater and a journal devoted to East European and Slavic theater and drama. He serves on the editorial boards of Books Abroad and Comparative Drama. Recipient of a Fulbright Senior Research Grant in 1968 and an International Research Exchange Grant to Czechoslovakia in 1969, Professor Czerwinski has visited almost every theater in Eastern Europe. He has just completed a book, Dialog: The Polish Theater of the Absurd. A number of his plays have been produced in various universities and off-Broadway.

Professor Czerwinski has translated the plays of Aleksandar Popovic, Jovan Hristic, Tadeusz Rozewicz, and other Slavic playwrights, and he has just completed translating an anthology of Yugoslav poetry.

JAROSLAW PIEKALKIEWICZ is Associate Professor of Political Science and of Slavic and Soviet Area Studies, University of Kansas, and Associate Director, University of Kansas-Adam Mickiewicz University, Poznan, Poland, Exchange Program. He is the author of Public Opinion Polling in Czechoslovakia, 1968-69: Results and Analysis of Surveys Conducted During the Dubcek Era, to be published in the Praeger Special Studies series. Professor Piekalkiewicz holds a Ph.D. from Indiana University and has traveled extensively throughout Eastern Europe.

HANA BENESOVA studied philosophy at Charles University in Prague and at the Sorbonne in Paris. During World War II she served as an editor in the News Bureau of the Overseas Branch of the Office of War Information. Having returned to Czechoslovakia in 1945, she became the foreign editor of the leading non-Communist daily Svobodne slovo. She remained in this position until the Communist seizure of power in Czechoslovakia in February, 1948. After having gone into exile, she worked for a year and a half in the International Division of the Canadian Broadcasting Corporation in Montreal as a script writer and broadcaster. Since 1962, Hana Benesova has been a lecturer in the Department of Slavic Languages and Literatures at Indiana University, teaching Czech literature and the Czech language.

GEORGE GOMORI was born in Budapest, Hungary, and has been living in England since 1956. His higher studies were completed at Oxford University where he did research on Polish and Hungarian literature. In 1963-64 he was a Lecturer at the University of California, Berkeley, in 1964-65 a Research Fellow at the Harvard Russian Research Center, and between 1965 and 1969 held research posts at Birmingham University. At present he is teaching Polish language and literature at Cambridge University. His publications include Polish and Hungarian Poetry 1945 to 1956, New Writing of East Europe, edited with Charles Newman, and numerous articles and essays in the East European and Slavonic Review, Survey, Books Abroad, Tri-Quarterly, and other journals.

ROGER E. KANET is Associate Professor of Political Science at the University of Kansas. He is Chairman of the Bibliography and Documentation Committee of the American Association for the Advancement of Slavik Studies. His publications include The Behaviorial Revolution and Communist Studies, which he edited, and he is co-editor of the forthcoming On the Road to Communism: Essays on Soviet Domestic and Foreign Politics. Professor Kanet has also written a number of articles that have appeared in Canadian-Slavic Studies, The Russian Review, Soviet Studies, and Internationale Spectator.

WERNER SICHEL is Associate Professor of Economics at Western Michigan University. He received his B.S. degree from New York University and his M.A. and Ph.D. degree from Northwestern University. Before joining the faculty at WMU in 1960, Dr. Sichel taught at Lake Forest College and Roosevelt University. He serves as a business consultant and is a member of the American Economics Association. Dr. Sichel was a Fulbright-Hays lecturer at the University of Belgrade, Yugoslavia, for the academic year 1968-69. He has written articles for several Yugoslav journals including Gledista and Anali Pravnog Fakulteta u Beogradu, for Conferences on Public Finance, a publication of the University of Istanbul, and for American journals including the Journal of Risk and Insurance, The Antitrust Bulletin, MSU Business Topics, and the St. John's Law Review. Dr. Sichel is also the editor of two books: Industrial Organization and Public Policy: Selected Readings, and Antitrust Policy and Economic Welfare.

IVAN SVITAK is Professor in the Department of Philosophy at Chico State College, California. Author of over a dozen books and hundreds of articles, Professor Svitak's latest publication is The Czechoslovak Experiment. Professor Svitak was one of the leaders of the intellectual movement in Prague prior to the Soviet invasion. His books include Human Sense of Culture (1968), Hundred Faces of Love (1968), Human Meaning of Marxism (1969), Film in a Manipulated World (1969), and Unscientific Anthropology (1969).

RUDOLF L. TOKES, born in Hungary, is Associate Professor of Political Science at the University of Connecticut. He received his Ph.D. from Columbia University. Professor Tokes, was the recipient of an ACLS-SSRC Faculty Research Fellowship in 1966-67 and a Senior Fellowship at the Research Institute on Communist Affairs at Columbia University. His publications include Bela Kun and the Hungarian Soviet Republic of 1919 and the just-completed The Communist Party and the Hungarian Left, 1920-1944— An Intellectual History. He has contributed to various symposia and articles and book reviews in the Journal of Contemporary History, The Review, and the Slavic Review.

IVAN VOLGYES, Associate Professor of Political Science and Coordinator of Slavic Studies at the University of Nebraska, was born in Budapest, Hungary. He received his Ph.D. from the School of International Service of the American University in Washington, D.C. He has taught at the University of Maryland, Denison University, and the University of Nebraska and has lectured in Germany, Spain, Turkey, Italy, and Hungary.

E. BENNETT WARNSTROM is Instructor of French at Indiana University. He was a recipient of a Fulbright-Hays Grant for study at the University of Bucharest, Romania, from 1967 to 1969. Mr. Warnstrom is presently compiling an anthology of Romanian poetry in prose translation. He has written about Romanian television and films and has acted as guide and interpreter for the Department of State.

DATE DUE

MAY 9 1980			
GAYLORD			PRINTED IN U.S.A.